Machine Learning

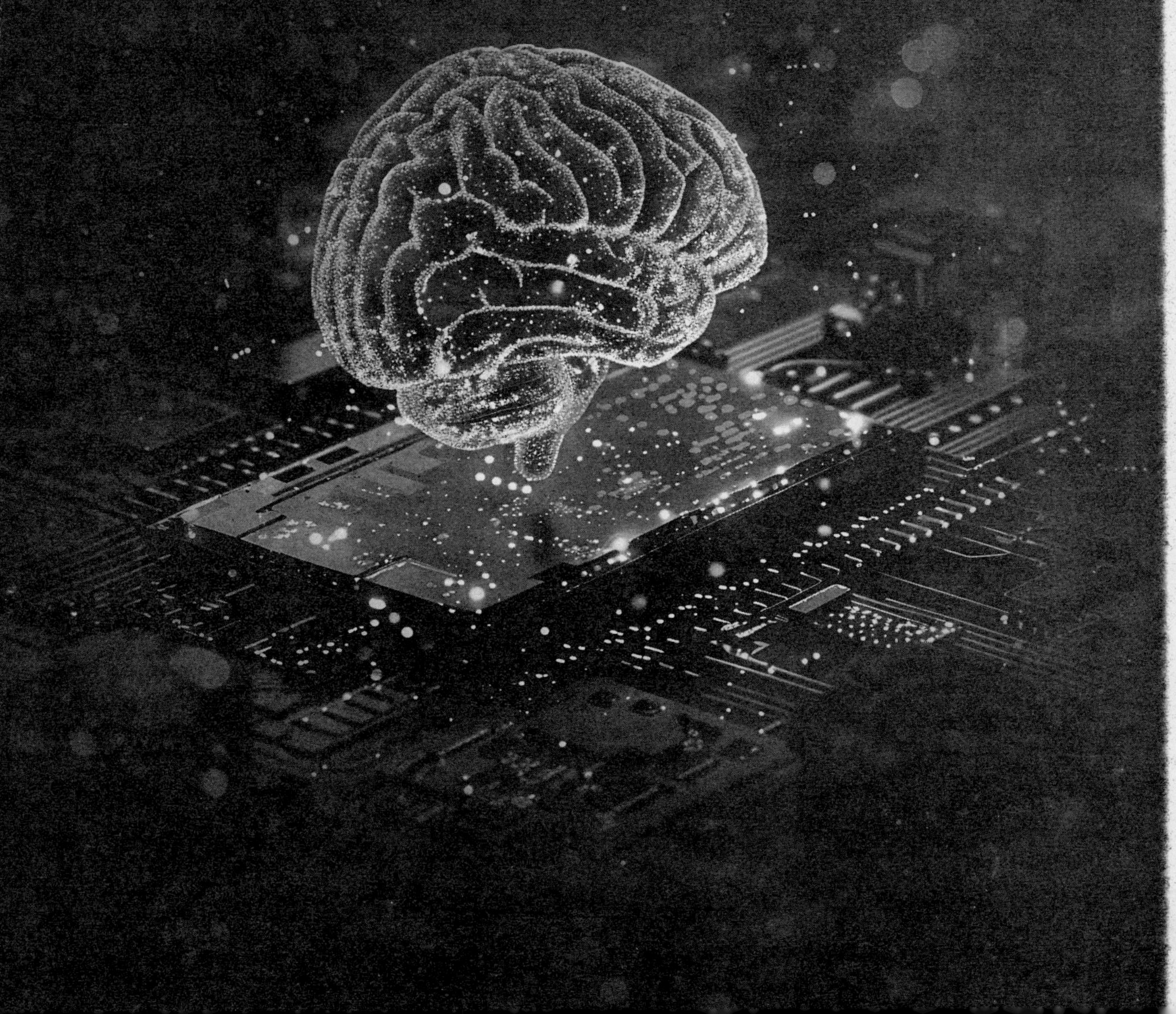

Machine Learning

N. Bhaskar
K.L. Vasundhara
Monalisha Pattnaik
G. Mahesh Kumar

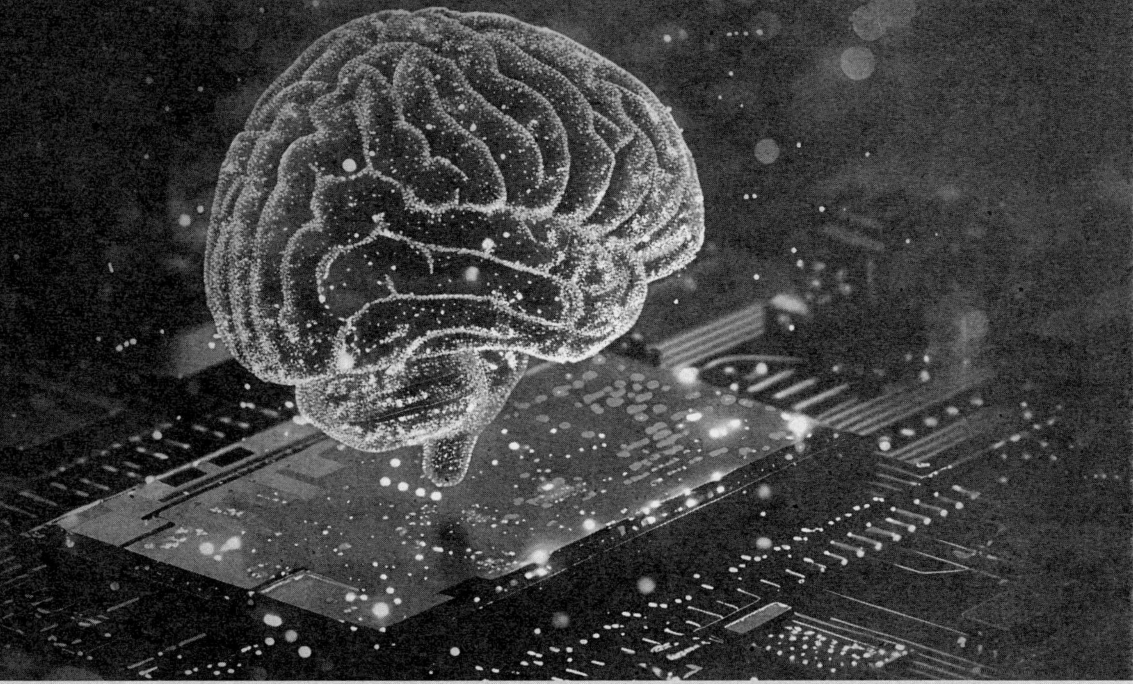

KHANNA BOOK PUBLISHING CO. (P) LTD.

PUBLISHER OF ENGINEERING AND COMPUTER BOOKS

4C/4344, Ansari Road, Darya Ganj, New Delhi-110002

Phone : 011-23244447-48 Mobile: +91-99109 09320

E-mail : contact@khannabooks.com; Website : www.khannabooks.com

Dear Readers,

To prevent the piracy, this book is secured with HIGH SECURITY HOLOGRAM on the front title cover. In case you don't find the hologram on the front cover title, please write us to at contact@khannabooks.com or whatsapp us at +91-99109 09320 and avail special gift voucher for yourself.

Specimen of Hologram on front Cover title:

Moreover, there is a SPECIAL DISCOUNT COUPON for you with EVERY HOLOGRAM.

How to avail this SPECIAL DISCOUNT:

Step 1: Scratch the hologram
Step 2: Under the scratch area, your "coupon code" is available
Step 3: Logon to www.khannabooks.com
Step 4: Use your "coupon code" in the shopping cart and get your copy at a special discount
Step 5: Enjoy your reading!

Thanks,
Khanna Publishing House

ISBN: 978-93-5538-498-0

Machine Learning

by Dr. N. Bhaskar, Dr. K.L. Vasundhara, Prof. Monalisha Pattnaik and Dr. G. Mahesh Kumar

First Edition: 2025
Reprint: 2026

To view complete list of books, please scan the QR Code:

Published by:
Khanna Book Publishing Co. (P) Ltd.
CIN: U22110DL1998PTC095547

Visit us at: www.khannabooks.com
Write us at: contact@khannabooks.com

Printed in Bharat.

ACKNOWLEDGEMENT

I, **Dr. N. Bhaskar**, Head &Asst. Professor, Dept. of Computer Science take pleasure to express my sincere thanks to my research supervisor Prof. MV Ramana Murthy, Former Head and BOS Chairman, Dept. of Mathematics and Computer Science, Osmania University, Hyderabad. It is my immense pleasure to associate with Prof. MV Ramana Murthy and his continuous guidance and task oriented mind setup to complete this task very soon. I am also thankful to Bhavan's Vivekananda College of Science Humanities and Commerce, Management,Principal-Dr. GSVRK Choudary, Mrs. KVB Saraswathi Devi for given me the support and encouraging me to achieve goals successfully.I co-authored books on"Computer Fundamentals", Data Science with Machine Learning using R.

I, **Dr.K.L. Vasundhara**, HOD & Assoc. Professor, Dept of Mathematics, Thank my Mentor Prof. M.V Ramana Murthy (Former Head and BOS Chairman, Dept. of Mathematics and Computer Science, OU, Hyderabad) for his guidance, time, ideas and help. I am greatly indebted to Sri K. Krishna Rao (Correspondent, Stanley college of Engineering and Technology for Women, Hyderabad) for his support. It is imperative on my behalf to remember my beloved Mother Late Smt. K. Varalakshmi and my Father-in-Law Late Sri. Yerasuri Gopala Krishna Murthy for their divine blessings.

Recipient of "UTTAMA ADYAPIKA AWARD" 2022, "JYSTA ACH ARNA AWARD" 2024 and authored 16 papers in various National & International Journals, Co-authored books on "Engineering Mathematics-IV", "Data Science with Machine Learning using R". AICTE nominated expert for Data Analytics and having 6 Patents.

I, **Prof. Monalisha Pattnaik,** currently serving as the Head of Department in the Department of Statistics, at Sambalpur University holds her D.Litt. in Supply Chain Management from Sambalpur University and her Ph.D. in Operations Research from Utkal University. Additionally, she holds the position of Deputy Director of the Research and Development Cell, at Sambalpur University. Apart from that, she actively conducts training programs, and seminars, and delivers talks at Faculty Development Programmes conducted by HRDC. In association with the mentioned, she is an avid researcher and has devoted her time to urging young minds into research. Her dedication to research is evident from her extensive list of publications in reputed international and national journals. Prof. Pattnaik boasts an impressive publication record with over 50 papers indexed in SCOPUS and WoS. In addition to her articles, Prof. Pattnaik has authored eight books, edited five books of international repute, and contributed numerous book chapters, solidifying her expertise in her fields of interest. As a highly regarded reviewer for prestigious publishers such as Elsevier, Taylor & Francis, IEEE Access, and Springer, she actively contributes to the academic community. She has an active role to play as a Member of the Editorial Board of reputed international journals. She is also associated with independent projects conducted by both Govt. of India and Govt. of Odisha. Presently, she is associated with Sambalpur University funded project based on Predictive Analytics. In her 16 years of teaching experience, she has covered topics such as Artificial Intelligence, Bibliometrics, Advanced Operations Research, Financial Time Series Analysis, Co-integration, ARIMA Modelling, Production and Operations Management, Security Analysis and Portfolio Management, Logistics and Supply Chain Management, Optimization Techniques, Research Methodology, and Advanced Multivariate Analysis. Her name has been included as an active reviewer in the online library of reputed international journals such as British Academy of Management and John Wiley & Sons Ltd. One of her article published in the journal Statistics Optimization and Information Computing has been included in the CAM-Digest Magazine, China. She has been getting invitation for conducting track chair session of international conferences in South Korea, Bangkok and France (Online). Recently, she has developed a new algorithm of Transportation Problem and it is published in a reputed journal of Log Forum, Poland. She has published a case study which is available online in an academic website "studymode.com". Very recently, she has published three preprints on COVID-19 in the medRxiv org. USA, the preprint server health sciences, world reputed free online archive and distribution server for complete but preprints in the medical, clinical, and related health sciences. With a notable number of citations, an h-index of 14, and an i10-index of 26 from 2018 until the present, Prof. Pattnaik continues to be a prominent figure in the academic and research world, contributing her vast experience and expertise to various domains within Management, Statistics, and Artificial Intelligence. Her work was acknowledged in the AD Scientific Index 2024, a prestigious research database curated by Stanford University, where she was listed among the world's top scientists. Her latest accomplishment adds another feather to her cap, i.e. the successful granting of a patent by the Intellectual Property Office, UK, for her innovative design. Recently she has been awarded the prestigious "JYESTA ACHARYA AWARD" 2021-2022, All India Level on 4th Dec organised by "Bharat Education Excellence Awards-2022" team of Skill, Swadesh, LACE, Brainovision, Cito Health Care & Lions Club, Hyderabad. She has also the recipient of the "Distinguished Woman Researcher in Operations Research", (OPERATIONS RESEARCH – 2024 (Management)) by Venus International Women Awards: Chennai, Tamil Nadu, India.

I, **Dr. G Mahesh Kumar** holds the position of Assistant Professor, Department of Computer Science, Bhavan's Vivekananda College of Science, Humanities and Commerce, Sainikpuri, Secunderabad, Telangana, India. He has completed his Ph.D. in Computer Science & Engineering from JNTU Hyderabad. He has done his Masters in Information Systems, M.Tech (CSE) from Osmania University. He has qualified UGC-NET in Computer Applications. He has presented papers in national and international conferences. He has published research papers international and national journals. He has published one patent. His research areas include Grid Computing, Cloud Computing, Internet of Things, Blockchain Technology, and Machine Learning.

–Authors

Prof. M.V. RamanaMurthy, Ph.D,
Former Head and BOS Chairman,Mathematics and Computer Science, Osmania University, Hyderabad, India. Former Professor in Computer Science, King Abdul Azeez university, Rabigh Campus, Jeddah. K S A., George Mason University UAE .

Dr. Sureshkumar Lokhande, Ph.D.
Chairman CSE, Osamania University, Hyderabad.

Prof. K. Jayashankar, Ph.D,
Dean(R&D), Methodist Engg. College, Former Principal, Vasavi Engg. College and Mahathma Gandhi Institute of Techonology, Hyderabad.

Prof. Y.V.K. RaviKumar, Ph.D,
Professor, BITS, Hyderabad.

Prof. RavindraHegde, Ph.D,
Dean, Computer Science, Karnataka Central University, Gulburga-Karnataka.

CONTENTS

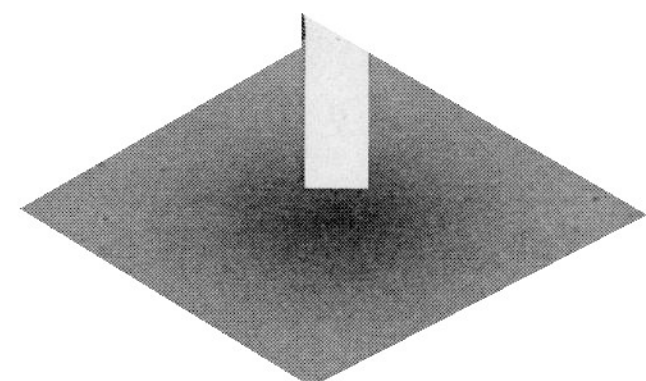

1.0 INTRODUCTION

Objectives

1. To provide Knowledge of Probability distributions.
2. To study the matrix algebra and its uses in solving eigen value problems and single value decomposition problems.
3. To explain the basic concepts in Number theory.

Outcomes

At the end of this chapter, the student will be able to

1. Apply probability theory to solve practical problems.
2. Solve the eigne values, eigen vectors and single value decomposition problems.
3. Apply Cryptographic algorithms to Practical problems.

Machine Learning

Machine learning is a field that involves studying algorithms and statistical models used by computers to perform tasks through pattern recognition and deduction. It builds mathematical models from sample data, employing techniques like supervised and unsupervised learning. Computational statistics, a bridge between statistics and computer science, is closely related to machine learning. Linear algebra and probability theory are Mathematical tools in machine learning. Statistics, a science focused on collecting and analyzing data plays a crucial role in understanding and interpreting results in machine learning.

Artificial Intelligence (*AI*) and Machine Learning (*ML*) are forefront technologies in the 21st century, mimicking human intelligence in problem-solving and learning. *AI*'s capabilities, including strategic game performance, autonomous driving, and simulations, make it a key interest for the new generation. Statistical methods, linear algebra, and partial differential equations form the foundation of AI and ML, enabling advancements in tasks like image processing and intelligent routing.

Cyber security for Machine Learning: Cyber security is increasingly vital due to growing technological dependence on the internet. It involves protecting computer systems, networks, and programs from cyber-attacks, which are becoming more sophisticated. Cryptanalysis is employed to crack cryptographic systems, focusing on deciphering encrypted data. Traditional cryptanalysis has challenges such as exponential time complexity, but machine learning may reduce computational complexity in cryptanalysis. Number theory serves as the backbone of cryptography.

Mathematical Preliminaries in Machine Learning

Following Mathematical concepts are principle drivers in implementation of Machine Learning:

1. Probability
2. Linear Algebra
3. Number Theory

1.1 PROBABILITY

There are several definitions available to understand probability. Among them two of the mostly used definitions are:

1. Relative frequency definition
2. Axiomatic definition.

Relative Frequency

Suppose that an experiment is repeated '*n*' times and one of the possible outcome '*A*' occurs n_A times. Now, the relative frequency of occurrence of *A* is (n_A/n).

This ratio (n_A/n) is not predictable unless *n* is very large.

For example, in the rolling of a die, let the outcome *A* corresponds to the appearance of 3 on the die. In four tosses, the number 3 may not appear at all or it may appear all the four times, or any number of times in between. Thus with

$$n = 4, (n^A/n) = 0 \text{ or } 1/6, \text{etc., upto } 1$$

On the other hand, we know from experience that when an experiment (whose outcomes are determined by chance) is repeated too many times, the relative frequency of a particular outcome approaches a fixed limit. Thus, if we were to roll a die too many times, we would expect that (n_A/n) would turn out to be very close to ¼. This limiting value of the relative frequency of occurrence is called the probability of outcome A,

i.e;

$$P(A) = \log_{n \to \infty} (n_A/n)$$

This probability, determined as the limit of the relative frequency of occurrence, is known as **a posteriori probability**, i.e., probability determined after the event.

Axiomatic Probability

The probability of an event *A* consisting of n_A outcomes equals the ratio n_A/n provided the outcomes are equally likely to occur, i.e.

$$P(A) = \frac{\text{Number of possible favorable outcomes}}{\text{Total number of possible equally likely outcomes}} = (n_A/n)$$

For example, assume that a bag contains 9 balls out of which 5 are red and 4 are white. Then, in a single draw, the probability to select a white ball is 4/9. This is arrived because out of 9 possible outcomes of the experiment, i.e., any one of 9 balls may be drawn; 4 are favorable to our interest. Thus, the probability of the event is determined with out conducting the event, i.e., prior to the event and is also known as **apriori probability**.

From the above two definitions, it is clear that

(i) The probability of occurrence of an event is a positive number

(ii) $0 \leq P(A) \leq 1$

(iii) If an outcome A is not possible $P(A) = 0$, while if the outcome is very certain $P(A) = 1$.

1.1.1 Terms in Probability

(i) **Outcome:** The end result of an experiment.

(ii) **Randomexperiment:** An experiment whose outcome is not known in advance.

(iii) **Randomevent:** A random event is an outcome or a set of outcomes of a random experiment.

(iv) **Occurrence:** An event of a random experiment is said to have occurred if the experiment terminates in an outcome that belongs to that event.

(v) **Equally likely:** A set of events is said to be equally likely if one of them cannot be expected to happen in preference to any other.

For example, in tossing a coin, the turning up of the head or tail is equally likely.

(vi) **Mutually exclusive:** A set of events is said to be mutually exclusive, if the occurrence of one of them does not prevent the occurrence of the others.

For example, in tossing a coin, either the head or the tail will turn up. Both cannot happen at the same time.

(vii) **Exhaustive:** A set of events is said to be exhaustive if it includes all the possible outcomes. In tossing a coin, either the head or the tail turns up.

For example, in tossing a coin, there are two Exhaustive elementary events.

i.e., head and tail.

1.1.2 Axioms of Probability

The probability of an event A, denoted by $P(A)$ is so chosen as to satisfy the following **three** axioms.

(i) $P(A) \geq 0 \Rightarrow$ This axiom states that the probability of occurrence of an event A in a random experiment may be zero or any positive number and it must not be a negative number.

(ii) $P(S) = 1 \Rightarrow$ this states that the sample space, S, it self is an event and since it is the event comprising all possible outcomes, it should have the highest possible probability, i.e. one.

(iii) If $A \cap B = 0$, Then $P(AUB) = P(A) + P(B) \Rightarrow$ this axiom states that the probability of the event equal to the union of any number of mutually exclusive events is equal to the sum of the individual event probabilities.

1.1.3 Use full Laws of Probability

1. $P(AUB) = P(A) + P(B) - P(A \cap B)$
2. If $AU\bar{A} = S$ and $A \cap \bar{A} = \phi$, then $\bar{A}$ is called the complement of A,

   i.e. $(\bar{A}) = 1 - P(A)$.

3. If $A_1, A_2, A_3, ..., A_n$ are 'n' random events such that $A_i \cap A_j = 0$, for $i = j$

   and $\quad A_1 \cap A_2 \cap ... \cap A_n = S$

1.2 DIFFERENCE BETWEEN INDEPENDENT EVENTS AND DEPENDENT EVENTS

Independent Events	Dependent Events
Independent events are events that are not affected by the occurrence of other events.	Dependent events are events that are affected by the occurrence of other events.
The formula for the Independent Events is, **P(A and B) = P(A) × P(B)**	The formula for the Dependent Events is, **P(B and A) = P(A) × P(B after A)**
Examples of Independent Events are, Tossing one coin was not affected by the tossing of other coins	Examples of Dependent Events are, The probability of finding a red ball from a box of 4 red balls and 3 green balls changes if we take out two balls from the box.

1.3 USEFUL INEQUALITIES

In applications it is often not possible to get precise expressions for a probability we are interested in, most often because we don't know the exact distribution we are dealing with and only have access to parameters such as the expectation or the variance. There are several useful inequalities that help us bound the tail or deviation probabilities. For the following, we assume $X \subset R$.

Jensen's inequality: Let $f : R \rightarrow R$ be a convex function, that is,

$f(\lambda x + (1 - \lambda) y) \leq \lambda f(x) + (1 - \lambda) f(y)$ for $\lambda \in [0, 1]$. Then $f(E[X]) \leq E[f(X)]$.

Markov's Inequality ("first moment method") For $X \geq 0$ and $\lambda > 0$,

$P(X \geq \lambda) \leq E[X]/\lambda$

Chebyshev's Inequality ("second moment method") for $\lambda > 0$,

$P(|X - E[X] \geq \alpha) \leq \text{Varience}(X)/\lambda^2$

Exponential Moment Inequality for any $S, \lambda > 0$,

$P(X \geq \lambda) \leq e^{-s\lambda} E(e^{SX})$.

Note that both the Chebyshev and the exponential moment inequality follow from the Markov inequality applied to certain transformations of X.

1.4 MULTIPLICATION THEOREM

Considering two experiments A and B with outcomes $|A_1, A_2 ... A_n|$ and $|B_1, B_2 ... B_m|$ respectively, sometimes the probability of occurrence of an event Bj may depend on the occurrence of a related event Ai.

For instance, assume that a box contains five green colour pens and one red colour pen. Let us take a pen from the box. Then, **without replacing the first pen**, if we take another pen, the probability of getting a red pen in the second time depends on the outcome of the first draw, i.e., if we had taken a red pen on the first time itself, there is no more red pen in the box. Thus, we have a situation in which the outcome of the second experiment is **conditional** on the outcome of the first experiment.

The probability of the outcome *Bj* given that *Ai* is known is called the **Conditional probability** or **transition probability** and it is written as *P (Bj/Ai)*.

If *NA* represents the number of times an event *A* happens, *NB* represent the number of times event *B* happens and *NAB* represent the number of timesof joint happening, then

$$P\left(\frac{B}{A}\right) = \frac{NAB}{NA} = \frac{NAB/N}{NA/N} = \frac{P(AB)}{P(A)}, \text{ for } p(A) > 0$$

Similarly,

$$P\left(\frac{B}{A}\right) = \frac{NAB}{NB} = \frac{NAB/N}{NA/N} = \frac{P(AB)}{P(A)}, \text{ for } p(B) > 0$$

This may be simply written as

$$\boxed{\begin{array}{l} P(A \cap B) = P(A).P(B/A) \\ P(B \cap A) = P(B).P(A/B) \end{array}}$$

These expressions represent **Chain rule** or **theorem of multiplication.** This is also called as law of multiplication of probability.

1.5 CONDITIONAL PROBABILITY AND EXPECTATION

Given events *A*, *B* in a sample space *S* and $P(A) \neq 0$, then the probability of *B*, after the event *A* has occurred, is called the **conditional probability** of the event of *B* given *A* and is denoted by

$$P(B|A) = P(A \cap B)/P(A)$$

or

$$P(B|A) = \frac{\text{Number elements in } A \cap B}{\text{Number of elements of } A}$$

We can rearrange the expression for conditional probability to

$$P(A \cap B) = P(B|A)\, P(A),$$

Similarly

$$P(A|B) = P(A \cap B)/P(B)$$

1.6 BAYE'S THEOREM

$E_1, E_2 \ldots E_n$ are *n* mutually exclusive and exhaustive events such that P(Ei)>0(i=1,2,.....n) in a sample space *S* and *A* is any other event in *S* intersecting with every E_i (i.e., A can only in combination with any of the events $E_1, E_2 \ldots E_n$) such that $P(A) > 0$ If E_i is any of the events of $E_1, E_2 \ldots E_n$ where $P(E_1), P(E_2) \ldots P(E_n)$ and $P(A/E_1), P(A/E_2) \ldots P(A/E_n)$ are known then

$$P(E_k/A) = \frac{P(E_k), P\left(\frac{A}{E_k}\right)}{P(E_1), P\left(\frac{A}{E_1}\right) + P(E_2), P\left(\frac{A}{E_1}\right) \ldots P(E_n), P\left(\frac{A}{E_n}\right)}$$

Problems on Baye's Theorem

Question 1: Three persons A, B and C have applied for a job in a private company. The chance of their selections is in the ratio 1:2:4. The probabilities that A, B and C can introduce changes to improve the profits of the company are 0.8, 0.5 and 0.3, respectively. If the change does not take place, find the probability that it is due to the appointment of C.

Solution: Let E_1: person A get selected

E_2: person B get selected

E_3: person C get selected

A: Changes introduced but profit not happened

Now, $P(E_1) = 1/(1 + 2 + 4) = 1/7$

$P(E_2) = 2/7$ and $P(E_3) = 4/7$

$P(A|E_1) = P$ (Profit not happened by the changes introduces by A)

$= 1 - P$ (Profit happened by the changes introduces by A)

$= 1 - 0.8 = 0.2$

$P(A|E_2) = P$ (Profit not happened by the changes introduces by B)

$= 1 - P$ (Profit happened by the changes introduces by B)

$= 1 - 0.5 = 0.5$

$P(A|E_3) = P$ (Profit not happened by the changes introduces by C)

$= 1 - P$ (Profit happened by the changes introduces by C)

$= 1 - 0.3 = 0.7$

We have to find the probability of not happening profit due to selection of C

$$P(E_3/A) = \frac{(p(A/E_3)\,p(E_3))}{p(A/E_1)\,p(E_1) + p(A/E_2)\,p(E_2) + p(A/E_3)\,p(E_3)}$$

$p(E_3/A) = 0.7\,(4/7) \,/\, 0.2\,(1/7) + 0.5\,(2/7) + 0.7\,(4/7)$

∴ The required probability is 0.7.

Question 2: A bag contains 4 balls. Two balls are drawn at random without replacement and are found to be blue. What is the probability that all balls in the bag are blue?

Solution: Let E_1 = Bag contains two blue balls

E_2 = Bag contains three blue balls

E_3 = Bag contains four blue balls

A = event of getting two white balls

$P(E_1) = P(E_2) = P(E_3) = ⅓$

$P(A|E_1) = 2\,C_2/4C_2 = 1/6$

$P(A|E_2) = 3\,C_2/4C_2 = ½$

$P(A|E_3) = 4\,C_2/4C_2 = 1$

$$P(E_3/A) = \frac{(p(A/E_3)\,p(E_3))}{p(A/E_1)\,p(E_1) + p(A/E_2)\,p(E_2) + p(A/E_3)\,p(E_3)}$$

$$= (1/3 \times 1)/((1/3 \times 1/6) + (1/3 \times 1/2) + (1/3 \times 1) = 3/5$$

The above concepts (**conditional probability**) clearly extend to random variable where we can define, for example

$$P(X\in A \mid Y\in B) = P(X\in A,\, Y\in B)/P(X\in B).$$

Note that if X and Y are independent, then the conditional probability is just the normal probability of X: knowing that Y

B does not give us any additional information about X! If we fix an event such as $\{Y\in B\}$, then we can define the **conditioning** of the random variable X to this event as the random variable X' with distribution

$$P(X'\in A) = P(X\in A \mid Y\in B).$$

In particular, $P(X\in A \mid Y\in B) + P(X\notin A \mid Y\in B) = 1$ Approximating functions is by using optimization methods.

Optimization is a key tool in machine learning, where the goal is to achieve the best possible objective function value in a minimum amount of time.

1.7 OPTIMIZATION

The notion of best fit is formalized by using a **loss function**. A loss function $L{:}Y * Y \rightarrow R^+$ measures the mismatch between a prediction on a given input $x\in X$ and an element $y\in Y$. The **empirical risk** of a function h: $X\rightarrow Y$ is the average loss

$L(h(x^i), y^i)$ over the training data,

$\check{R}(h){:} = 1/n\, \Sigma^n{}_{i=1}\, L(h(x^i), y^i))$

One would then aim to find a function h among a set of candidate function H that minimizes the loss when applying the function to the training data:

Minimize $\check{R}(h)$.

$h \in H$

Optimization problem

Minimizing over a set of functions my look abstract, but functions in H are typically parameterized by few parameters. For example, when the class H consists of linear functions of the form

$\beta_0 + \beta_{1\times 1} + \ldots + \beta_{p\times p}$,

Minimizing a function over R^{p+1}.

In the case of neural networks, Example, one optimizes over the weights $w_{ij}{}^k$ and bias terms $b_i{}^k$ as terms $b_i{}^k$.

The form of the loss function depends on the problem at hand and is usually derived from statistical considerations. Two common candidates are the square error for regression problems, which applied to function $h{:}R^d\rightarrow R$ takes the form $L(h(x), y) = (h(x) - y)^2$, and the **indicator loss function**, which takes the general form

$L(h(x), y) = 1\{h(x) \neq y\} = \{(1 \text{ if } h(x) = y \text{ @ } 0 \text{ if } h(x) \neq y)\}$

As this function is not continuous, in practice one often encounters continuous approximations. A binary classifier is often implemented by a function

$h : X \rightarrow [0, 1]$ that provides a probability of an input belonging to a class.

If $h(x) > 1/2$, then x is assigned to class 1,

while if $h(x) \leq 1/2$, then x is assigned to class 0.

A common loss function for this setting is the **log-loss** function, or **cross-entropy**,

$L(h(x), y) = -y \log(h(x)) - (1 - y) \log(1 - h(x))$

$= \{-\log(h(x)) \text{ if } y = 1 \text{ @ } -\log(1 - h(x)) \text{ if } y = 0)\}$

The function is designed to take on large values if the class predicted by $h(x)$ does not match y, and can be interpreted in the context of maximum-like lihoodestimation.

Finding or approximating a minimize of a function falls into the real m of Numerical-optimization.

While for linear regression we can solve the relevant optimization problem (least-squares minimization) in closed form, for more involved problems such as neural networks we use optimization algorithms such as **gradient descent**: we start withan initial guess and try to minimize our function by taking steps indirection of steepest descent, that is, along the negative gradient of the function. In the case of composite functions such as neural networks, computing the gradient requires the chain rule, which leads to the famous **back propagation** algorithm for training a neural network that will be discussed in detail.

There are many challenges related to optimization models and algorithms. The function to be minimized may have many local minima or saddle points, and algorithms that look for minimizes may find any one of these, instead of a global minimize. The functions to be minimized may not be differentiable, and methods from the field **non-smooth optimization** come into play. The biggest challenge for optimization algorithms in the context of machine learning, however, lies in the particular form of the objective function: it is given as a sum of many terms, one for each data point. Evaluating such a function and computing its gradient can be time and memory consuming. An old class of algorithms that includes **stochastic gradient descent** circumvents this issue by not computing the gradient of the whole function at each step, but only of a small random subset of the terms. These algorithms work surprisingly well, considering that they do not make use of all the information available at every step.

1.8 LINEAR ALGEBRA

Type's of Matrices

Definition: A rectangular arrangement of elements In m rows and n columns Is an $m \times n$ matrix.

Example:

$$\begin{bmatrix} a_{11} & a_{12} & \cdots & a_{1n} \\ a_{21} & a_{22} & \cdots & a_{2n} \\ \vdots & \vdots & \cdots & \vdots \\ a_{m1} & a_{m2} & \cdots & a_{mn} \end{bmatrix}$$

Row matrix: A matrix having a single row.

Column matrix: A matrix having a single column.

Square matrix: A matrix having equal number of rows and columns is a square matrix of size $m \times n$ when $m = n$ the matrix is called a square matrix.

Singular Matrix: A square matrix A is said to be singular if

Determinant $(A) = |A| = 0$.

Non-Singular Matrix: A square matrix A is said to be non-singular if

Determinant $(A) = |A| \neq 0$.

Unit Matrix: A square matrix A of order n, in which elements in the leading diagonals are 1 and all other elements are 0 is called a unit matrix. It is denoted by I.

Transpose of a Matrix: The matrix obtained from an $m \times n$ matrix A, by inter changing the rows and columns of A, is called the transpose of A. It is denoted by A^T.

Example: If $A = \begin{bmatrix} 2 & 3 & 4 \\ 5 & 6 & 7 \end{bmatrix}$, then $A^T = \begin{bmatrix} 2 & 5 \\ 3 & 6 \\ 4 & 7 \end{bmatrix}$

Symmetric Matrix: A square matrix A is said to be symmetric, if $A^T = A$.

A symmetric Matrix: A square matrix A is said to be A symmetric, if $A^T = -A$

Hermitain Matrix: A square matrix A is said to be Hermitain Matrix, if $A^T = \overline{A}$

Illustration: Computer Graphics

Let P be a point in the plane having Cartesian coordinates (x, y) Assume O (0, 0) be the origin and OP makes an angle a (say) with the x-axis. Suppose that OP is rotated about O in anti clockwise direction through an angle θ so that the point P moves to P' (x_1, y_1). Let $OP = OP' = r$ (say),We have

$$x = r \cos a, y = r \sin a,$$

$$x_1 = r \cos (\theta + a), \text{ and } y_1 = r \sin (\theta + a).$$

$$x_1 = x \cos \theta - y \sin \theta).$$

$$y_1 = x \sin \theta + y \cos \theta).$$

Using matrix notation, we can write

$$\begin{bmatrix} x_1 \\ y_1 \end{bmatrix} \begin{bmatrix} \cos\theta - \sin\theta \\ \sin\theta \quad \cos\theta \end{bmatrix} \begin{bmatrix} x \\ y \end{bmatrix}$$

Illustration: Apply the following geometric operations on vector $(x, y, z)^T$:

1. Identity operation

$$\begin{bmatrix} 1 & 0 & 0 \\ 0 & 1 & 0 \\ 0 & 0 & 1 \end{bmatrix} \begin{bmatrix} x \\ y \\ z \end{bmatrix} = \begin{bmatrix} x \\ y \\ z \end{bmatrix}$$

2. Reflection operation

$$\begin{bmatrix} 1 & 0 & 0 \\ 0 & 1 & 0 \\ 0 & 0 & -1 \end{bmatrix} \begin{bmatrix} x \\ y \\ z \end{bmatrix} = \begin{bmatrix} x \\ y \\ -z \end{bmatrix}$$

3. Inverse operation

In version of single coordinate

$$\begin{bmatrix} 1 & 0 & 0 \\ 0 & -1 & 0 \\ 0 & 0 & 1 \end{bmatrix} \begin{bmatrix} x \\ y \\ z \end{bmatrix} = \begin{bmatrix} x \\ -y \\ z \end{bmatrix}$$

In version of all three coordinates

$$\begin{bmatrix} -1 & 0 & 0 \\ 0 & -1 & 0 \\ 0 & 0 & -1 \end{bmatrix} \begin{bmatrix} x \\ y \\ z \end{bmatrix} = \begin{bmatrix} -x \\ -y \\ -z \end{bmatrix}$$

4. Proper rotation about a coordinate axis

Counter clockwise axis rotation about z-axis. Assume angle of rotation = ϕ

$$\begin{bmatrix} \cos\phi & \sin\phi & 0 \\ -\sin\phi & \cos\phi & 0 \\ 0 & 0 & 1 \end{bmatrix} \begin{bmatrix} x \\ y \\ z \end{bmatrix} = \begin{bmatrix} x' \\ y' \\ z' \end{bmatrix}$$

Illustration: Graph Theory

Consider a directed graph as shown in Fig. There is one self-loop but no parallel edges. The adjacency matrix of this graphics **X** The sum of the elements in the ith row of **X** represents the number of edges existing from vertex v_i, i.e., the out-degree of vertex v

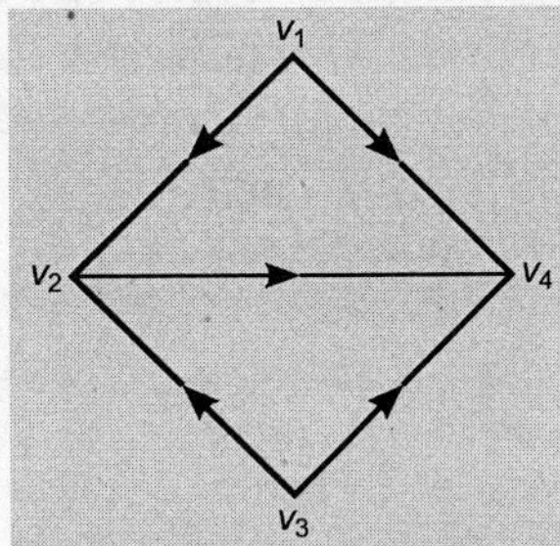

Fig. 1.1: A directed graph with one-self loop and no parallel edges.

Here $$\mathbf{X} = \begin{bmatrix} 0 & 1 & 0 & 1 \\ 0 & 0 & 0 & 1 \\ 0 & 1 & 0 & 1 \\ 0 & 0 & 0 & 1 \end{bmatrix}$$

Therefore, the sum of all out-degrees is equal to the sum of elements in **X**. The sum of the in the jth column of **X** is the number of edges incident on vertex v_1 or the in-degree of vertex v_1. The sum of the elements of **X**, therefore also equals the sum of all in-degrees.

1.9 EIGEN VALUES AND EIGEN VECTORS

Let A be an $n \times n$ matrix. A number is called as the eigen value of A if there exists

A non-zero vector $$X = \begin{bmatrix} x_1 \\ x_2 \\ \vdots \\ x_n \end{bmatrix}$$

Such that $AX = \lambda X$ and X is called as an Eigenvector

Corresponding to the eigen value λ.

Note:

1. If X is an eigen vector corresponding to the eigen values λ of, then α is any non-zero number, is also an eigen vector corresponding to λ.
2. Let X is an eigen vector corresponding to the eigen value λ of A.

Then $AX = \lambda X$ so that $(A - \lambda I) = 0$.

Thus X is a non-trivial solution of the system of homogeneous linear equations $(A - \lambda I) = 0$.

Hence $|A - \lambda I| = 0$, which is the characteristic polynomial of A.

Let $V\,|A - \lambda I| = 0$, which is the characteristic polynomial of

Let $|A - \lambda I| = a_0\lambda^n + a_1\lambda^{n-1} + \ldots + a_n$

The roots of this polynomial give the eigen values of A. Hence eigen values are also called characteristics roots.

Properties of Eigen value of an Eigen vectors

Some properties of Eigen values and Eigen vectors are as follows:

(i) The sum of the eigenvalues of a matrix is equal to the trace of the matrix, where the trace of the matrix as the sum of the elements of its principal diagonal.

(ii) If λ is an eigen value of matrix A, then $1/\lambda$ is the eigen value of A^{-1}.

(iii) If λ is an eigen value of an or thogonal matrix, then $1/\lambda$ is also its eigen value.

(iv) If $\lambda_1, \lambda_2, \ldots, \lambda_n$ are the eigen values of a matrix A, then A^m has the eigen values $\lambda^m{}_1, \lambda^m{}_2, \ldots, \lambda^m{}_n$. (Where m is a positive integer).

(v) (In variance if Eigen values). The eigen values of A are in variant under a linear transformation, i.e., the characteristic polynomials $|\lambda I - A|$ and $|\lambda I - P^{-1} AP|$ are identical

(vi) If the eigen values of a matrix are distinct, then the associate deigen vectors of A associate deigen vectors are linearly independent.

(vii) If the eigen values of a matrix are distinct, then the associated eigen vectors of are linearly independent.

(viii) If A is real symmetric matrix, then the eigen values of A are real and the eigen vectors of A associated with distinct eigen values are mutually or thogonal vectors.

(ix) A matrix is singular if and only if it has a zero eigen value.

(x) The eigen values of an upper (or lower) triangular matrix are the elements on the main diagonal.

(xi) If λ is an eigen value of A, then $\alpha\lambda$ is an eigen value of αA, where α is any arbitrary scalar.

(xii) If λ is an eigen value of A, then λ is an eigen value of A^T.

Example 1: Computer Graphics

Show that the equation of a two dimensional ellipse is $8x^2 - 4xy + 5y^2 = 1$ can be written as:

$$\begin{bmatrix} x & y \end{bmatrix} \begin{bmatrix} 8 & -2 \\ -2 & 5 \end{bmatrix} \begin{bmatrix} x \\ y \end{bmatrix}$$

Or $\qquad X^T AX = 1$

Solution: $\qquad X = \begin{bmatrix} x \\ y \end{bmatrix}$ and $A = \begin{bmatrix} 8 & -2 \\ -2 & 5 \end{bmatrix}$

Now, diagonalize the matrix A, then the eigen values of A are $\lambda_1 = 9, \lambda_2 = 4$.

$$|\lambda I - A| = \begin{bmatrix} \lambda - 8 & 2 \\ 2 & \lambda - 5 \end{bmatrix} = (\lambda - 8)(\lambda - 5) - 4$$

$$= \lambda^2 - 13\lambda + 36$$

$$= (\lambda - 9)(\lambda - 4)$$

Therefore, the diagonal matrix is given by

$$A = \begin{bmatrix} 9 & 0 \\ 0 & 4 \end{bmatrix}$$

And the normalized vector is given by

$$p = \begin{bmatrix} \frac{-2}{\sqrt{5}} & \frac{1}{\sqrt{5}} \\ \frac{1}{\sqrt{5}} & \frac{2}{\sqrt{5}} \end{bmatrix} \quad U = PX$$

Or $$\begin{bmatrix} u \\ y \end{bmatrix} = \begin{bmatrix} \frac{-2}{\sqrt{5}} & \frac{1}{\sqrt{5}} \\ \frac{1}{\sqrt{5}} & \frac{2}{\sqrt{5}} \end{bmatrix} \begin{bmatrix} x \\ y \end{bmatrix}$$

or $$u = 1/\sqrt{5(y-2x)},\ v = 1/\sqrt{5(x+2y)}.$$

Now, with respect to the new coordinate system

we shift $u = 0$, $v = 0$. The equation of the minor and major axes of the ellipse are corresponding to the large and small latent root. The equations are $y - 2x = 0$, $x + 2y = 0$.

Now the transformed equation of the ellipse in the new coordinate system is $U^T AU = 1$ i.e;

$$[u \ \ v] \begin{bmatrix} 9 & 0 \\ 0 & 4 \end{bmatrix} \begin{bmatrix} x \\ y \end{bmatrix} = [u \ \ v] \begin{bmatrix} 9u \\ 4u \end{bmatrix} = 1$$

$$9u^2 + 4v^2 = 1$$

1.10 NATURE OF THE EIGEN VALUES

Convexity of quadratic forms

In general, there are five ways to decide the nature of a given square matrix based on the signs of the eigen values, for example

1. If the Eigen values are positive then the nature is positive definite.
2. If the Eigen values are negative then the nature is negative definite.
3. If the Eigen values are non negative then the nature is Positive semi definite.

4. If the Eigen values are non positive then the nature is negative semi definite.
5. If the Eigen values are positive and negative then the nature is indefinite.

The positive definite matrices are generally diagonalizable.

For examplea Matrix is Positive Definite

$$A = \begin{bmatrix} 4 & 2 & 2 \\ 2 & 4 & 2 \\ 2 & 2 & 4 \end{bmatrix}$$

The characteristic equation of A is

$$\det(\lambda I - A) = \det\begin{bmatrix} \lambda-4 & -2 & -2 \\ -2 & \lambda-4 & -2 \\ -2 & -2 & \lambda-4 \end{bmatrix} = (\lambda - 2)^2 - (\lambda - 8) = 0$$

Here λ is 2, 2 and 8. All the Eigen values are positive. *A symmetric matrix A is positive definite if and only if the determinant of every leading principal minor is positive.*

A quantity which has zero dimensions is a Scalar (magnitude), one dimension is a Vector (magnitude and direction), two dimensions is a Matrix and more than two dimensions is called as Tensors. A data set is frequently and conveniently represented as a Matrix.

1.11 SINGLE VALUE DECOMPOSITION

In linear algebra Single Value decomposition abbreviated as *SVD* is used to factorize a real or complex matrix. It generalizes the eigen decomposition of a square normal matrix with an orthonormal eigen basis to any $m \times n$ matrix.

The singular value decomposition of a matrix A is the factorization of A into the product of three matrices namely two orthonormal matrices U & V and a diagonal matrix D.

$$A = UDV^T$$

The matrix A is $m \times n$ matrix, U is $m \times m$ complex unitary matrix , D is $m \times n$ rectangular diagonal matrix with non-negative real numbers on the diagonal, V is $n \times n$ complex unitary matrix and V^T is conjugate V.

Hence the above Single value decomposition of matrix A can be written as

$$[A]_{m \times n} = [U]_{m \times m}\,[D]_{m \times n}\,[V^T]_{n \times n}$$

Applications of SVD

1. The singular value decomposition can be used for computing the pseudoinverse of a matrix.
2. It is sued to solve set of linear homogenous equations with no vanishing single value.
3. Total Least square minimization.
4. Explicit representation of Range and Null space of a Matrix can be obtained by *SVD*.
5. It is used for decomposing a matrix into weighted and ordered sum of separable matrices.
6. It is used to determine the nearest orthogonal matrix.

7. It is used to assess the optimal rotation that will align a set of points with corresponding set of points.
8. In signal processing and image processing, *SVD* is exhaustively used for compression algorithm, and it is more apt while dealing with BIG DATA.
9. *SVD* is used in Principal Component's analysis and clustering a mixture of spherical gaussians, a dimensional reduce technique.
10. It is applicable in discrete optimization problems.

Procedural steps in calculating the Single Value Decomposition (SVD)

1. Write the given Matrix A in Matrix form
2. Determine the Transpose of Matrix *A*, i.e., A^T
3. Determine the Matrix $A.A^T$
4. Determine the Eigen values of the Matrix $A.A^T$ and sort the eigen vales in the descending order.
5. Determine the square root of these eigen values will give the single value.
6. Construct the diagonal matrix by placing the singular values on diagonal.
7. Determine the eigen vectors of the matrix $A.A^T$
8. Place these as columns of matrix *V* and determine the V^T.
9. Determine Matrix $U = AVD^{-1}$

Step-1: Let us consider the Matrix $A = \begin{bmatrix} -5 & 0 \\ 3 & 4 \end{bmatrix}$

Step-2: Determine the Transpose of the Matrix *A*, $A^T = \begin{bmatrix} -5 & 3 \\ 0 & 4 \end{bmatrix}$

Step-3: Determine the Matrix $A.A^T = \begin{bmatrix} -5 & 0 \\ 3 & 4 \end{bmatrix} \times \begin{bmatrix} -5 & 3 \\ 0 & 4 \end{bmatrix} = \begin{bmatrix} 25 & -15 \\ -15 & 25 \end{bmatrix}$

Step-4: Determine the Eigen Values of the Matrix $A.A^T$. Let the Eigen values be denoted by λ.

$$|A.A^T - \lambda I| = 0 \Rightarrow \begin{bmatrix} 25-\lambda & -15 \\ -15 & 25-\lambda \end{bmatrix} = (25 - \lambda)\,(125 - \lambda) - 225 = 0.$$

The Eigen values of λ is obtained by the quadratic equation, $\lambda^2 - 50\lambda + 225 = 0$.

The Values of $\lambda = 40$ & $\lambda = 10 \Rightarrow$ the eigen vales of the matrix are 40 and 10.

Step-5: The single value of the Matrix *A* are square root of $\lambda^1 = 40$ and $\lambda^2 = 10$ are

Singular value of $\lambda^1 = \sqrt{\lambda_1} = \sqrt{40} = 6.324$ and singular value of $\lambda_2 = \sqrt{\lambda_2} = \sqrt{10} = 3.162$

Step-6: The diagonal Matrix $D = \begin{bmatrix} 6.324 & 0 \\ 0 & 3.162 \end{bmatrix}$ and the inverse of the Diagonal matrix D^{-1} is

$$D^{-1} = \begin{bmatrix} 0.1581 & 0 \\ 0 & 0.3162 \end{bmatrix}$$

Step-7: Determination of Eigen vectors of the matrix $A.A^T$

For $\lambda_1 = 40 \Rightarrow (A.A^T - \lambda_1 I)\, X = 0$

$$\Rightarrow \begin{bmatrix} 25-40 & -15 \\ -15 & 25-40 \end{bmatrix}\begin{bmatrix} x_1 \\ x_2 \end{bmatrix} = 0$$

$$\Rightarrow \begin{bmatrix} -15 & -15 \\ -15 & -15 \end{bmatrix}\begin{bmatrix} x_1 \\ x_2 \end{bmatrix} = 0$$

The Eigen vectors are

$$-15 \times 1 - 15 \times 2 = 0;$$
$$-15 \times 1 - 15 \times 2 = 0$$

Solving the above eigen vectors will give : $x_1 = -x_2$

Hence the $x_1 = \begin{bmatrix} x_1 \\ x_2 \end{bmatrix} = \begin{bmatrix} x_1 \\ -x_1 \end{bmatrix}$

The Length of the Matrix $x_1 = \sqrt{x_1^2 + x_2^2} = \sqrt{x_1^2 + (-x_1)^2}$

$$= x_1\sqrt{2}$$

The matrix $x_1 = \begin{bmatrix} \dfrac{x_1}{L} \\ \dfrac{x_2}{L} \end{bmatrix} = \begin{bmatrix} \dfrac{x_1}{x_1\sqrt{2}} \\ \dfrac{-x_1}{x_1\sqrt{2}} \end{bmatrix} = \begin{bmatrix} \dfrac{1}{\sqrt{2}} \\ \dfrac{-1}{\sqrt{2}} \end{bmatrix}$

For $\lambda_1 = 10 \Rightarrow (A.A^T - \lambda_1 I)\, X = 0$

$$\Rightarrow \begin{bmatrix} 25-10 & -15 \\ -15 & 25-10 \end{bmatrix}\begin{bmatrix} x_1 \\ x_2 \end{bmatrix} = 0$$

$$\Rightarrow \begin{bmatrix} 15 & -15 \\ -15 & 15 \end{bmatrix}\begin{bmatrix} x_1 \\ x_2 \end{bmatrix} = 0$$

The Eigen vectors are

$$15x_1 - 15x_2 = 0;$$
$$-15x_1 + 15x_2 = 0$$

Solving the above eigen vectors will give : $x_1 = x_2$

Hence the $x_2 = \begin{bmatrix} x_1 \\ x_2 \end{bmatrix} = \begin{bmatrix} x_1 \\ x_1 \end{bmatrix}$

The Length of the Matrix $x_1 = \sqrt{x_1^2 + x_2^2} = \sqrt{x_1^2 + (x_1)^2}$

$$= x_1\sqrt{2}$$

The matrix $x_2 = \begin{bmatrix} \dfrac{x_1}{L} \\ \dfrac{x_2}{L} \end{bmatrix} = \begin{bmatrix} \dfrac{x_1}{x_1\sqrt{2}} \\ \dfrac{x_1}{x_1\sqrt{2}} \end{bmatrix} = \begin{bmatrix} \dfrac{1}{\sqrt{2}} \\ \dfrac{1}{\sqrt{2}} \end{bmatrix}$

Step-8: Determine the Matrix $V = [X_1\ X_2]$

$$V = \begin{bmatrix} 1/\sqrt{2} & 1/\sqrt{2} \\ -1/\sqrt{2} & 1/\sqrt{2} \end{bmatrix}$$

and

$$V^T = \begin{bmatrix} 1/\sqrt{2} & -1/\sqrt{2} \\ 1/\sqrt{2} & 1/\sqrt{2} \end{bmatrix}$$

Step-9: Determine the Matrix $U = AVD^{-1}$

$$U = \begin{bmatrix} -5 & 0 \\ 3 & 4 \end{bmatrix} \times \begin{bmatrix} 1/\sqrt{2} & 1/\sqrt{2} \\ 1/\sqrt{2} & 1/\sqrt{2} \end{bmatrix} \times \begin{bmatrix} 0.1581 & 0 \\ 0 & 0.3162 \end{bmatrix}$$

$$= \begin{bmatrix} -0.55902 & 0-1.118 \\ -0.1118 & 1.1562 \end{bmatrix}$$

1.12 LOW-RANK APPROXIMATION

In mathematics, **low-rank approximation** is a minimization problem, in which the costfunction measures the fit between a given matrix (the data) and an approximating matrix, subject to a constraint that the approximating matrix has reduced rank. The problem is used for mathematical modeling and data compression. The rank constraint is related to a constraint on the complexity of a model that fits the data. In applications, often there are other constraints on the approximating matrix apart from the rank constraint, e.g., non-negativity and Hankel structure.

Low-rank approximation is closely related to numerous other techniques, including principal component analysis, factor analysis, total least squares, orthogonal regressionlatent semantic analysis, and dynamic modede composition.

Definition

Given Structure specification $\boldsymbol{S}: \boldsymbol{R}^{np} \rightarrow \boldsymbol{R}^{m \times n}$

Vector of structure parameters $\boldsymbol{p} \in \boldsymbol{R}^{np}$

Norm $||\cdot||$, and desired rank $\boldsymbol{r}$,

minimize over $\hat{p} \| p - \hat{p} \|$ subject to rank $(S(\hat{p})) \leq r$.

Applications

Linear system identification, in which case the approximating matrix is **Hankel** structured. Machine learning, in which case the approximating matrix is nonlinearly structured.

Recommender systems, in which cases the data matrix has missing values and the approximation is categorical. Distance matrix completion, in which case there is a positive definiteness constraint. Natural language processing in which case the approximation is non-negative. Computer algebra, in which case the approximation is Sylvester structured.

Problem based on Basic low-rank approximation

The unstructured problem with fit measured by the Frobeniusnorm,

i.e., minimize over $\widehat{D} \| D-\widehat{D} \| |F$ subject to rank $(\widehat{D}) \leq r$

has analytic solution in terms of the singular value decomposition of the data matrix. The result is referred to as the matrix approximation **Eckart – Young – Mirsky theorem**. This problem was originally solved by Erhard Schmidt in the infinite dimensional context of integral operators and later rediscovered by C. Eckart and G. Young. L. Mirsky generalized the result to arbitrary unitarily invariant norms. Let

$$D = U\Sigma V^T \in R^{mxn}, m \leq n$$

be the singular value decomposition of, where $\Sigma =: \text{diag}(\sigma_1, ..., \sigma_m)$ is the $m \times n$ rectangular diagonal matrix with the singular values $\sigma_1 \geq ... \geq \sigma_m$.

For a given $r \in \{1, ..., m - 1\}$

partition U, Σ, and V as follows:

$$U =: [U_1 \;\; U_2], \Sigma =: \begin{bmatrix} \Sigma_1 & 0 \\ 0 & \Sigma_2 \end{bmatrix}, \text{ and } V =: [V_1 \;\; V_2],$$

Where $\boldsymbol{U_1}$ is $\boldsymbol{m \times r}$, $\boldsymbol{\Sigma_1}$ is $\boldsymbol{r \times r}$, and $\mathbf{V_1}$ is $\boldsymbol{r \times n}$. Then the rank-$\boldsymbol{r}$ matrix, obtained from the truncated singular value decomposition

$$\widehat{D^*} = U_1 \Sigma_1 V_1^T,$$

is such that

$$\|D-\widehat{D^*}\|_F = \min \text{rank}(\widehat{D}) \leq r \|D-\widehat{D}\|_F = \sqrt{(\sigma_{r+1}^2 + ... + \sigma_m^2)}$$

The minimize $\widehat{D^*}$ is unique if and only if $\boldsymbol{\sigma_{r+1} \neq \sigma_r}$

Eckart–Young–Mirsky theorem

Let $\boldsymbol{A} \in \boldsymbol{R^{m \times n}}$ be a real (possibly rectangular) matrix with $\boldsymbol{m \leq n}$. Suppose that

$$A = U\Sigma V^T$$

is the singular value decomposition of $\boldsymbol{A}$. Recall that U and V are orthogonal matrices, and Σ is an $\boldsymbol{m \times n}$ diagonal matrix with entries $(\boldsymbol{\sigma_1, \sigma_2, ..., \sigma_m})$ such that $\boldsymbol{\sigma_1 \geq \sigma_2 \geq ... \geq \sigma_m \geq 0}$.

We claim that the best rank-approximation to in the spectral norm, denoted by $\|\cdot\|_F$ is given by

$$A^k = \sum_{i=1}^{k} \sigma_i u_i v_i$$

Where $\boldsymbol{u_i}$ and $\boldsymbol{v_i}$ denote $\boldsymbol{i^{th}}$ column of $\boldsymbol{U}$ and $\boldsymbol{V}$, respectively.

First, note that we have

$$\|A - A_k\|_F^2 = \left\| \sum_{i=k+1}^{n} \sigma_1 u_i v_i^T \right\|_F^2$$

Therefore, we need to show that if $\boldsymbol{B_k = XY^T}$ where $\boldsymbol{X}$ and $\boldsymbol{Y}$ have $\boldsymbol{k}$ columns then

$$\|A - A_k\|_F^2 \leq \|A - B_k\|_F^2$$

Since Y has k columns, then there must be a nontrivial linear combination of the first $k + 1$ columns of V, i.e.

$$\omega = \gamma_1 \upsilon_1 + ... + \gamma_k + 1\upsilon_{k+1},$$

Such that $Y^T \omega = 0$. Without loss of generality,

we can scale ω so that $||\omega||_2 = 1$ or (equivalently)

$$\gamma_1^2 + ... + \gamma_{k+1}^2 = 1.$$

Therefore,

$$\|A - B\|_2^2 \geq \|(A - B_k)\omega\|_2^2 = \|A\omega\|_2^2 = \gamma_1^2\sigma_1^2 + \gamma_{k+1}^2\sigma_{k+1}^2 \geq \sigma_{k+1}^2$$

The result follows by taking the square root of both sides of the above inequality

Eckart-Young-Mirsky Theorem

Let $A \in R^{m*n}$ be a real (possible rectangular) matrix with $m \leq n$. Suppose that $A = U\Sigma V^T$

Is the singular value decomposition of A.

We claim that the best rank k approximation to A in the Forbenius norm, denoted by $||\,.\,||_F$ is given by

$$A_k = \sum_{i=1}^{k} \sigma_1 u_i v_i^T$$

Where u_i and v_i denote the Ith column U and V, respectively. First, note that we have

$$||A - A_k||F^2 = \left\|\sum_{i=k+1}^{n} \sigma_1 u_i v_i^T\right\| F^2 = \sum_{i=k+1}^{n} \sigma_i^2$$

Therefore, we need to show that if $B_k = XY^T$ where X and Y have k columns then

$$||A - A_k||F^2 = \sum_{i=k+1}^{n} \sigma_i^2 \leq ||A - B||F^2$$

By the triangle inequality with the spectral norm, if $A = A' + A''$ then $\sigma_1 (A) \leq \sigma_1 (A') + \sigma_1 (A'')$. Suppose A'_k and A''_k respectively denote the rank k approximation to A' and A'' by *SVD* method described above. Then, for any $i, j \geq 1$.

$$\sigma_i (A') + \sigma_j (A'') = \sigma_1 (A' - A'_{i-1}) + \sigma_1 (A'' - A''_{j-1})$$

$$\geq \quad \sigma_1 (A - A'_{I-1} - A''_{j-1})$$

$$\geq \quad \sigma_1 (A - A_{I+j-2}) \qquad \text{(since rank } (A'_{i-1} + A''_{j-1}) \leq \text{rank } (A_{i+j-2}))$$

$$= \sigma_{i+j-1} (A).$$

Since $\sigma_{k+1} (B_k) = 0$, when $A' = A - B_k$ and $A'' = B_k$ we conclude that for $i \geq 1$,

$$j = k + 1$$

$\sigma i\ (A - B_k) \geq \sigma_{k+I} (A)$. Therefore,

$$||A - B_k||F^2 = \sum_{i-1}^{n} \sigma_i (A - B_k)^2 \geq \sigma_{i=k-1}^{n}\ \sigma_i(A)^2 = ||A - A_k||^2_F,$$ As required

1.13 GRADIENT DESCENT

Gradient Descent is an optimization algorithm for finding a local minimum of a differentiable function. Gradient descent in machine learning is simply used to find the values of a function's parameters (coefficients) that minimize a cost function as far as possible.

In this we will derive a convergence result for gradient descent applied to a convex function $f \in C^1(R^d)$. Convergence results in optimization are often stated in terms of the difference $f(x^k) - f^*$, where $f^* = f(x^*)$ and x^* is a minimize of f. By the convexity of f, we have

$$f(x^k) - f(x^*) \le (\nabla f(x^k), x^k - x^*) \le ||\nabla f(x^k)|| \cdot ||x^k - x^*||,$$

Which allows to relate the convergence of $f(x^k) - x^*$ to the convergence of $||x^k - x^*||$. In order to guarantee good convergence rates, we need some additional smoothness and boundedness conditions.

Gradient descent for smooth convex functions

The most common smoothness condition in optimization is Lips chitz continuity, applied to a function or to its gradient.

Definition: A function $f: R^l \to R^k$ is called Lipschitz continuous with Lipschitz constant $L > 0$, if for all $x, y \in R^n$,

$$||f(x) - f(y)|| \le L\,||x - y||.$$

A function f : $R^n \to R$ is called β-smooth for some $\beta > 0$ if the gradient is called Lipschitz constant:

$$||\nabla f(x) - \nabla f(y)|| \le \beta\,||x - y||$$

For all $x, y \in R^n$.

Lipschitz continuity lies somewhere between continuity and differentiability. If $f \in C^1(R^n)$ is Lipschitz continuous with Lipschitz constant L, then $||\nabla f(x)|| \le L$. Similarly,

β-smoothness implies that $||\nabla^2 f(x)|| \le \beta$. Recall from that a function

$f \in C^1(R^n)$ is convex if and only if $f(y) + (\nabla f(y), x - y) \le f(x)$

For all $x, y \in R^n$. The following shows that β-smoothness is equivalent to quadratic upper bound on the difference between the function value $f(x)$ and its linear bound

Lemma: Let $f \in C^1(R^n)$ β-smooth and convex. Then for any $\boldsymbol{x}, \boldsymbol{y} \in R^n$

$$f(x) \le f(y) + (\nabla f(y), x - y) + \beta/2\,||x - y||^2$$

Conversely, if a convex function $f \in C^1(R^n)$ satisfies, then for all $\boldsymbol{x}, \boldsymbol{y} \in R^n$

$$1/\beta\,||\nabla f(x) - \nabla f(y)||^2 \le (\nabla f(x) - f(y), x - y).$$

In particular, f is β-smooth.

Proof: The first inequality follows from the convexity assumption. For the second inequality, represent $f(x) - f(y)$ as an integral

$$f(x) - f(y) = \int_0^1 \nabla (\nabla f(y + t(x - y))\,dt,$$

We can then write

$$f(x) - f(y) - \{\nabla f(y), x - y\} = \int_0^1 \{\nabla f(y + t(x - y)), x - y\} - \{\nabla f(y), x - y\}\,dt$$

$$\le \int_0^1 ||\nabla f(y + t(x - y)) - \nabla f(y)||\,||x - y||\,dt$$

$$\le \beta \int_0^1 t\,||x - y||^2\,dt = \beta/2\,||x - y||^2,$$

Where the first inequality follows from applying Cauchy-Schwartz, and the second from the assumption of β-smoothness.

For the second claim, assume that f satisfies the bound. For any $x, y, z \in R^n$ we have

$$f(x) - f(y) = f(x) - f(z) + f(z) - f(y) \leq \{\nabla f(x), x - z\} + \{\nabla f(y), z - y\} + \beta/2\, ||z - y||^2,$$

Where we used the convexity of f to bound $f(x) - f(z)$ and the β-smoothness to bound $f(z) - f(y)$. If we now set $z = y - (1/\beta)(\nabla f(y) - \nabla f(x))$ and simplify the resulting expression,

we get $f(x) - f(y) \leq \{\nabla f(x), x - y\} - 1/2\beta\, ||\nabla f(x) - \nabla f(y)||^2$

Adding this expression to the same one with the roles of x and y exchanged, we get $0 \leq \{\nabla f(x) - \{\nabla f(y)\}, x - y\} - 1/\beta\, ||\nabla f(x) - \nabla f(y)||^2$

The fact that this implies β-smoothness off follows from the Cauchy-Schwartz inequality.

We can, and will, use this as alternative definition of β-smoothness.

1.14 THE BAYES CLASSIFIER

While in Example we could choose (at least in principle) $h(x) = f(x)$ and get

$R(h) = 0$, in the presence of noise this is not possible. However, we could define a classified h^* by setting

$$1\, f(x) > ½$$
$$h^*(x) = 0\, f(x) \leq ½$$

We call this **Bayes classifier.** The following result shows that this is the best possible classifier.

Theorem: The Bayes classifier h^* satisfies

$$R(h^*) = \text{in}\, fr\,(h),$$

Where the infinity is overall measurable h. Moreover, $R(h^*) \leq ½$

Proof: Let h be any classifier. To compute the risk $R(h)$, we first condition on X and then average over X:

$$R(h) = E[1\{h(X) \neq Y\}] = E[E[1\{h(X) \neq Y\}]\, X]\}$$

For the inner expectation, we have

$$E[1\{h(X) \neq Y\}|\, X] = E\{1\{h(X) = 1, Y = 0\} + 1\{h(X) = 0, Y = 1\}|\, X]$$
$$= E[\{1 - Y\}1\{h(X) = 1\}|\, X] + E[Y1\{h(X) = 0\}|\, X]$$
$$1\{h(X) = 1\}\, E|(1 - Y)|\, X] + 1\{h(X) = 0\}\, E|Y|X|$$
$$= 1\{h(X) = 1\}(1 - f(X)) + 1\{h(X) = 0\} f(X)$$

To see why it holds, recall that the random variable $E|Y_1\{h(X) = 0\}|\, X]$ takes values $E|Y1\{h(x) = 0\}|X = x|$, and will therefore only be non-zero if $h(x) = 0$. We can therefore pull the indicates functions out of the expectation.

Hence,

We decompose

$$R(h) = E|1\{h(X) = 1\}\{1 - f(X)) + 1\{h(X) = 0\} f(X)].$$
$$1\{h(X) = 1\}(1 - f(X)) = 1\{h(X) = 1, f(X) > ½\}\{1 - f(X)) + 1\{h(X)$$
$$= 1, f(X) \leq 1/2\}\{1 - f(X)) \geq 1\{h(X)$$
$$= 1, f(X) > ½\}\{1 - f(X)) + 1\{h(X) = 1, f(X) \leq 1/2\} f(X),$$

Where the inequality follows since $\{1 - f(X)\} \geq f(X)$ if $f(X) \leq ½$.

By the same reasoning, for this we get

$$1\{h(X) = 0\} f(X) \geq \{h(X) = 0, f(X) > ½\}\{1 - f(X)\} + 1\{h(X) = 0, f(X) \leq 1/2\} f(X),$$

Combining the inequalities within the bound and collecting the terms that are multiplied with $f(X)$ and those that are multiplied with $(1 - f(X))$, we arrive at

$$R(h) \geq E[1\{f(X) \geq ½\} f(X) + 1\{f(X) > ½\}\{1 - f(X)\}]$$
$$= E[1\{h^*(X) = 0\} f(X) + 1\{h^*(X) = 1\}\{1 - f(X)\}] = R(h^*)$$

Where the equality follows from here applied to $h = h^*$. The characterizational so shows that

$$R(h^*) = E[1\{f(X) > ½\}\{1 - f(X)\}] + 1\{f(X) \leq ½\} f(X)]$$
$$= E[\min\{f(X), 1 - f(X)\}] \leq 1/2$$

At the other extreme, if the response Y does not depend on X at all, then the Bayes risk is ½. This means that for every input, the best possible classifier consists of "guessing" without any prior information, which means that we have 50% chance of being correct!

The error

$$\varepsilon(h) = R(h) - R(h^*)$$

is called the excess risk or error of h with respect to the best possible classifier.

Approximation and Estimation

We conclude this lecture by relating notions of risk. In what follows, we assume that aclass of classifiers H is given from which we are allowed to choose. We denote by h_m the classifier obtained by minimizing the empirical risk $R(h)$ over H, that is

$$R(h) = \text{in}\, f_{n \in N} \Sigma_1 (h(X_1) \neq Y_1)$$

Where the (X_1, Y_1) are *i.i.d* copies of random variables (X, Y) on $X \times Y$. Note that hnis what we will typically obtain by computation from samples (x_1, y_1). The way it is defined, it depends on n, the class of function H and the random variables (X_1, Y_1) and as such is itself a random variable.

We want h_n to generalize well, that is, we want

$$R(h_n) = P(h_n(X) \neq Y)$$

To be small. We know that the smallest possible value this risk can attain is given by $R(h^*)$, where h^* is bayes classifier. We can decompose the difference between the risk of hnand that of the Bayes classifier as follows:

$$R(h_n) - R(h^*) = R(h_n) - inf_{n \in N} R(h) + inf_{n \in N} R(h) - R(h^*)$$

The first compares the performance of h_n against the best possible classifier within the class H while the second is a statement about the power of class H.

We can reduce the estimation error by making the class H smaller, but then approximation error increases. Ideally, we would like to find bounds on the estimation error that converges to 0 as the number of sample n increases.

1.15 NUMBER THEORY

Number theory is used to find out if a given integer '*m*' is divisible with the integer '*n*' and this is used in many divisibility tests. This theory is not only used in Mathematics, but also applied in cryptography, device authentication, websites for e-commerce, coding, security systems, and many more.

For the most part, number theory remains a purely abstract area of mathematical study, but applications do exist in the field of cryptography, where number theory can create simple yet highly secure codes. This is a first post in which I intend to explain the basic ingredients needed to understand the cryptography for privacy preserving machine learning topics.

Privacy preserving machine learning (PPML) is a relatively new field of study that aims to protect data privacy as well as intellectual property in the field of machine learning.

Cryptography, a word with Greek origins, means "secret writing" is the science of devising methods that allow for information to be sent in a secure form in such a way that the only person able to retrieve this information is the intended recipient. The message to be sent through an unreliable medium is known as plaintext, which is encrypted before sending over the medium. The encrypted message is known as cipher text, which is received at the other end of the medium and decrypted to get back the original plaintext message. Hence a cryptosystem is a collection of algorithms and associated procedures for hiding and revealing information.

Cryptographic Algorithms

Cryptographic algorithms have evolved over time to answer various needs. Cryptography algorithms can be divided into two broad categorizes. Symmetric key cryptography and asymmetric key cryptography. For example a study of two well known asymmetric key cryptographic algorithms is done. In asymmetric key cryptography, different keys are used for encryption and decryption; hence it is called as public key encryption. The two keys are a private key and a public key. The public key is announced to the public; whereas the private key is kept by the receiver. The sender uses the public key of the receiver for encryption and the receiver uses his private key for decryption. Here the number of keys required is small, but it is not efficient for long messages. In asymmetric key encryption Rivest-Shamir-Adlemann (RSA) and Elliptic-Curve cryptographic (ECC) algorithms, different factors are studied.

Rivest-Shamir-Adlemann (RSA)

RSA is based on the use of two large prime numbers according to the mathematical fact that it is easy to find to large prime numbers but difficult to factorize their product.

RSA generates two keys: Public key for encryption and Private key for decryption. The public key consists of public-key modulus and public-key exponent. The private-key consists of private-key modulus and private-key exponent.

Algorithm:

- Take two prime numbers, p and q.
- Calculate, $n = p^*q$. n is called the modulus of both public and private keys.
- Calculate, $\varphi(n) = (p - 1)(q - 1) = n - (p + q - 1)$, where φ is Euler's totient function and its value is kept secret.

- Choose an integer e, $1 < e < \varphi(n)$ and $gcd(e, \varphi(n)) = 1$. e and $\varphi(n)$ are co-prime. e is called the public key exponent.
- Calculate, $d \equiv e - 1 \pmod{\varphi(n)}$. d is called the private key exponent.

EXAMPLE

To demonstrate the RSA public key encryption algorithm, let's start it with 2 smaller prime numbers 5 and 7.

Generation the public key and private key with prime numbers of 5 and 7 can be illustrated as:

- Given p as 5
- Given q as 7
- Compute $n = p*q : n = 5*7 = 35$
- Compute $m = (p - 1)* (q - 1): m = 4*6 = 24$
- Select e, such that e and m are co prime numbers: $e = 5$
- Compute d, such that $d*e \bmod m = 1: d = 29$
- The public key $\{n, e\}$ is $= \{35, 5\}$
- The private key $\{n, d\}$ is $= \{35, 29\}$

With the public key of {35, 5}, encryption of a clear text M represented as number 23 can be illustrated as:

Given public key $\{n, e\}$ as {35, 5}

Given clear text M represented in number as 23

Divide B into blocks: 1 block is enough

Compute encrypted block $C = M^e \bmod n$:

$C = 23^5 \bmod 35 = 6436343 \bmod 35 = 18$

The ciphertext C represented in number is 18

With the private key of {35, 29}, decryption of the cipher text C represented as number 18 can be illustrated as:

Given private key $\{n, e\}$ as {35, 29}

Given ciphertext C represented in number as 18

Divide C into blocks: 1 block is enough

Compute encrypted block $M = C^d \bmod n$:

$$
\begin{aligned}
M &= 18^{29} \bmod 35 \\
&= 18*18^{28} \bmod 35 \\
&= 18* (18^4)^7 \bmod 35 \\
&= 18* (104976)^7 \text{ mode } 35 \\
&= 18* (104976 \bmod 35)^7 \bmod 35 \\
&= 18* (11)^7 \bmod 35 \\
&= 18*19487171 \bmod 35
\end{aligned}
$$

$$= 350769078 \bmod 35$$

$$= 23$$

The clear text M represented in number is 23

Elliptic-Curve Cryptographic Algorithms(ECC)

The primary advantage of using Elliptic Curve based cryptography is reduced key size and hence speeds. Elliptic curve based algorithms use significantly smaller key sizes than the non-elliptic curve equivalents. The difference in equivalent key sizes increases dramatically as the key sizes increase. ECC is a public key cryptography (PKC) which has public and private keys for authentication. It is based on elliptic curves over finite fields.

A field is a set of elements with operations defined for the elements of that set that equate to operations like addition, subtraction, multiplication and division. The elements could be numbers, or they could be something else entirely. The following conditions should meet in order to be a field:

- Both addition and multiplication are closed over the set, so for example if a and b are in the set then so are $a + b$ and $a * b$
- Addition and multiplication must be associative: so $a + (b + c) = (a + b) + c$ and similarly for multiplication
- Addition and multiplication must be commutative: so $a + b = b + a$ and similarly for multiplication
- Both addition and multiplication must have identity elements. So, for example 0 and 1 where: $a + 0 = a$, and $a * 1 = a$
- There must be additive and multiplicative inverses for all elements in the set. So, for example, for every element a in the set there is $-a$ so that $a + (-a) = 0$ (where 0 is the identity element for addition). Similarly, for multiplication.
- Multiplication distributes over addition: if a, b and c are in the set then $a * (b + c) = (a * b) + (a * c)$

A finite field is simply a field where the set has a finite number of elements. So, for example, the set of all integers could not be used as the basis for a finite field because there are an infinite number of them. However, the set of integers from 0 to 100 could form the basis of a finite field.

Quiz Questions

1. Maximum value of Probability is

   (*a*) 0 (*b*) 1

   (*c*) 10 (*d*) none

2. Which of the following statement is not true about probability?

   (*a*) The probability of an impossible event is 0.

   (*b*) Probability can be greater than 1 or less than 0.

   (*c*) Probability cannot be greater than 1.

   (*d*) None of the above.

3. If $P(A) \neq 0$ and $P(B|A) = \dfrac{\text{Number elements in } A \cap B}{\text{Number of elements of } A}$ then it is called as

(*a*) Coditional Probability
(*b*) Multiplication theorem
(*c*) Addition theorem
(*d*) None of the above

4. A square matrix A is said to be non-singular if
(*a*) $|A| \neq 0$
(*b*) $|A| = 0$
(*c*) A is an $m \times n$ matrix
(*d*) None of the above

5. The eigen values of an idempotent matrix are
(*a*) 0 only
(*b*) 0 and 1 only
(*c*) 0 and –1 only
(*d*) None of the above

6. If the eigen values are positive and negative then the nature is
(*a*) Indefinite
(*b*) Positive definite
(*c*) Negative definite
(*d*) None of the above

7. Discrete optimization problems can be Solve by using
(*a*) Singular Matrix
(*b*) Single value decomposition
(*c*) Non singular matrix
(*d*) None of the above

8. Find the *gcd* of 621 and 483
(*a*) 49
(*b*) 69
(*c*) 29
(*d*) None of the above

9. Elliptic-Curve Cryptography is based on...
(*a*) Infinite curves
(*b*) Finite curves
(*c*) Infinite curves as well as Finite curves
(*d*) None of the above

ANSWERS

1.(*b*)	2.(*b*)	3.(*a*)	4.(*a*)	5.(*b*)	6.(*a*)	7.(*b*)	8.(*b*)	9.(*b*)

Objectives

1. To Provide Knowledge of probability and its application.
2. To predict a probability distribution over a set of classes given an observation of input, instead of simply outputting the most likely class to which the observation should belong.
3. To match predicted probabilities with class labels.

Outcomes

At the end of this chapter the student will be able to

1. Evaluate classification models, both linear and non-linear model structures.
2. Optimize the model's performance, such as improving accuracy or reducing false positives.
3. Build a strong foundation in data science and analytics, enabling them with data preparation and analysis.

2.1 INTRODUCTION

Classification is used to identify a category of new observations (testing datasets) based on a classification model built from the training dataset of which the categories are already known. Similar to regression, classification is categorized as a supervised learning method as it employs known answers (label) of a training dataset to predict the answer (label) of the testing dataset. The main difference between regression and classification is that regression is used to predict continuous values. In contrast to this, classification is used to identify the category of a given observation. For example, one may use regression to predict the future price of a given stock based on historical prices. However, one should use the classification method to predict whether the stock price will rise or fall. In this chapter, we will illustrate how to use *R* to perform classification. We first build a training dataset and a testing dataset from the different dataset, and then apply different classification methods to classify the churn dataset. In the following recipes, we will introduce the three different classification methods out of which two methods are using a probabilistic-based method with the training dataset to build up a classification model, and then use the model to predict the category (class label) of the testing dataset. We will also use a confusion matrix to measure the performance. Building a classification model requires a training dataset to train the classification model, and testing data is needed to then validate the prediction performance. Discriminant analysis is used to distinguish distinct sets of observations and allocate new observations to previously defined groups. The main goals of discriminant analysis are discrimination and classification. The assumptions regarding discriminant analysis are multivariate normality, equality of variance-covariance within group and low multicollinearity of the variables. In the following recipe, we will demonstrate how to split the different datasets into training and testing datasets, respectively.

2.2 NAIVE BAYES CLASSIFIERS

The Naive Bayes classifier is also a probability-based classifier, which is based on applyingthe Bayes theorem with a strong independent assumption. This method is relatively simple andstraightforward to use, it is suitable when the training set isrelativly small, it can deal with some noisy andmissing data and it can easily obtain the probabilityfor a prediction.

In this recipe, we will introducehow to classify data with the Naive Bayes classifier.

2.2.1 Case – I: Fitting of Naive Bayes Classification

The Naive Bayes classifier is also a probability-based classifier, which is based on applying the Bayes theorem with a strong independent assumption. In this recipe, we will introduce how to classify data with the Naive Bayes classifier. In *R*, we can fit a Naive Bayes model to data with the naive Bayes function.

2.2.1a Getting Ready

You need to have the first recipe completed by generating training and testing datasets.

2.2.1b How to do it

Perform the following steps to classify the Outcome data with the Naive Bayes classifier:

1. You should install the following packages and load libraries:

```
>install.packages("C50")
>install.packages("caret")
>install.packages("e1071")
>library(caret)
>library(e1071)
>library(C50)
```

2. From the package, you can load the Outcome dataset:

```
>url="https://drive.google.com/file/d/1epnX2w3aImgJ7u35VNl0Zp99Rlw6Ndfm/
view?usp=sharing"
>data1=read.csv(url)
```

3. You can use the str function to display the structure of the Outcome dataset:

```
>str(data1)
```

Output:

```
'data.frame':        980 obs. of 4 variables:
```

$ Ind_Exp_Act_Score: num 6.2 2.6 9.5 2.6 10 0.2 2.5 0.4 0.2 8.9 ...

$ Tran_Speed_Score: num 9.3 2.2 1.5 5 7.7 2.3 2.8 1.6 9.8 6.1 ...

$ Peer_Comb_Score: num 7.4 8.7 8.2 0.4 7.2 3.4 4.6 5.3 0.8 9.2 ...

$ Outcome: int 1 1 1 0 1 0 0 0 0 1 ...

>set.seed(1)

4. Use 70% of dataset as training set and remaining 30% as testing set

   >sample = sample (*c* (TRUE, FALSE), *n* row (data1), replace = TRUE, prob = *c* (0.7, 0.3)

   >train = data1 [sample,]

   >test = data1 [!sample,]

5. View dimensions of training set

   >dim(train)

   Output:

   [1] 679 4

   >dim (test)

   Output:

   [1] 301 4

6. Building the naives Bayes classifier by specifying the indicators. The naive Bayes() function will be used. It uses the Bayes rule to compute posterior probabilities for a givenset of class variables given independent predictor variables. The function assumes a Gaussian distribution of metric predictors. Employ the naive Bayes function to build the classifier:

   >fit = naive Bayes (Outcome~., data = train)

7. Displaying the Naive Bayes classifier result:

   >fit

   Output:

   Naive Bayes Classifier for Discrete Predictors

   Call:

   naive Bayes.default (*x* = *X*, *y* = *Y*, laplace = laplace)

   A-priori probabilities:

   Y 0 1

   0.2665685 0.7334315

   Conditional probabilities:

   Ind_Exp_Act_Score

Y	[,1]	[,2]
0	3.407182	2.582614
1	5.806024	2.708286

   Tran_Speed_Score

   Y [,1] [,2]

0 3.291713 2.572588

1 5.680321 2.730190

Peer_Comb_Score

Y	[,1]	[,2]
0	2.481768	1.822224
1	5.883936	2.637034

8. Next, you can generate a classification table for the testing dataset:

```
>bayes.table = table(predict(fit, test[,
+ !names(test) %in% c("Outcome")]), test$Outcome)
>bayes.table
```

Output:

	0	1
0	74	1
1	16	210

9. Lastly, you can generate a confusion matrix from the classification table:

```
>confusion Matrix(bayes.table)
```

Output:

Confusion Matrix and Statistics

	0	1
0	74	1
1	16	210

Accuracy : 0.9435

95% CI : (0.9111, 0.9668)

No Information Rate : 0.701

P-Value [Acc> NIR] : < 2.2e – 16

Kappa : 0.8585

Mcnemar's Test P-Value : 0.000685

Sensitivity : 0.8222

Specificity : 0.9953

Pos Pred Value : 0.9867

Neg Pred Value : 0.9292

Prevalence : 0.2990

Detection Rate : 0.2458

Detection Prevalence : 0.2492

Balanced Accuracy : 0.9087

'Positive' Class : 0

The rows in the output correspond to the groups specified in the original data and the columns correspond to the classification made by the Naive Bayes classifier. In a perfect classification, large values would lie along the diagonal, with zeroes off the diagonal, which would indicate that all samples that belong to group 1 were classified by the Naive Bayes as belonging to group 2, and so on. The form of this table can give you considerable insight into which groups are reliably classsified. It can also show which groups are likely to be confused and which types of misclassification are more common than others.

Here the predictive accuracy is almost 94.35%, quite a success. This approach measures what is called the resubstitution error, how well the samples are classified when all the samples are used.

Table 2.1: Coding of Naive Bayes Classification Model

```
>install.packages("C50")
>install.packages("caret")
>install.packages("e1071")
>library(caret)
>library(e1071)
>library(C50)
>url="https://drive.google.com/file/d/1epnX2w3aImgJ7u35VNl0Zp99Rlw6Ndfm/view?usp=sharing"
>data1=read.csv(url)
>str(data1)
>set.seed(1)
>sample = sample(c(TRUE, FALSE), nrow(data1), replace=TRUE, prob=c(0.7,0.3))
>train = data1[sample, ]
>test = data1[!sample, ]
>dim(train)
>dim(test)
>fit = naiveBayes(Outcome~.,data=train)
>fit
>bayes.table = table(predict(fit, test[,
!names(test) %in% c("Outcome")]), test$Outcome)
>bayes.table
>confusionMatrix(bayes.table)
```

2.2.2 Case – II: Fitting of Naive Bayes Classification

The Naive Bayes classifier is also a probability-based classifier, which is based on applying the Bayes theorem with a strong independent assumption. In this recipe, we will introduce how to classify data with the Naive Bayes classifier. In *R*, we can fit a Naive Bayes model to data with the naiveBayes function.

2.2.2a Getting Ready

You need to have the first recipe completed by generating training and testing datasets.

2.2.2b How to do it

Perform the following steps to classify the Churn data with the Naive Bayes classifier:

1. You should install the following packages and load libraries:

```
> install.packages("C50")
> install.packages("caret")
> install.packages("e1071")
> library(caret)
> library(e1071)
> library(C50)
```

2. From the package, you can load the Churn dataset:

```
>url="https://drive.google.com/file/d/1PmsZsiKck64FyQcvOf3vZdfnA06C64Np/view?usp=sharing"
>data2=read.csv(url)
```

3. You can use the str function to display the structure of the Churn dataset:

```
> str(data2)
```

Output:

```
'data.frame':                2666 obs. of 17 variables:
$ International.plan:        int 0 0 0 1 1 1 0 1 1 0 ...
$ Voice.mail.plan:           int 1 1 0 0 0 0 1 0 1 0 ...
$ Number.vmail.messages:     int 25 26 0 0 0 0 24 0 37 0 ...
$ Total.day.minutes:         num 265 162 243 299 167 ...
$ Total.day.calls:           int 110 123 114 71 113 98 88 79 84 127 ...
$ Total.day.charge:          num 45.1 27.5 41.4 50.9 28.3 ...
$ Total.eve.minutes:         num 197.4 195.5 121.2 61.9 148.3 ...
$ Total.eve.calls:           int 99 103 110 88 122 101 108 94 111 148 ...
$ Total.eve.charge:          num 16.78 16.62 10.3 5.26 12.61 ...
$ Total.night.minutes:       num 245 254 163 197 187 ...
$ Total.night.calls:         int 91 103 104 89 121 118 118 96 97 94 ...
$ Total.night.charge:        num 11.01 11.45 7.32 8.86 8.41 ...
$ Total.intl.minutes:        num 10 13.7 12.2 6.6 10.1 6.3 7.5 7.1 11.2 9.1 ...
$ Total.intl.calls:          int 3 3 5 7 3 6 7 6 5 5 ...
$ Total.intl.charge:         num 2.7 3.7 3.29 1.78 2.73 1.7 2.03 1.92 3.02 2.46 ...
$ Customer.service.calls:    int 1 1 0 2 3 0 3 0 0 0 ...
$ Churn:                     int 0 0 0 0 0 0 0 0 0 0 ...
>set.seed(2)
```

4. Use 70% of dataset as training set and remaining 30% as testing set

   >sample = sample(c(TRUE, FALSE), nrow(data2), replace=TRUE, prob=c(0.7,0.3))

   >train = data2[sample,]

   >test = data2[!sample,]

5. View dimensions of training set

   >dim(train)

   Output:

   [1] 1836 17

   >dim(test)

   Output:

   [1] 830 17

6. Building the naives Bayes classifier by specifying the indicators. The naiveBayes() function will be used. It uses the Bayes rule to compute posterior probabilities for a given set of class variables given independent predictor variables. The function assumes a Gaussian distribution of metric predictors. Employ the naiveBayes function to build the classifier:

   >fit1 = naiveBayes(Churn~.,data=train)

7. Displaying the NaiveBayesclassifier result:

   >fit1

   Output:

   Naive Bayes Classifier for Discrete Predictors

   Call:

   naiveBayes.default(*x* = X, *y* = Y, laplace = laplace)

   A-priori probabilities:

Y	0	1
	0.8529412	0.1470588

   Conditional probabilities:

   International.plan

Y	[,1]	[,2]
0	0.06194125	0.2411258
1	0.30370370	0.4607102

   Voice.mail.plan

Y	[,1]	[,2]
0	0.2962963	0.4567691
1	0.1592593	0.3665972

   Number.vmail.messages

Y	[,1]	[,2]
0	8.505747	13.73281
1	4.940741	11.69200

   Total.day.minutes

Y	[,1]	[,2]
0	176.1100	49.86216
1	204.7289	69.77990

Total.day.calls

Y	[,1]	[,2]
0	100.1622	19.54833
1	101.0630	22.34554

Total.day.charge

Y	[,1]	[,2]
0	29.93928	8.476486
1	34.80459	11.862908

Total.eve.minutes

Y	[,1]	[,2]
0	197.6782	51.29958
1	208.1096	51.61649

Total.eve.calls

Y	[,1]	[,2]
0	100.05556	20.14703
1	99.73333	19.88076

Total.eve.charge

Y	[,1]	[,2]
0	16.80292	4.360404
1	17.68948	4.387263

Total.night.minutes

Y	[,1]	[,2]
0	200.8810	51.79730
1	203.1737	48.02443

Total.night.calls

Y	[,1]	[,2]
0	100.2886	18.91548
1	101.2963	20.34848

Total.night.charge

Y	[,1]	[,2]
0	9.039738	2.330840
1	9.143111	2.161381

Total.intl.minutes

```
Y    [,1]       [,2]
0    10.09061   2.819779
1    10.83000   2.833514
Total.intl.calls
Y    [,1]       [,2]
0    4.479566   2.379740
1    4.107407   2.415782
Total.intl.charge
Y    [,1]       [,2]
0    2.724949   0.7612921
1    2.924852   0.7651721
Customer.service.calls
Y    [,1]       [,2]
0    1.445083   1.166294
1    2.214815   1.858909
```

8. Next, you can generate a classification table for the testing dataset:

```
>bayes.table = table(predict(fit1, test[,
+ !names(test) %in% c("Churn")]), test$Churn)
>bayes.table
```

Output:

```
0    1
0    645    56
1    67     62
```

9. Lastly, you can generate a confusion matrix from the classification table:

```
>confusionMatrix(bayes.table)
```

Output:

```
Confusion Matrix and Statistics
0    1
0    645    56
1    67     62
Accuracy : 0.8518
95% CI : (0.8258, 0.8753)
No Information Rate : 0.8578
P-Value [Acc> NIR] : 0.7105
Kappa : 0.4152
Mcnemar's Test P-Value : 0.3672
```

Sensitivity : 0.9059

Specificity : 0.5254

Pos Pred Value : 0.9201

Neg Pred Value : 0.4806

Prevalence : 0.8578

Detection Rate : 0.7771

Detection Prevalence : 0.8446

Balanced Accuracy : 0.7157

'Positive' Class : 0

The rows in the output correspond to the groups specified in the original data and the columns correspond to the classification made by the Naive Bayes classifier. In a perfect classification, large values would lie along the diagonal, with zeroes off the diagonal, which would indicate that all samples that belong to group 1 were classified by the Naive Bayes as belonging to group 2, and so on. The form of this table can give you considerable insight into which groups are reliably classified. It can also show which groups are likely to be confused and which types of misclassification are more common than others.

Here the predictive accuracy is almost 85.18%, quite a success. This approach measures what is called the resubstitution error, how well the samples are classified when all the samples are used.

Table 2.2: Coding of Naive Bayes Classification Model

```
>install.packages("C50")
>install.packages("caret")
>install.packages("e1071")
> library(caret)
> library(e1071)
> library(C50)
>url="https://drive.google.com/file/d/1PmsZsiKck64FyQcvOf3vZdfnA06C64Np/view?usp=sharing"
>data2=read.csv(url)
> str(data2)
>set.seed(2)
> sample = sample(c(TRUE, FALSE), nrow(data2), replace=TRUE, prob=c(0.7,0.3))
>train = data2[sample, ]
> test = data2[!sample, ]
> dim(train)
> dim(test)
> fit1 = naiveBayes(Churn~.,data=train)
> fit1
>bayes.table = table(predict(fit1, test[,
!names(test) %in% c("Churn")]), test$Churn)
>bayes.table
>confusionMatrix(bayes.table)
```

2.2.2c How it works

Naive Bayes assumes that features are conditionally independent, which the effect of a predictor (x) to class (c) is independent of the effect of other predictors to class(c). It computes the posterior probability, $P(c|x)$, as the following formula:

Where $P(x|c)$ is called likelihood, $p(x)$ is called the marginal likelihood, and $p(c)$ is called the prior probability. If there are many predictors, we can formulate the posterior probability as follows:

The advantage of Naive Bayes is that it is relatively simple and straightforward to use. It is suitable when the training set is relative small, and may contain some noisy and missing data. Moreover, you can easily obtain the probability for a prediction. The drawbacks of Naive Bayes are that it assumes that all features are independent and equally important, which is very unlikely in real-world cases. In this recipe, we use the Naive Bayes classifier from the e1071 package to build a classification model. First, we specify all the variables (excluding the Outcome or Churn class label) as the first input parameters, and specify the Outcome or Churn class label as the second parameter in the naiveBayes function call. Next, we assign the classification model into the variable classifier. Then, we print the variable classifier to obtain information, such as function call, A-priori probabilities, and conditional probabilities. We can also use the predict function to obtain the predicted outcome and the table function to retrieve the classification table of the testing dataset. Finally, we use a confusion matrix to calculate the performance measurement of the classification model.

2.3 LOGISTIC REGRESSION MODEL

Logistic regression is the most favorable white-box model used for binary classification. White-box models are defined as models providing visibility into theentire reasoning done for the prediction. For each prediction made, we can leveragethe model's mathematical equation and decode the reasons for the prediction made. There are also a set of classification models that are entirely black-box, that is, by no means can we understand the reasoning for the prediction leveraged by the model. In situations where we want to focus only on the end outcome, we should prefer blackbox models as they are more powerful. Though the name ends with regression, logistic regression is a technique used to predict binary categorical outcomes and is hence a good choice for classification problems. As discussed in the previous section, we need a different approach to model for a categorical outcome. This can be done by transforming the outcome into the log of the odds ratio or the probability of the event to happen.

2.3.1 Case – I: Fitting of Logistic Regression

Logistic regression is a form of probabilistic statistical classification model, which can be used to predict class labels based on one or more features. The classification is done by using the logit function to estimate the outcome probability. One can use logistic regression by specifying the family as a binomial while using the glm function. In this recipe, we will introduce how to classify data using logistic regression. In *R*, we can fit a logistic regression model to data with the glm function.

2.3.1a Getting Ready

You need to have the first recipe completed by generating training and testing datasets.

2.3.1b How to do it

Perform the following steps to classify the Outcome data with the glm classifier:

1. You should install the following packages and load libraries:
```
>install.packages("C50")
>install.packages("caret")
>install.packages("e1071")
> library(caret)
> library(e1071)
> library(C50)
```
2. From the package, you can load the Outcome dataset:
```
>url="https://drive.google.com/file/d/1epnX2w3aImgJ7u35VNl0Zp99Rlw6Ndfm/view?usp=sharing"
>data1=read.csv(url)
```
3. You can use the str function to display the structure of the Outcome dataset:
```
>str(data1)
```
Output:
```
'data.frame':           980 obs. of 4 variables:
$ Ind_Exp_Act_Score: num 6.2 2.6 9.5 2.6 10 0.2 2.5 0.4 0.2 8.9 ...
$ Tran_Speed_Score:  num 9.3 2.2 1.5 5 7.7 2.3 2.8 1.6 9.8 6.1 ...
$ Peer_Comb_Score:   num 7.4 8.7 8.2 0.4 7.2 3.4 4.6 5.3 0.8 9.2 ...
$ Outcome:           int 1 1 1 0 1 0 0 0 0 1 ...
```
4. You need to have completed the first recipe by generating training and testing datasets. Use 70% of dataset as training set and remaining 30% as testing set
```
>set.seed(2)
>sample = sample(c(TRUE, FALSE), nrow(data1), replace=TRUE, prob=c(0.7,0.3))
>train = data1[sample, ]
>test = data1[!sample, ]
```
5. View dimensions of training set
```
>dim(train)
```
Output:
```
[1] 683 4
>dim(test)
```
Output:
```
[1] 297 4
```
6. With the specification of family as a binomial, we apply the glm function on thedataset trainset, by using Outcome as a class label and the rest of the variables asinput features. Perform the following steps to classify the Outcome data with logistic regression:
```
>fit = glm(Outcome~.,data = train,family = binomial)
```

7. Displaying the logistic regression model result:

```
>summary(fit)
Output:
Call:
glm(formula = Outcome ~ ., family = binomial, data = train)
Deviance Residuals:
    Min        1Q     Median       3Q        Max
-2.34013  -0.00022  0.00002   0.00676   2.29662
Coefficients:
Estimate Std. Error z value Pr(>|z|)
(Intercept)         -33.9964   4.9024  -6.935  4.07e-12 ***
Ind_Exp_Act_Score    2.6235    0.3907   6.714  1.89e-11 ***
Tran_Speed_Score     2.7230    0.3962   6.872  6.32e-12 ***
Peer_Comb_Score      3.3345    0.4758   7.007  2.43e-12 ***
---
Signif. codes:  0 '***' 0.001 '**' 0.01 '*' 0.05 '.' 0.1 ' ' 1
(Dispersion parameter for binomial family taken to be 1)
Null deviance: 807.621 on 682 degrees of freedom
Residual deviance: 97.899 on 679 degrees of freedom
AIC: 105.9
Number of Fisher Scoring iterations: 10
```

8. Then, you can then use a fitted model, fit, to predict the outcome of test set.You can also determine the class by judging whether the probability is above 0.5:

```
>pred = predict(fit,test, type ="response")
>Class = pred >.5
```

9. Next, the use of the summary function will show you the binary outcome count, and reveal whether the probability is above 0.5:

```
>summary(Class)
Output:
Mode    FALSE    TRUE
logical   79      218
```

10. You can generate the counting statistics based on the testing dataset label andpredicted result:

```
>tb = table(test$Outcome,Class)
>tb
Output:
```

```
Class  FALSE  TRUE
  0      76     5
  1       3   213
```

11. You can turn the statistics of the previous step into a classification table, and thengenerate the confusion matrix:

```
>data1.mod = ifelse(test$Outcome>0.5,1,0)
>pred_class = data1.mod
>pred_class[pred<=.5] = 1- pred_class[pred > .5]
>ctb = table(data1.mod,pred_class)
>ctb
Output:
pred_class
data1.mod   0    1
    0      79    2
    1       3  213
>confusionMatrix(ctb)
Output:
Confusion Matrix and Statistics
pred_class
data1.mod   0    1
    0      79    2
    1       3  213
Accuracy : 0.9832
95% CI : (0.9612, 0.9945)
No Information Rate : 0.7239
P-Value [Acc> NIR] :<2e-16
Kappa : 0.9577
Mcnemar's Test P-Value : 1
Sensitivity : 0.9634
Specificity : 0.9907
Pos Pred Value : 0.9753
Neg Pred Value : 0.9861
Prevalence : 0.2761
Detection Rate : 0.2660
Detection Prevalence : 0.2727
Balanced Accuracy : 0.9771
```

'Positive' Class : 0

The rows in the output correspond to the groups specified in the original data and the columns correspond to the classification made by the logistic regression model classifier. In a perfect classification, large values would lie along the diagonal, with zeroes off the diagonal, which would indicate that all samples that belong to true were classified by the logistic regression model as belonging to true, and so on. The form of this table can give you considerable insight into which groups are reliably classified. It can also show which groups are likely to be confused and which types of misclassification are more common than others.

Here the predictive accuracy is almost 98.32%, quite a success. This approach measures what is called the resubstitution error, how well the samples are classified when all the samples are used.

Table 2.3: Coding of Logistic Regression Model

```
>install.packages("C50")
>install.packages("caret")
>install.packages("e1071")
>library(caret)
>library(e1071)
>library(C50)
>url="https://drive.google.com/file/d/1epnX2w3aImgJ7u35VNl0Zp99Rlw6Ndfm/view?usp=sharing"
>data1=read.csv(url)
>str(data1)
>set.seed(2)
>sample = sample(c(TRUE, FALSE), nrow(data1), replace=TRUE, prob=c(0.7,0.3))
>train = data1[sample, ]
>test = data1[!sample, ]
>dim(train)
>dim(test)
>fit = glm(Outcome ~., data = train, family = binomial)
>summary(fit)
>pred = predict(fit, test, type ="response")
>Class = pred >.5
>summary(Class)
>tb = table(test$Outcome, Class)
>tb
>data1.mod = ifelse(test$Outcome> 0.5, 1, 0)
>pred_class = data1.mod
>pred_class[pred <= .5] = 1- pred_class[pred > .5]
>ctb = table(data1.mod, pred_class)
>ctb
>confusionMatrix(ctb)
```

2.3.2 Case – I: Fitting of Logistic Regression

Logistic regression is a form of probabilistic statistical classification model, which can be used to predict class labels based on one or more features. The classification is done by using the logit function to estimate the outcome probability. One can use logistic regression by specifying the family as a binomial while using the glm function. In this recipe, we will introduce how to classify data using logistic regression. In *R*, we can fit a logistic regression model to data with the glm function.

2.3.2a Getting Ready

You need to have the first recipe completed by generating training and testing datasets.

2.3.2b How to do it

Perform the following steps to classify the Churn data with the glm classifier:

1. You should install the following packages and load libraries:

```
>install.packages("C50")
>install.packages("caret")
>install.packages("e1071")
> library(caret)
> library(e1071)
> library(C50)
```

2. From the package, you can load the Churn dataset:

```
>url="https://drive.google.com/file/d/1PmsZsiKck64FyQcvOf3vZdfnA06C64Np/view?usp
=sharing"
> churn=read.csv(url)
```

3. You can use the str function to display the structure of the Churn dataset:

```
> str(churn)
```

Output:

```
'data.frame':        2666 obs. of 17 variables:
$ International.plan : int 0 0 0 1 1 1 0 1 1 0 ...
$ Voice.mail.plan : int 1 1 0 0 0 0 1 0 1 0 ...
$ Number.vmail.messages : int 25 26 0 0 0 0 24 0 37 0 ...
$ Total.day.minutes :num 265 162 243 299 167 ...
$ Total.day.calls : int 110 123 114 71 113 98 88 79 84 127 ...
$ Total.day.charge :num 45.1 27.5 41.4 50.9 28.3 ...
$ Total.eve.minutes :num 197.4 195.5 121.2 61.9 148.3 ...
$ Total.eve.calls : int 99 103 110 88 122 101 108 94 111 148 ...
$ Total.eve.charge :num 16.78 16.62 10.3 5.26 12.61 ...
$ Total.night.minutes : num 245 254 163 197 187 ...
$ Total.night.calls : int 91 103 104 89 121 118 118 96 97 94 ...
```

```
$ Total.night.charge : num 11.01 11.45 7.32 8.86 8.41 ...
$ Total.intl.minutes : num 10 13.7 12.2 6.6 10.1 6.3 7.5 7.1 11.2 9.1 ...
$ Total.intl.calls : int 3 3 5 7 3 6 7 6 5 5 ...
$ Total.intl.charge : num 2.7 3.7 3.29 1.78 2.73 1.7 2.03 1.92 3.02 2.46 ...
$ Customer.service.calls: int 1 1 0 2 3 0 3 0 0 0 ...
$ Churn : int 0 0 0 0 0 0 0 0 0 0 ...
```

4. Make this example reproducible. You need to have completed the first recipe by generating training and testing datasets. Use 70% of dataset as training set and remaining 30% as testing set

```
>set.seed(1)
>sample = sample(c(TRUE, FALSE), nrow(churn), replace=TRUE, prob=c(0.7,0.3))
>train = churn[sample, ]
>test = churn[!sample, ]
```

5. View dimensions of training set

```
>dim(train)
Output:
[1] 1866 17
>dim(test)
Output:
[1] 800 17
```

6. With the specification of family as a binomial, we apply the glm function on the dataset trainset, by using Churn as a class label and the rest of the variables as input features. Perform the following steps to classify the Churn data with logistic regression:

```
> fit = glm(Churn ~., data = train, family = binomial)
```

7. Displaying the logistic regression model result:

```
> summary(fit)
Output:
Call:
glm(formula = Churn ~ ., family = binomial, data = train)
Deviance Residuals:
  Min       1Q      Median     3Q       Max
-2.0148  -0.5123  -0.3395  -0.2010   3.2628
Coefficients:
Estimate                  Std.       Error z     value      Pr(>|z|)
(Intercept)             -7.403052   0.944913   -7.835    4.7e-15 ***
International.plan       2.188237   0.189659   11.538<    2e-16 ***
Voice.mail.plan         -2.279898   0.777119   -2.934    0.003349 **
Number.vmail.messages    0.047618   0.024219    1.966    0.049280 *
```

```
Total.day.minutes         -2.732831    4.392631   -0.622    0.533850
Total.day.calls            0.001793    0.003696    0.485    0.627656
Total.day.charge          16.140264   25.839121    0.625    0.532204
Total.eve.minutes          0.981565    2.187649    0.449    0.653659
Total.eve.calls           -0.001658    0.003703   -0.448    0.654216
Total.eve.charge         -11.485020   25.737106   -0.446    0.655421
Total.night.minutes       -0.319365    1.170590   -0.273    0.784989
Total.night.calls          0.002686    0.003767    0.713    0.475817
Total.night.charge         7.166755   26.012643    0.276    0.782924
Total.intl.minutes        -5.654404    7.162919   -0.789    0.429879
Total.intl.calls          -0.137492    0.035447   -3.879    0.000105 ***
Total.intl.charge         21.270957   26.527284    0.802    0.422639
Customer.service.calls     0.536117    0.051381   10.434    < 2e-16 ***
---
Signif. codes:    0 '***'   0.001 '**'   0.01 '*'   0.05 '.' 0.1 ' ' 1
(Dispersion parameter for binomial family taken to be 1)
Null deviance: 1549.9 on 1865 degrees of freedom
Residual deviance: 1213.4 on 1849 degrees of freedom
AIC: 1247.4
Number of Fisher Scoring iterations: 6
>fit1 = glm(Churn ~ International.plan + Voice.mail.plan + Total.intl.calls + Customer.service.calls,data = train, family = binomial)
>summary(fit1)
Output:
Call:
glm(formula = Churn ~ International.plan + Voice.mail.plan + Total.intl.calls + Customer.service.calls, family = binomial, data = train)
Deviance Residuals:
   Min       1Q     Median      3Q      Max
-1.6701  -0.5385  -0.4019  -0.2836   2.8008
Coefficients:
Estimate                  Std        Error      z value    Pr(>|z|)
(Intercept)              -2.36119    0.19188   -12.305    < 2e-16 ***
International.plan        2.12137    0.17971    11.805    < 2e-16 ***
Voice.mail.plan          -0.74154    0.18062    -4.105    4.03e-05 ***
Total.intl.calls         -0.11423    0.03377    -3.382    0.000719 ***
Customer.service.calls    0.48019    0.04863     9.875    < 2e-16 ***
```

```
---
Signif. codes:  0 '***'  0.001 '**'  0.01 '*' 0.05 '.' 0.1 ' ' 1
(Dispersion parameter for binomial family taken to be 1)
Null deviance: 1549.9 on 1865 degrees of freedom
Residual deviance: 1308.2 on 1861 degrees of freedom
AIC: 1318.2
Number of Fisher Scoring iterations: 5
```

8. Then, you can then use a fitted model, fit, to predict the outcome of testset. You can also determine the class by judging whether the probability is above 0.5:

```
>pred = predict(fit1,test, type="response")
>Class = pred >.5
```

9. Next, the use of the summary function will show you the binary outcome count, and reveal whether the probability is above 0.5:

```
>summary(Class)
Output:
 Mode      FALSE    TRUE
 logical    771      29
```

10. You can generate the counting statistics based on the testing dataset label and predicted result:

```
> tb = table(test$Churn,Class)
> tb
Output:
Class      FALSE    TRUE
   0        673      11
   1         98      18
```

11. You can turn the statistics of the previous step into a classification table, and then generate the confusion matrix:

```
> churn.mod = ifelse(test$Churn>.5,1,0)
>pred_class = churn.mod
>pred_class[pred<=.5] = 1- pred_class[pred > .5]
>ctb = table(churn.mod, pred_class)
>ctb
Output:
pred_class
churn.mod    0      1
   0        426    258
   1         63     53
>confusionMatrix(ctb)
```

Output:

Accuracy : 0.5988

95% CI : (0.5638, 0.6329)

No Information Rate : 0.6112

P-Value [Acc> NIR] : 0.7772

Kappa : 0.0469

Mcnemar's Test P-Value :<2e-16

Sensitivity : 0.8712

Specificity : 0.1704

Pos Pred Value : 0.6228

Neg Pred Value : 0.4569

Prevalence : 0.6112

Detection Rate : 0.5325

Detection Prevalence : 0.8550

Balanced Accuracy : 0.5208

'Positive' Class : 0

The rows in the output correspond to the groups specified in the original data and the columns correspond to the classification made by the logistic regression model classifier. In a perfect classification, large values would lie along the diagonal, with zeroes off the diagonal, which would indicate that all samples that belong to true were classified by the logistic regression model as belonging to true, and so on. The form of this table can give you considerable insight into which groups are reliably classsified. It can also show which groups are likely to be confused and which types of misclassification are more common than others.

Here the predictive accuracy is almost 59.88%, quite a success. This approach measures what is called the resubstitution error, how well the samples are classified when all the samples are used.

Table 2.4: Coding of Logistic Regression Model

```
>install.packages("C50")
>install.packages("caret")
>install.packages("e1071")
> library(caret)
> library(e1071)
> library(C50)
>url="https://drive.google.com/file/d/1PmsZsiKck64FyQcvOf3vZdfnA06C64Np/view?usp=sharing”
> churn=read.csv(url)
> str(churn)
>set.seed(1)
> sample = sample(c(TRUE, FALSE), nrow(churn), replace=TRUE, prob=c(0.7,0.3))
>train = churn[sample, ]
```

```
> test = churn[!sample, ]
> dim(train)
> dim(test)
> fit = glm(Churn ~. , data = train, family = binomial)
> summary(fit)
> fit1 = glm(Churn ~ International.plan + Voice.mail.plan + Total.intl.calls + Customer.service.calls,data = train,
family = binomial)
> summary(fit1)
> pred = predict(fit1, test, type = "response")
> Class = pred > .5
>summary(Class)
> tb = table(test$Churn, Class)
> tb
> churn.mod = ifelse(test$Churn> .5, 1, 0)
>pred_class = churn.mod
>pred_class[pred<=.5] = 1- pred_class[pred > .5]
>ctb = table(churn.mod, pred_class)
>ctb
>confusionMatrix(ctb)
```

2.3.2c How it works

Logistic regression is very similar to linear regression; the main difference is that the dependent variable in linear regression is continuous but the dependent variable in logistic regression is dichotomous (or nominal). The primary goal of logistic regression is to use logic to yield the probability of a nominal variable being related to the measurement variable. We can formulate logic in the following equation: ln $(P/(1-P))$, where P is the probability that a certain event occurs. The advantage of logistic regression is that it is easy to interpret, it directs model logisticprobability, and provides a confidence interval for the result. Unlike the decision tree, which makes it difficult to update the model, you can quickly update the classification model to incorporate new data in logistic regression. The main drawback of the algorithm is that it suffers from multicol linearity and, therefore, the explanatory variables must be linear independent. glm provides a generalized linear regression model, which enables specifying the model in an option family. If the family is specified to a binomial logistic, you can setthe family as a binomial to classify the dependent variable of the category. The classification process begins by generating a logistic regression model with the use ofthe training dataset by specifying Outcome or Churn as the class label, the other variables as training features, and family set as binomial. We then use the summary function to generate the model's summary information. From the summary information, we may find some insignificant variables (p-values > 0.05), which may lead to misclassification. Therefore, we should consider only significant variables for the model. Next, we use the fit function to predict the categorical dependent variable of the testing dataset, testset. The fit function outputs the probability of a class label with a resultequal to 0.5 and below, suggesting that the predicted label does not match the label of thetesting dataset, and a probability above 0.5, which indicates that the predicted label matchesthe label of the testing dataset. Further, we can use the summary function to obtain the statistics of whether the predicted label matches the label of the testing dataset. Lastly, inorder to generate a confusion matrix, we first generate a classification table and then use confusion Matrix to generate the performance measurement.

2.4 LINEAR DISCRIMINANT CLASSIFIERS

Discriminant analysis is used to distinguish distinct sets of observations and allocate new observations to previously defined groups. For example, if a study was to be carried out in order to investigate the variables that discriminate between fruits eaten by (1) primates, (2) birds, or (3) squirrels, the researcher could collect data on numerous fruit characteristics of those species eaten by each of the animal groups. Most fruits will naturally fall into one ofthe three categories. Discriminant analysis could then be used to determine which variables are the best predictors of whether a fruit will be eaten by birds, primates, or squirrels. Discriminant analysis is commonly used in biological species classification, in medical classification of tumors, in facial recognition technologies, and in the credit card and insurance industries for determining risk. The main goals of discriminant analysis are discrimination and classification. The assumptions regarding discriminant analysis are multivariate normality, equality of variance-covariance within group and low multicol linearity of the variables.

2.4.1 Case – I: Classification by Linear Discriminant Analysis

Discriminant analysis is used to distinguish distinct sets of observations and allocate new observations to previously defined groups. On the collected samples in order to separate the samples from which they were excavated, DFA can be used as a function. The function can then be applied to classify and to predict. In *R*, we can fit a model to data with the *lda* function.

2.4.1a Getting Ready

In order to perform discriminant function analysis we shall be using a data set collected from Outcome.

2.4.1b How to do it

Perform the following steps to perform linear discriminate analysis with *lda*:

1. You should install the car package and load its library:
```
>install.packages("caret")
>install.packages("e1071")
>install.packages("MASS")
>library(caret)
>library(e1071)
>library(MASS)
```
2. From the package, you can load the Outcome dataset:
```
>url="https://drive.google.com/file/d/15Ij9jt_N4fgYtuESSaGzdQDq3NJWdQyF/view?usp=sharing"
>data1=read.csv(url)
```
3. Make this example reproducible. You can use the str function to display the structure of the Outcome dataset:

```
>str(data1)
Output:
'data.frame': 980 obs. of 4 variables:
$ Ind_Exp_Act_Score: num 6.2 2.6 9.5 2.6 10 0.2 2.5 0.4 0.2 8.9 ...
$ Tran_Speed_Score:  num 9.3 2.2 1.5 5 7.7 2.3 2.8 1.6 9.8 6.1 ...
$ Peer_Comb_Score:   num 7.4 8.7 8.2 0.4 7.2 3.4 4.6 5.3 0.8 9.2 ...
$ Outcome
>set.seed(2)
>head(data1)
Output:
 Ind_Exp_Act_Score Tran_Speed_Score Peer_Comb_Score Outcome
        1              6.2              9.3          7.4 1
        2              2.6              2.2          8.7 1
        3              9.5              1.5          8.2 1
        4              2.6              5.0          0.4 2
        5             10.0              7.7          7.2 1
        6              0.2              2.3          3.4 2
```

4. Pairs function produces a matrix of scatterplots. The cross-plots should only compare the measurement variables in columns 1-3. Consider the following:

   ```
   >pairs(data1[,1:3])
   ```

   Output:

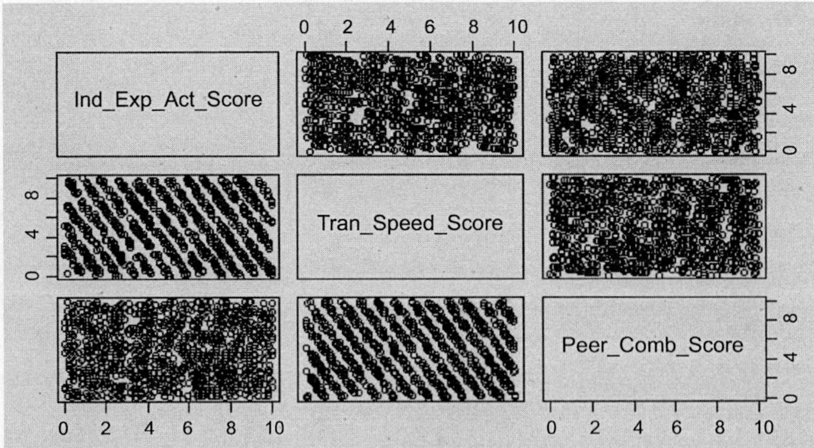

Fig. 2.1: A matrix of scatter plots

5. The next step is about training the model. This is carried out by discriminant function analysis. The lda() function is called to perform discriminant function analysis as follows:

   ```
   >lda=lda(Outcome~Ind_Exp_Act_Score+Tran_Speed_Score+Peer_Comb_Score,data=data1)
   ```

6. The format of this call is much like a linear regression or ANOVA, in that we specify a formula. Here, the GROUP variable should be treated as the dependent variable, with the geochemical measurements as the independent variables. In this case, no interactions between the variables are being modeled, so the variables are added with + instead of *. Because attach() was not called, the name of the data frame must be supplied to the data parameter. After running the DFA, the first step is to view the results, as follows:

   >lda

   Output:

   Call:

   lda(Outcome ~ Ind_Exp_Act_Score + Tran_Speed_Score + Peer_Comb_Score, data = data1)

   Prior probabilities of groups:

1	2
0.7234694	0.2765306

   Group means:

Ind_Exp_	Act_Score	Tran_Speed_Score	Peer_Comb_Score
1	5.729055	5.767278	5.863893
2	3.247601	3.122878	2.522878

   Coefficients of linear discriminants:

   LD1

   Ind_Exp_Act_Score –0.2709720

   Tran_Speed_Score -0.2806365

   Peer_Comb_Score -0.3510662

- The first part of the output displays the formula that was fitted.
- The second section is the prior probabilities of the groups, which reflects the proportion of each group within the dataset. In other words, if you had no measurements and the number of measured samples represented the actual relative abundances of the groups, the prior probabilities would describe the probability that any unknown sample would belong to each of the groups.
- The third section shows the group means, which is a table of the average value of each of the variables for each of your groups. Scanning this table can help you to see if the groups are distinctive in terms of one or more of the variables.
- The fourth section reports the coefficients of the discriminant function (*a*, and *b*). Because there are two groups, there are 2-1 linear discriminants (if you had only two groups, you would need only 1 [2-1] linear discriminants). For each linear discriminant LD1, there is one coefficient corresponding, in order, to each of the variables.

7. The predict() function, also part of the MASS package, uses the lda() results to assign the samples to the groups. In other words, since lda() derived a linear function that should classify the groups, predict() allows you to apply this function to the same data to see how successful the classification function is. Following the statistical convention that *x*-hat is the prediction of *x*, (hat is added to the object name to make it clear that these are the predictions). Consider the following:

   >pred=predict(lda)

   >pred

Output:

```
486    0.9980476539    1.952346e-03
487    0.9981698447    1.830155e-03
488    0.9890655703    1.093443e-02
489    0.0182872573    9.817127e-01
490    0.5701112782    4.298887e-01
491    0.7113910348    2.886090e-01
492    0.9999147720    8.522800e-05
493    0.9948612999    5.138700e-03
494    0.9998260538    1.739462e-04
495    0.1353221638    8.646778e-01
496    0.1081547897    8.918452e-01
497    0.1809089935    8.190910e-01
498    0.9964229890    3.577011e-03
499    0.0308811769    9.691188e-01
500    0.9974108305    2.589170e-03
[ reached getOption("max.print") -- omitted 480 rows ]
```

The output starts with the assigned classifications of each of our samples. Next, it lists the posterior probabilities of each sample to each group, with the probabilities in each row (that is, for each sample) summing to 1.0. These posterior probabilities measure the strength of each classification. If one of these probabilities for a sample is much greater than all the others, that sample is assigned to one group with a high degree of certainty. If two or more of the probabilities are nearly equal, the assignment is much less certain.

8. If there are many groups, the following command is a quick way to find the maximum probability for each sample:

```
> apply(pred$posterior,MARGIN=1,FUN=max)
```

Output:

```
        1         2         3         4         5         6         7         8
0.9998159 0.8910203 0.9974687 0.9678615 0.9999509 0.9869160 0.7785976 0.9509850
        9        10        11        12        13        14        15        16
0.7753839 0.9999448 0.9517511 0.9319962 0.8647043 0.5996989 0.6983882 0.7905112
       17        18        19        20        21        22        23        24
0.7129808 0.8649516 0.9999813 0.9999629 0.9500947 0.9870731 0.9031679 0.9052050
       25        26        27        28        29        30        31        32
0.7684331 0.9999479 0.9998536 0.6444637 0.8169487 0.9673279 0.9875913 0.9891927
       33        34        35        36        37        38        39        40
```

```
0.7487921 0.9991947 0.5163380 0.9997611 0.9952310 0.9928042 0.9984594 0.9996970
       41        42        43        44        45        46        47        48
0.5694634 0.9658146 0.9985762 0.8694793 0.9505015 0.9999870 0.9991380 0.9659520
       49        50        51        52        53        54
0.8992920 0.7650120 0.9848763 0.9999473 0.9988122 0.9999528
```

Since most of the probabilities in the dataset are large (>0.9), this indicates that most of the samples in the set have been assigned to one group.

9. If most of these probabilities are large, the overall classification is successful. The last part of the predict() output lists the scores of each sample for each discriminant function axis. These scores can be plotted to show graphically how the groups are distributed in the discriminant function, just as scores from a principal components analysis could be plotted, as follows:

   > plot(lda)

   The two groups occupy distinctly different and non-overlapping regions. There is just one case of group 1 being close to group 2, so one can clearly state that the discrimination has been successful. The plot is as shown in the following figure:

   Output:

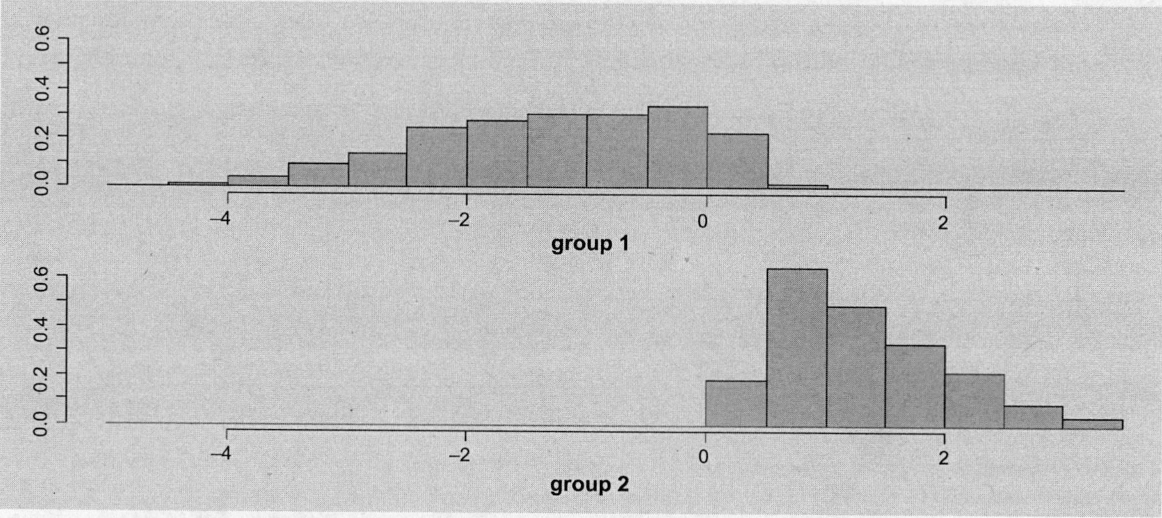

Fig. 2.2: Distribution of groups along a particular discriminant function

10. Again, note the good separation of the groups along discriminant function 1, andparticularly so for group 1.

    The effectiveness of DFA in classifying the groups must be evaluated, and this is done by comparing the assignments made by predict() to the actual group assignments. The table() function is most useful for this. By convention, it is called with the actual assignments as the first argument and the fitted assignments as the second argument, as follows:

    > tab=table(data1$Outcome,pred$class)

    > tab

Output:

	1	2
1	692	17
2	13	258

The rows in the output correspond to the groups specified in the original data and the columns correspond to the classification made by the DFA. In a perfect classification, large values would lie along the diagonal, with zeroes off the diagonal, which would indicate that all samples that belong to group 1 were discriminated by the DFA as belonging to group 1, and so on. The form of this table can give you considerable insight into which groups are reliably discriminated. It can also show which groups are likely to be confused and which types of misclassification are more common than others.

11. The following command will calculate the overall predictive accuracy, that is, the proportion of cases that lie along the diagonal:

    > sum(tab[row(tab)==col(tab)])/sum(tab)

    Output:

    [1] 0.9693878

    Here the predictive accuracy is almost 97%, quite a success. This approach measures what is called the resubstitution error, how well the samples are classified when all the samples are used to develop the discriminant function.

Table 2.5: Coding of Classification by Linear Discriminant Analysis

```
>install.packages("caret")
>install.packages("e1071")
>install.packages("MASS")
>library(caret)
>library(e1071)
>library(MASS)
>url="https://drive.google.com/file/d/15Ij9jt_N4fgYtuESSaGzdQDq3NJWdQyF/view?usp=sharing"
> data1=read.csv(url)
>str(data1)
>set.seed(2)
>head(data1)
>pairs(data1[,1:3])
>lda=lda(Outcome~Ind_Exp_Act_Score+Tran_Speed_Score+Peer_Comb_Score,data=data1)
>lda
>pred=predict(lda)
>pred
>apply(pred$posterior,MARGIN=1,FUN=max)
>plot(lda)
>tab=table(data1$Outcome,pred$class)
>tab
>sum(tab[row(tab)==col(tab)])/sum(tab)
```

2.4.2 Case – II: Classification by Linear Discriminant Analysis

Discriminant analysis is used to distinguish distinct sets of observations and allocate new observations to previously defined groups. On the collected samples in order to separate the samples from which they were excavated, DFA can be used as a function. The function can then be applied to classify and to predict. In *R*, we can fit a model to data with the lda function.

2.4.2a Getting Ready

In order to perform discriminant function analysis we shall be using a dataset collected from Obese.

2.4.2b How to do it

Perform the following steps to perform linear discriminate analysis with lda:

1. You should install the car package and load its library:

```
>install.packages("caret")
>install.packages("e1071")
>install.packages("MASS")
> library(caret)
> library(e1071)
>library(MASS)
```

2. From the package, you can load the Obese dataset:

```
>url="https://drive.google.com/file/d/1Ph1OmYAe0jRhfbibNSa7HnIU8UOYmyc1/view?usp
=sharing"
> data2=read.csv(url)
```

3. You can use the str function to display the structure of the Obese dataset:

```
> str(data2)
```

Output:

```
'data.frame':       4690 obs. of 6 variables:
$ sbp : int 112 136 130 132 138 128 125 108 136 128 ...
$ dbp : int 74 90 70 89 70 80 90 74 76 76 ...
$ scl : int 243 246 221 248 215 175 200 221 196 159 ...
$ age : int 30 31 31 31 31 31 31 32 32 32 ...
$ bmi :num 26.3 27.1 23.7 25.1 23 ...
$ obese: int 2 2 2 2 2 2 2 2 2 2 ...
>set.seed(1)
>head(data2)
```

Output:

	sbp	dbp	scl	age	bmi	obese
1	112	74	243	30	26.3	2
2	136	90	246	31	27.1	2

3	130	70	221	31	23.7	2
4	132	89	248	31	25.1	2
5	138	70	215	31	23.0	2
6	128	80	175	31	19.5	2

4. Pairs function produces a matrix of scatterplots. The cross-plots should only compare the measurement variables in columns 1-5. Consider the following:

   >pairs(data2[,1:5])

   Output:

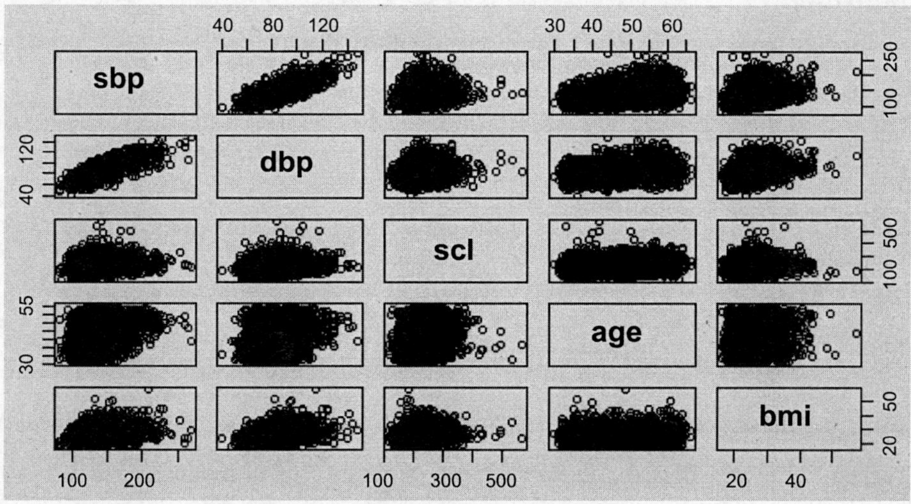

Fig. 2.3: A matrix of scatter plots

5. The next step is about training the model. This is carried out by discriminant function analysis. The lda() function is called to perform discriminant function analysis as follows:

   >lda=lda(obese ~ sbp + dbp + scl + age + bmi,data=data2)

6. The format of this call is much like a linear regression or ANOVA, in that we specify a formula. Here, the GROUP variable should be treated as the dependent variable, with the geochemical measurements as the independent variables. In this case, no interactions between the variables are being modeled, so the variables are added with + instead of *. Because attach() was not called, the name of the data frame must be supplied to the data parameter. After running the DFA, the first step is to view the results, as follows:

   >lda

   Output:

   Call:

   lda(obese ~ sbp + dbp + scl + age + bmi, data = data2)

   Prior probabilities of groups:

1	2
0.128145	0.871855

Group means:

	sbp	dbp	scl	age	bmi
1	146.2097	90.77205	237.7903	48.24293	33.05324
2	130.7816	81.31890	226.8271	45.70482	24.54089

Coefficients of linear discriminants:

LD1

sbp -0.0022810944

dbp 0.0031513130

scl 0.0005935947

age 0.0066235199

bmi -0.3424252993

- The first part of the output displays the formula that was fitted.
- The second section is the prior probabilities of the groups, which reflects the proportion of each group within the dataset. In other words, if you had no measurements and the number of measured samples represented the actual relative abundances of the groups, the prior probabilities would describe the probability that any unknown sample would belong to each of the groups.
- The third section shows the group means, which is a table of the average value of each of the variables for each of your groups. Scanning this table can help you to see if the groups are distinctive in terms of one or more of the variables.
- The fourth section reports the coefficients of the discriminant function (a, and b). Because there are two groups, there are 2-1 linear discriminants (if you had only two groups, you would need only 1 [2-1] linear discriminants). For each linear discriminant LD1, there is one coefficient corresponding, in order, to each of the variables.

7. The predict() function, also part of the MASS package, uses the lda() results to assign the samples to the groups. In other words, since lda() derived a linear function that should classify the groups, predict() allows you to apply this function to the same data to see how successful the classification function is. Following the statistical convention that *x*-hat is the prediction of *x*, (hat is added to the object name to make it clear that these are the predictions). Consider the following:

```
> pred=predict(lda)
> pred
```

Output:

```
3    5.244257e-01
4    1.163703e-01
5    7.423134e-01
6    1.971382e+00
7   -7.490665e-01
8   -4.334373e-01
```

```
9     1.617192e+00
10    1.990146e+00
11    7.203804e-01
12    3.354372e-01
13    1.668904e+00
14    4.792581e-01
15   -1.290156e+00
16    2.423466e+00
17   -3.826094e-01
18   -1.766145e-01
19   -7.919215e-01
```

The output starts with the assigned classifications of each of our samples. Next, it lists the posterior probabilities of each sample to each group, with the probabilities in each row (that is, for each sample) summing to 1.0. These posterior probabilities measure the strength of each classification. If one of these probabilities for a sample is much greater than all the others, that sample is assigned to one group with a high degree of certainty. If two or more of the probabilities are nearly equal, the assignment is much less certain.

8. If there are many groups, the following command is a quick way to find the maximum probability for each sample:

   >apply(pred$posterior,MARGIN=1,FUN=max)

   Output:

```
        1         2         3         4         5         6         7         8
0.9845157 0.9667714 0.9985824 0.9953916 0.9992454 0.9999785 0.9462493 0.9777412
        9        10        11        12        13        14        15        16
0.9999401 0.9999797 0.9991959 0.9975516 0.9999484 0.9983845 0.7859446 0.9999942
       17        18        19        20        21        22        23        24
0.9807300 0.9892973 0.9395737 0.9979921 0.9973038 0.9999478 0.9941827 0.9709362
       25        26        27        28        29        30        31        32
0.9165835 0.7376082 0.9999969
       33        34        35        36
```

   Since most of the probabilities in the dataset are large (>0.9), this indicates that most of the samples in the set have been assigned to one group.

9. If most of these probabilities are large, the overall classification is successful. The last part of the predict() output lists the scores of each sample for each discriminant function axis. These scores can be plotted to show graphically how the groups are distributed in the discriminant function, just as scores from a principal components analysis could be plotted, as follows:

   > plot(lda)

   The two groups occupy distinctly different and non-overlapping regions. There is just one case of group 1 being close to group 2, so one can clearly state that the discrimination has been successful.

The plot is as shown in the following figure:

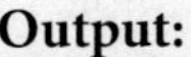

Output:

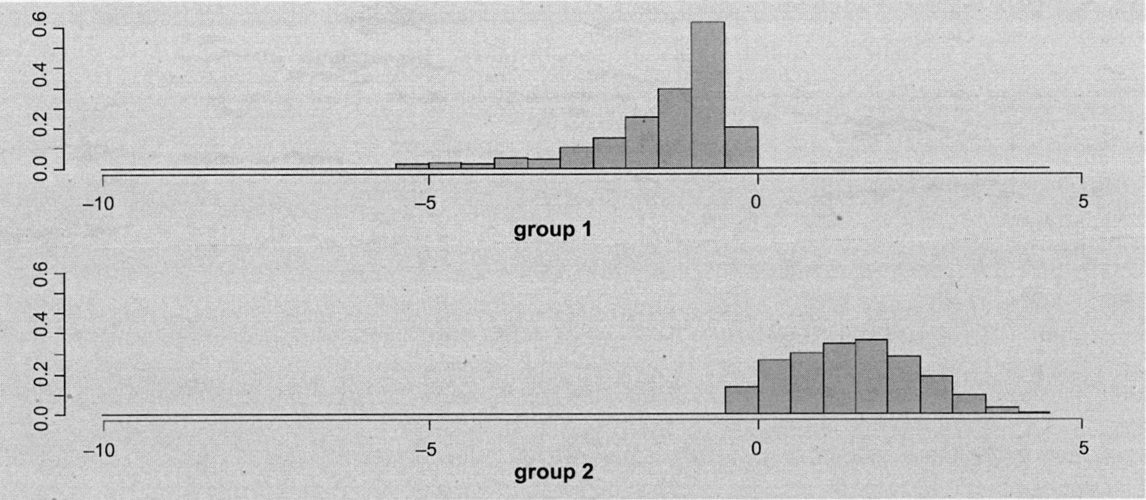

Fig. 2.4: Distribution of groups along a particular discriminant function

10. Again, note the good separation of the groups along discriminant function 2, and particularly so for group 2.

    The effectiveness of DFA in classifying the groups must be evaluated, and this is done by comparing the assignments made by predict() to the actual group assignments. The table() function is most useful for this. By convention, it is called with the actual assignments as the first argument and the fitted assignments as the second argument, as follows:

    ```
    >tab=table(data2$obese,pred$class)
    >tab
    ```

    Output:

	1	2
1	452	149
2	0	4089

    The rows in the output correspond to the groups specified in the original data and the columns correspond to the classification made by the DFA. In a perfect classification, large values would lie along the diagonal, with zeroes off the diagonal, which would indicate that all samples that belong to group 1 were discriminated by the DFA as belonging to group 1, and so on. The form of this table can give you considerable insight into which groups are reliably discriminated. It can also show which groups are likely to be confused and which types of misclassification are more common than others.

11. The following command will calculate the overall predictive accuracy, that is, the proportion of cases that lie along the diagonal:

    ```
    >sum(tab[row(tab)==col(tab)])/sum(tab)
    ```

    Output:

    [1] 0.9682303

Here the predictive accuracy is almost 97%, quite a success. This approach measures what is called the resubstitution error, how well the samples are classified when all the samples are used to develop the discriminant function.

Table 2.6: Coding of Classification by Linear Discriminant Analysis

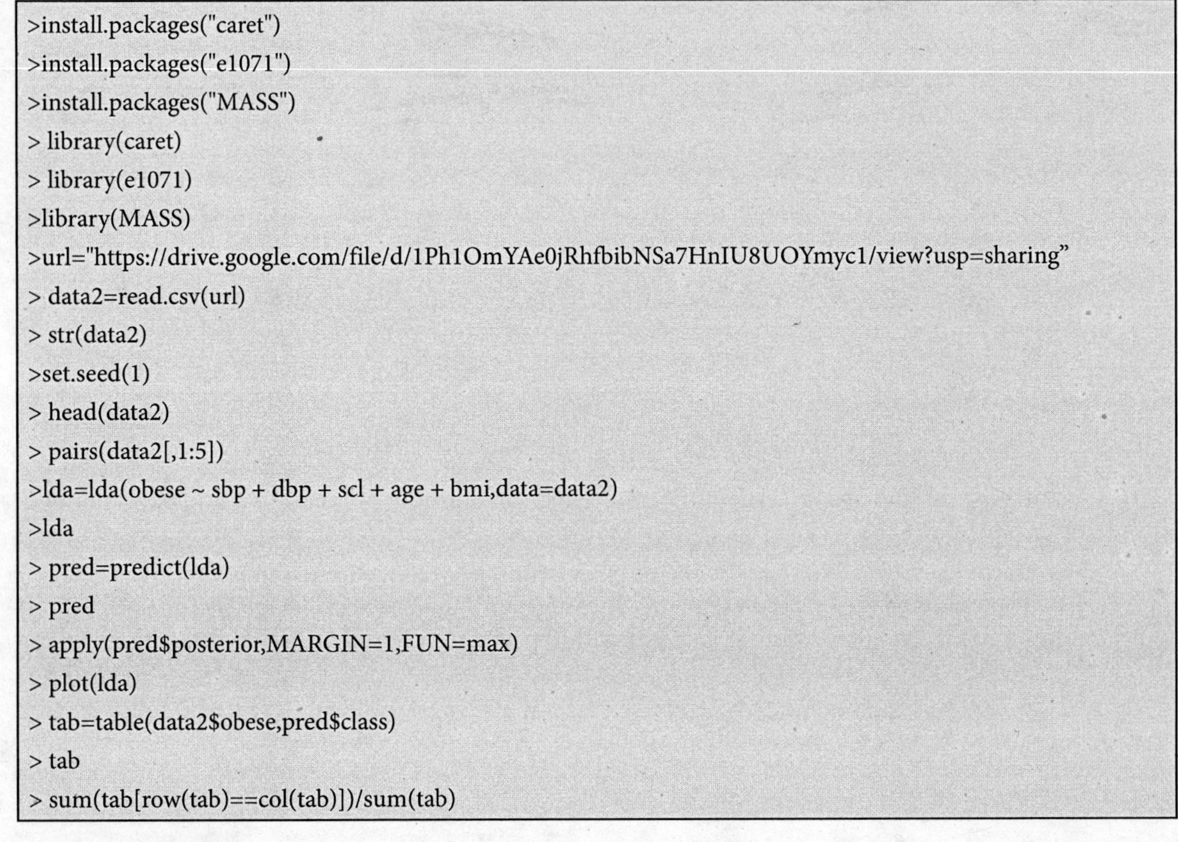

```
>install.packages("caret")
>install.packages("e1071")
>install.packages("MASS")
> library(caret)
> library(e1071)
>library(MASS)
>url="https://drive.google.com/file/d/1Ph1OmYAe0jRhfbibNSa7HnIU8UOYmyc1/view?usp=sharing"
> data2=read.csv(url)
> str(data2)
>set.seed(1)
> head(data2)
> pairs(data2[,1:5])
>lda=lda(obese ~ sbp + dbp + scl + age + bmi,data=data2)
>lda
> pred=predict(lda)
> pred
> apply(pred$posterior,MARGIN=1,FUN=max)
> plot(lda)
> tab=table(data2$obese,pred$class)
> tab
> sum(tab[row(tab)==col(tab)])/sum(tab)
```

Quiz Questions

1. A confusion matrix is a matrix that summarizes the .... of a machine learning model on a set of test data.
   (*a*) Results (*b*) Performance
   (*c*) Conclusion (*d*) None of the above
2. .... is an approach used in supervised machine learning to solve multi-class classification problems and it separates multiple classes with multiple features through data dimensionality reduction.
   (*a*) Linear discriminant analysis (*b*) Regression analysis
   (*c*) Correlation analysis (*d*) None of the above
3. Naive Bayes classifiers are a collection of .... algorithms based on Bayes' Theorem.
   (*a*) Prediction (*b*) Estimation
   (*c*) Classification (*d*) None of the above

4. Logistic regression is a process of modelling the probability of a .... outcome given an input variable.
   (*a*) Continuous (*b*) Discrete
   (*c*) Numeric (*d*) None of the above
5. The most common logistic regression models a .... outcome.
   (*a*) Categorical (*b*) Binary
   (*c*) Nonmetric (*d*) None of the above
6. In regression analysis, logistic regression model is otherwise known as .... regression model which is estimating the parameters of a logistic model.
   (*a*) Discriminant (*b*) Logit
   (*c*) Probit (*d*) None of the above
7. Linear discriminant analysis (LDA) is a generalization of ....
   (*a*) Normal disriminant analysis (*b*) Fisher's linear discriminant
   (*c*) Pearson's linear discriminant (*d*) None of the above
8. Linear discriminant analysis (LDA) is otherwise known as ....
   (*a*) Normal disriminant analysis (*b*) Fisher's linear discriminant
   (*c*) Discriminant function analysis (*d*) None of the above
9. .... models are known under a variety of names, including simple Bayes and independence Bayes.
   (*a*) Bayesian (*b*) Naive Bayes
   (*c*) Thomas Bayes (*d*) None of the above
10. In statistics, naive Bayes classifiers are a family of linear "........................ classifiers" which assumes that the features are conditionally independent, given the target class.
   (*a*) Probabilistic (*b*) Stochastic
   (*c*) Random (*d*) None of the above

ANSWERS

1.(*b*)	2.(*a*)	3.(*c*)	4.(*b*)	5.(*b*)	6.(*b*)	7.(*b*)	8.(*c*)	9.(*b*)	10. (*a*)

Objectives

1. The objective of a simple regression course is to teach students the fundamental concepts and techniques of regression analysis, focusing on models with one independent variable.
2. This includes understanding the assumptions of regression, interpreting regression coefficients, assessing model fit, making predictions and using regression for inference and hypothesis testing.
3. Students typically learn how to perform regression analysis using statistical software and how to interpret and communicate the results effectively.

Outcomes

Upon Completing a simple regression course, students should be able to:

1. Understand the theoretical foundations of simple regression analysis.
2. Identify and articulate the assumptions underlying simple regression models.
3. Critically evaluate and apply simple regression techniques to real-world problems in various fields such as economics, sociology, psychology and business.

3.1 INTRODUCTION

Regression is a supervised learning method, which is employed to model and analyze the relationship between a dependent (response) variable and one or more independent (predictor) variables. One can use regression to build a prediction model, which can first be used to find the best fitted model with minimum squared errors of the fitted values. The fitted model can then be further applied to data for continuous value predictions. There are many types of regression. If there is only one predictor variable, and the relationship between the response variable and independent variable is linear, we can apply a linear model. However, if there is more than one predictor variable, a multiple linear regression method should be used. When the relationship is nonlinear, one can use a nonlinear model to model the relationship between the predictor and response variables. In this chapter, we will introduce how to fit a linear model into data with the lm function.

3.2 LINEAR REGRESSION MODEL

This is the oldest type and most widely known type of regression. In this the dependent variable is continuous and the independent variable can be discrete or continuous and the regression line is linear. Linear regression is very sensitive to outliers and cross-correlations.

3.2.1 Case – I: Fitting of Linear Regression

The simplest model in regression is linear regression, which is best used when there is only one predictor variable, and the relationship between the response variable and the independent variable is linear. In *R*, we can fit a linear model to data with the lm function.

3.2.1*a* Getting Ready

We need to prepare data with one predictor and response variable, and with a linear relationship between the two variables.

3.2.1*b* How to do it

Perform the following steps to perform linear regression with *lm*:

1. You should install the car package and load its library:

   ```
   >install.packages("car")
   > library(car)
   ```

2. From the package, you can load the Prestige dataset:

   ```
   >url="https://drive.google.com/file/d/1zZuozCHlX5nddUVUkBNrGbCJXL55QZPj/view?usp
   =sharing"
   > data1=read.csv(url)
   ```

3. You can use the str function to display the structure of the prestige dataset:

   ```
   > str(data1)
   ```

   Output:

   ```
   'data.frame': 102 obs. of 7 variables:
   $ job : chr "gov.administrators" "general.managers" "accountants" "purchasing.officers" ...
   $ education: num 13.1 12.3 12.8 11.4 14.6 ...
   $ income:    int 12351 25879 9271 8865 8403 11030 8258 14163 11377 11023 ...
   $ women:     num 11.16 4.02 15.7 9.11 11.68 ...
   $ prestige:  num 68.8 69.1 63.4 56.8 73.5 77.6 72.6 78.1 73.1 68.8 ...
   $ census:    int 1113 1130 1171 1175 2111 2113 2133 2141 2143 2153 ...
   $ type:      chr "prof" "prof" "prof" "prof" ...
   ```

   ```
   >head(data1)
   ```

   Output:

   ```
   job education income women prestige census type
   1. gov.administrators 13.11   12351   11.16   68.8   1113 prof
   2. general.managers   12.26   25879    4.02   69.1   1130 prof
   3. accountants        12.77    9271   15.70   63.4   1171 prof
   ```

4. Draw a scatter plot of the *x* and *y* variables with plot, and append a fitted line through the *lm* and abline functions:

   ```
   > plot (data1)
   ```

Output:

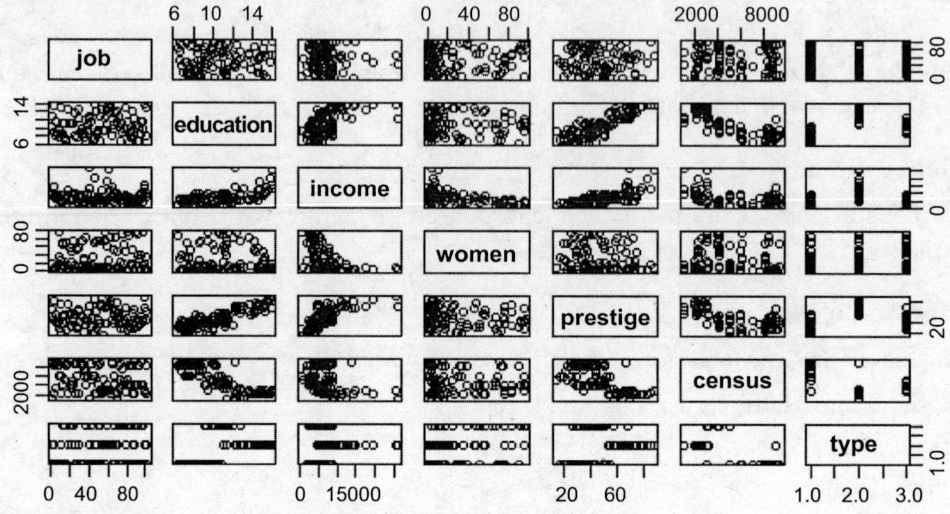

Fig. 3.1: A matrix of scatter plots

```
>plot(data1$prestige, data1$income)
> model1 = lm(income~prestige,data1)
>abline(model1, col="red")
```

Output:

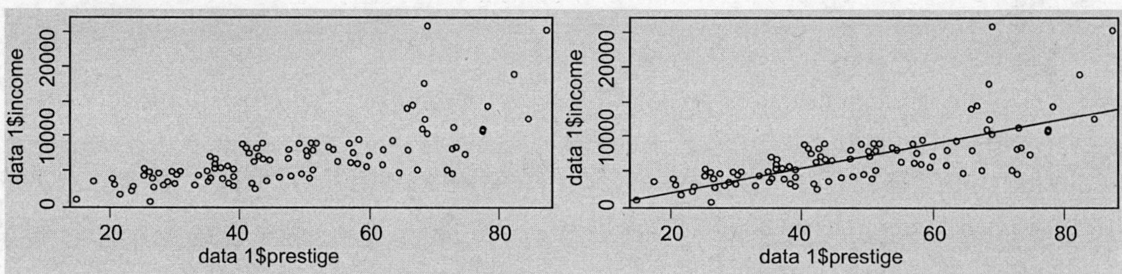

Fig. 3.2: Scatter plot of prestige versus income of linear regression model

Fig. 3.3: Scatter plot of actual versus predicted of linear regression model

5. To view the fit model, execute the following:

```
> model1
Output:
Call:
lm(formula = income ~ prestige, data = data1)
Coefficients:
(Intercept)  prestige
  -1465.0     176.4
```

3.2.1*c* How it works

The regression model has the response ~ terms form, where response is the response vector, and terms is a series of terms that specifies a predictor. We can illustrate a simple regression model with the formula $y = \alpha + \beta x$, where α is the intercept while the slope, β, describes the change in y when x changes. By using the least squares method, we can estimate and (where indicates the mean value of y and denotes the mean value of x).

3.2.1*d* There's more

To perform linear regression, we first prepare the data that has a linear relationship between the predictor variable and response variable. In this example, we load prestige dataset from the package car. Within the dataset, the x and y_1 variables have a linear relationship, and we prepare a scatter plot of these variables. To generate the regression line, we use the lm function to generate a model of the two variables. Furthermore, we use abline to plot a regression line on the plot. As per the previous screenshot, the regression line illustrates the linear relationship of x and y_1 variables. We can see that the coefficient of the fitted model shows the intercept equals –1465.0 and coefficient equals 176.4. As a result, we can use the intercept and coefficient to infer the response value. For example, we can infer the response value when x at 3 is equal to –935.8 (3 * 176.4 – 1465.0).

```
Linear Regression Model-2
>plot(data1$women, data1$income)
> model2 = lm(income~women,data1)
>abline(model2, col="red")
```

Output:

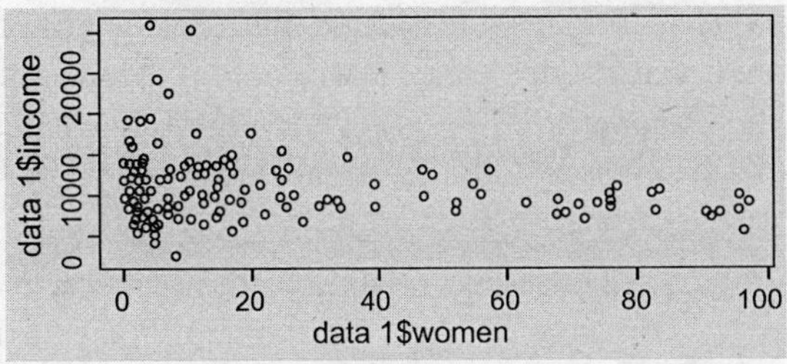

Fig. 3.4: Scatter plot of women versus income of linear regression model

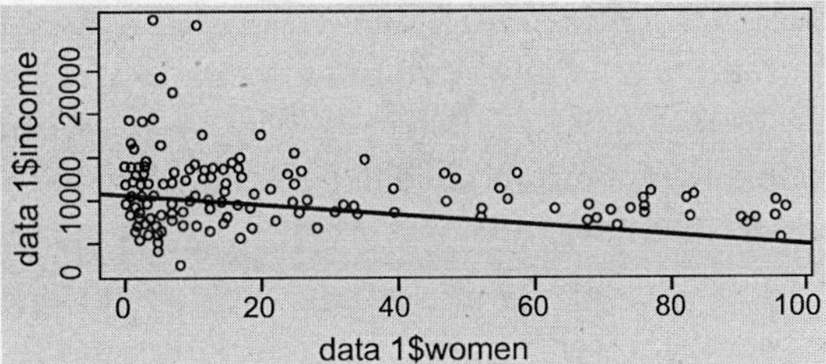

Fig. 3.5: Scatter plot of actual versus predicted of linear regression model

3.2.1*e* Summarizing Linear Model Fits

The summary function can be used to obtain the formatted coefficient, standard errors, degree of freedom, and other summarized information of a fitted model. This recipe introduces how to obtain overall information on a model through the use of the summary function.

3.2.1*f* Getting Ready

You need to have completed the previous recipe by computing the linear model of the x and y1 variables from the prestige, and have the fitted model assigned to the model 1 variable.

3.2.1*g* How to do it

Perform the following step to summarize linear model fits:

1. Compute a detailed summary of the fitted model:

   > summary (model1)

   Output:

   Call:

   lm(formula = income ~ prestige, data = data1)

   Residuals:

Min	1Q	Median	3Q	Max
–6693.3	–1434.9	136.5	1251.8	15152.5

   Coefficients:

   Estimate Std. Error *t* value *Pr* (>|*t*|)

(Intercept)	–1465.03	860.47	–1.703	0.0918.
prestige	176.43	17.26	10.224	<2e-16 ***

   Signif. codes: 0 '***' 0.001 '**' 0.01 '*' 0.05 '.' 0.1 ' ' 1

   Residual standard error: 2984 on 100 degrees of freedom

   Multiple *R*-squared: 0.5111, Adjusted *R*-squared: 0.5062

   F-statistic: 104.5 on 1 and 100 *DF*, *p*-value: < 2.2*e* – 16

3.2.1*h* How it works

The summary function is a generic function used to produce summary statistics. In this case, it computes and returns a list of the summary statistics of the fitted linear model. Here, it will output information such as residuals, coefficient standard error *R*-squared, f-statistic, and a degree of freedom. In the Call section, the function called to generate the fitted model is displayed. In the Residuals section, it provides a quick summary (Min, 1Q, Median, 3Q, Max) of the distribution.

In the Coefficients section, each coefficient is a Gaussian random variable. Within this section, Estimate represents the mean distribution of the variable; Std. Error displays the standard error of the variable; the *t* value is Estimate divided by Std.Error and the *p* value indicates the probability of getting a value larger than the *t* value. In this sample, the *p* value of intercept (0.0918) and prestige (2*e* – 16) have a 95 percent level of confidence. Residual standard error outputs the standard deviation of residuals, while the degree of freedom indicates the differences between the observation in training samples and the number used in the model. Multiple *R*-squared is obtained by dividing the sum of squares. One can use *R*-squared to measure how close the data is to fitting into the regression line. Mostly, the higher the *R*-squared, the better the model fits your data. However, it does not necessarily indicate whether the regression model is adequate. This means you might get a good model with a low *R*-squared or you can have a bad model with a high *R*-squared. Since multiple *R*-squared ignores a degree of freedom, the calculated score is biased. To make the calculation fair, an adjusted *R*-squared (0.5062) uses an unbiased estimate, and will be slightly less than multiple *R*-squared (0.5111). *F*-statistic is retrieved by performing an *f*-test on the model. A *p* value equal to 2.2*e* – 16 (< 0.05) rejects the null hypothesis (no linear correlation between variables) and indicates that the observed F is greater than the critical F value. In other words, the result shows that there is a significant positive linear correlation between the variables.

3.2.1*i* See also

For more information on the parameters used for obtaining a summary of the fitted model, you can use the help function or ? to view the help page:

```
> ?summary.lm
```

Alternatively, you can use the following functions to display the properties of the model:

```
>coefficients(model1) # Extract model coefficients
>confint(model1, level = 0.95) # Computes confidence intervals for model parameters.
>fitted(model1) # Extract model fitted values
>residuals(model1) # Extract model residuals
>anova(model1) # Compute analysis of variance tables for fitted model object
>vcov(model1) # Calculate variance-covariance matrix for a fitted model object
>influence(model1) # Diagnose quality of regression fits
```

3.2.1*j* Using Linear Regression to Predict Unknown Values

With a fitted regression model, we can apply the model to predict unknown values. For regression models, we can express the precision of prediction with a prediction interval and a confidence interval. In the following recipe, we will introduce how to predict unknown values under these two measurements.

3.2.1*k* Getting Ready

You need to have completed the previous recipe by computing the linear model of the prestige and income variables from the prestige dataset.

3.2.1*l* How to do it

Perform the following steps to predict values with linear regression:

1. Fit a linear model with the prestige and income variables:

   ```
   >model1 = lm(income~prestige, data1)
   ```

2. Assign values to be predicted into newdata:

   ```
   >newdata = data.frame(prestige = c(35.6,60.2,55.3))
   ```

3. Compute the prediction result using the confidence interval with level set as 0.95:

   ```
   >predict(model1, newdata, interval="confidence", level=0.95)
   ```

   Output:

   ```
          fit      lwr      upr
   1 4815.975 4114.951 5516.998
   2 9156.219 8412.617 9899.822
   3 8291.699 7637.825 8945.572
   ```

4. Compute the prediction result using this prediction interval:

   >predict(model1, newdata, interval="predict")

   Output:

	fit	lwr	upr
1	4815.975	-1144.85	10776.81
2	9156.219	3190.230	15122.21
3	8291.699	2336.228	14247.17

3.2.1*m* How it works

We first build a linear fitted model with x and y_1 variables. Next, we assign values to be predicted into a DataFrame, newdata. It is important to note that the generated model is in the form of $y_1 \sim x$.

Next, we compute the prediction result using a confidence interval by specifying confidence in the argument interval. From the output of row 1, we get fitted y_1 of the $x = 35.6$ input, which equals to 4815.975, and a 95 percent confidence interval (set 0.95 in the level argument) of the y_1 mean for $x = 35.6$ is between 4114.951 and 5516.9985. In addition to this, row 2 and 3 give the prediction result of y_1 with an input of $x = 60.2$ and $x = 55.3$.

Next, we compute the prediction result using a prediction interval by specifying prediction in the argument interval. From the output of row 1, we can see fitted y_1 of the $x = 35.6$ input is equal to 4815.975, and a 95 percent prediction interval of y_1 for $x = 35.6$ is between –1144.857 10776.81. Row 2 and 3 output the prediction result of y_1 with an input of $x = 60.2$ and $x = 55.3$.

3.2.1*n* Generating a diagnostic Plot of a Fitting Model

Diagnostics are methods to evaluate assumptions of the regression, which can be used to determine whether a fitted model adequately represents the data. In the following recipe, we will introduce how to diagnose a regression model through the use of a diagnostic plot.

3.2.1*o* Getting Ready

You need to have completed the previous recipe by computing a linear model of the x and y_1 variables from the prestige, and have the model assigned to the model1 variable.

3.2.1*p* How to do it

Perform the following step to generate a diagnostic plot of the fitted model:

1. Plot the diagnostic plot of the regression model:

   > par(mfrow=c(2,2))

   > plot(model1)

Output:

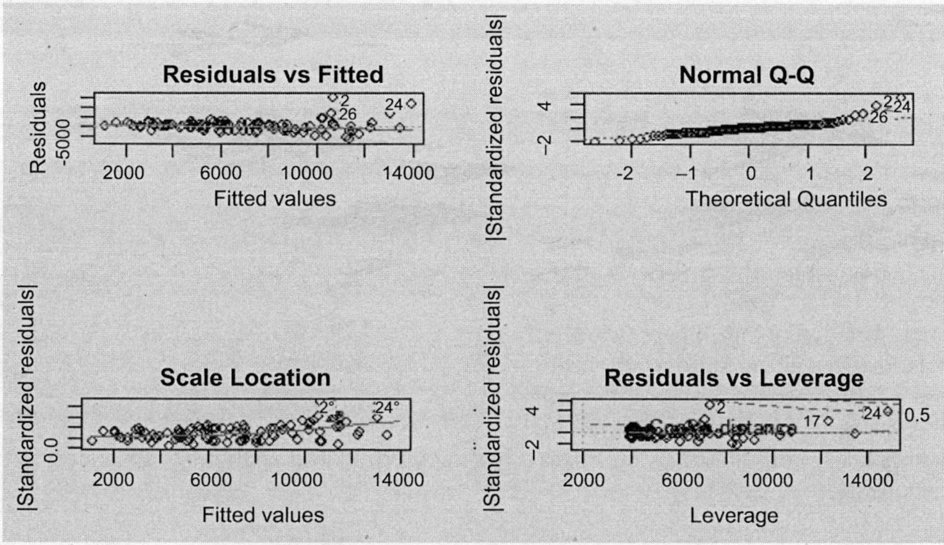

Fig. 3.6: Diagnostic plot of fitted linear regression model

3.2.1*q* How it works

The plot function generates four diagnostic plots of a regression model:

The upper-left plot shows residuals versus fitted values. Within the plot, residuals represent the vertical distance from a point to the regression line. If all points fall exactly on the regression line, all residuals will fall exactly on the dotted gray line. The red line within the plot is a smooth curve with regard to residuals, and if all the dots fall exactly on the regression line, the position of the red line should exactly match the dotted gray line.

The upper-right shows the normal for the residuals. This plot verifies the assumption that residuals were normally distributed. Thus, if the residuals were normally distributed, they should lie exactly on the gray dotted line. The Scale-Location plot on the bottom-left is used to measure the square root of the standardized residuals against the fitted value. Therefore, if all dots lie on the regression line, the value of y should be close to zero. Since it is assumed that the variance of residuals does not change the distribution substantially, if the assumption is correct, the red line should be relatively flat.

The bottom-right plot shows standardized residuals versus leverage. The leverage is a measurement of how each data point influences the regression. It is a measurement of the distance from the centroid of regression and level of isolation (measured by whether it has neighbors). Also, you can find the contour of Cook's distance, which is affected by high leverage and large residuals. You can use this to measure how regression would change if a single point is deleted. The red

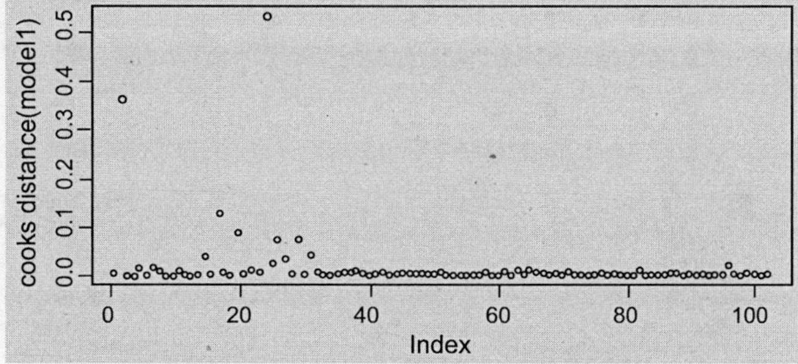

Fig. 3.7: Distribution of Cook's distance from linear regression model

line is smooth with regard to standardized residuals. For a perfect fit regression, the red line should be close to the dashed line with no points over 0.5 in Cook's distance.

3.2.1*r* There's more

To see more of the diagnostic plot function, you can use the help function to access further information:

Output:

> ?plot.lm

In this case, where the point on index 2 and 24 show greater Cook's distance than other points, one can investigate whether these points might be an outlier. In order to discover whether there are points with large Cook's distance, one can use the cooks.distance function to compute the Cook's distance of each point, and analyze the distribution of distance through visualization:

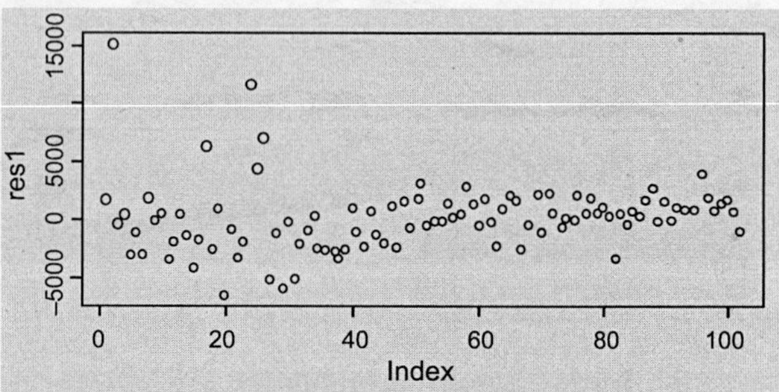

Fig. 3.8: Distribution of residuals of linear regression model

> plot(cooks.distance(model1))

Output:

To evaluate residuals of model1, you can use the resid function for obtaining this:

> res1=resid(model1)

> res1

> plot(res1)

Output:

To evaluate the fitted valyes of the model1, you can use the fitted function for obtaining this:

> fmodel1=fitted(model1)

> plot(fmodel1)

Output:

To evaluate the ANOVA table of model1, you can use the anova function for obtaining this:

>anova(model1)

Output:

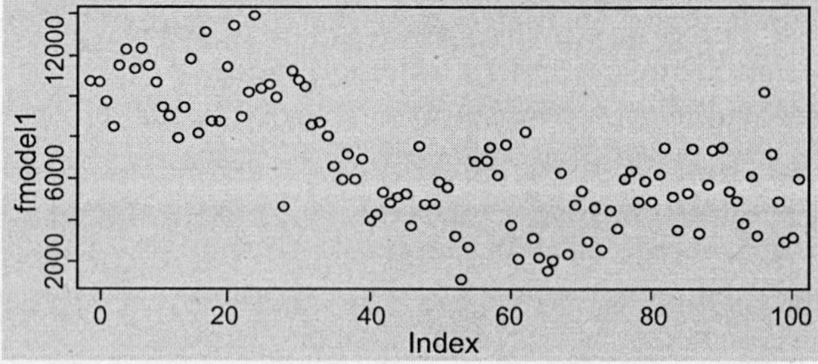

Fig. 3.9: Distribution of predicted values of linear regression model

Analysis of Variance Table

Response: income

Df Sum Sq Mean Sq F valuePr(>F)

prestige 1 930599714 930599714 104.54< 2.2e-16 ***

Residuals 100 890213697 8902137

Signif. codes: 0 '***' 0.001 '**' 0.01 '*' 0.05 '.' 0.1 ' ' 1

From ANOVA table it is concluded that the present regression model is statistically significant.

Table 3.1: Coding of Linear Regression Model

```
>install.packages("car")
> library(car)
>url="https://drive.google.com/file/d/1zZuozCHlX5nddUVUkBNrGbCJXL55QZPj/view?usp=sharing"
> data1=read.csv(url)
> str(data1)
> head(data1)
> plot(data1)
>plot(data1$prestige, data1$income)
> model1 = lm(income~prestige,data1)
>abline(model1, col="red")
> model1
> summary (model1)
>newdata = data.frame(prestige = c(35.6,60.2,55.3))
>predict(model1, newdata, interval="confidence", level=0.95)
>predict(model1, newdata, interval="predict")
> par(mfrow=c(2,2))
> plot(model1)
> plot(cooks.distance(model1))
> res1=resid(model1)
> res1
> plot(res1)
> fmodel1=fitted(model1)
> plot(fmodel1)
>anova(model1)
```

3.2.2 Case – II: Fitting of Linear Regression

The simplest model in regression is linear regression, which is best used when there is only one predictor variable, and the relationship between the response variable and the independent variable is linear. In *R*, we can fit a linear model to data with the *lm* function.

3.2.2a Getting Ready

We need to prepare data with one predictor and response variable, and with a linear relationship between the two variables.

3.2.2*b* How to do it

Perform the following steps to perform linear regression with lm:

1. You should install the car package and load its library:

   ```
   >install.packages("car")
   > library(car)
   ```

2. From the package, you can load the Salary dataset:

   >url="https://drive.google.com/file/d/18ssBdfTpFhl1OgWmAjqDKzC6QJfG_oMX/view?usp=sharing"

   > data2=read.csv(url)

3. You can use the str function to display the structure of the Salary dataset:

   > str(data2)

   Output:

   'data.frame': 30 obs. of 3 variables:

   $ X: int 0 1 2 3 4 5 6 7 8 9 ...

   $ YearsExperience: num 1.2 1.4 1.6 2.1 2.3 3 3.1 3.3 3.3 3.8 ...

   $ Salary : int 39344 46206 37732 43526 39892 56643 60151 54446 64446 57190 ...

   >head(data2)

   Output:

X	Years	Experience	Salary
1	0	1.2	39344
2	1	1.4	46206
3	2	1.6	37732
4	3	2.1	43526
5	4	2.3	39892
6	5	3.0	56643

4. Draw a scatter plot of the *x* and *y* variables with plot, and append a fitted line through the *lm* and abline functions:

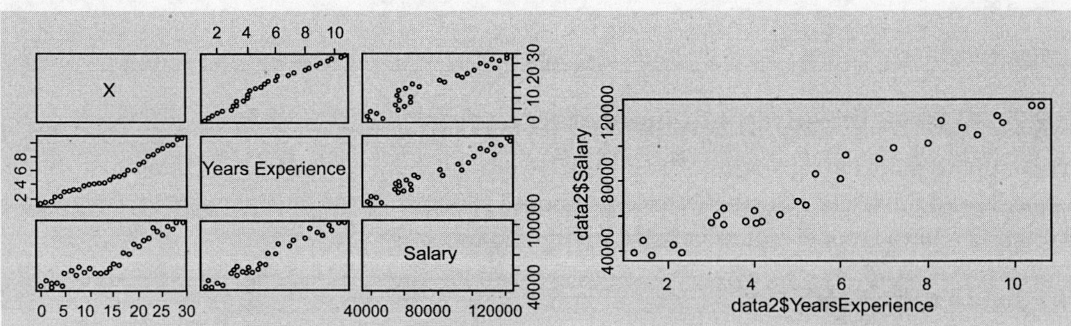

Fig. 3.10: A matrix of scatter plots

Fig. 3.11: Scatter plot of YearsExperience versus salary of linear regression model

> plot(data2)

Output:

> plot(data2$YearsExperience,data2$Salary)

Output:

> model2 = lm(Salary~YearsExperience,data2)

Output:

> abline(model2, col="red")

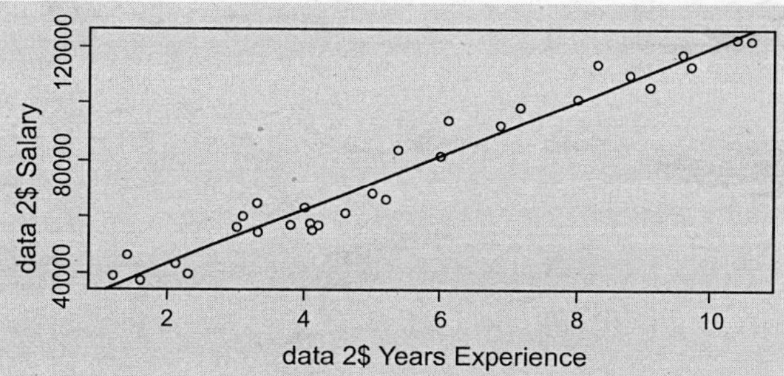

Fig. 3.12: Scatter plot of actual versus predicted of linear regression model

5. To view the fit model, execute the following:

   > model2

   Output:

   Call:

   lm(formula = Salary ~ YearsExperience, data = data2)

   Coefficients:

   (Intercept) Years Experience

   24848 9450

3.2.2*c* How it works

The regression model has the response ~ terms form, where response is the response vector, and terms is a series of terms that specifies a predictor. We can illustrate a simple regression model with the formula $y = \alpha + \beta x$, where α is the intercept while the slope, β, describes the change in y when x changes. By using the least squares method, we can estimate and (where indicates the mean value of y and denotes the mean value of x).

3.2.2*d* There's more

To perform linear regression, we first prepare the data that has a linear relationship between the predictor variable and response variable. In this example, we load Salary dataset from the package car. Within the dataset, the x and y_1 variables have a linear relationship, and we prepare a scatter plot of these variables. To generate the regression line, we use the lm function to generate a model of the two variables. Furthermore, we use abline to plot a regression line on the plot. As per the previous screenshot, the regression line illustrates the linear relationship of x and y_1 variables. We can see that the coefficient of the fitted model shows the intercept equals 24848 and coefficient equals 9450. As a result, we can use the intercept and coefficient to infer the response value. For example, we can infer the response value when x at 3 is equal to 53198 (3 *9450 + 24848).

3.2.2*e* Summarizing Linear Model Fits

The summary function can be used to obtain the formatted coefficient, standard errors, degree of freedom, and other summarized information of a fitted model. This recipe introduces how to obtain overall information on a model through the use of the summary function.

3.2.2*f* Getting Ready

You need to have completed the previous recipe by computing the linear model of the x and y_1 variables from the quartet, and have the fitted model assigned to the model2 variable.

3.2.2g How to do it

Perform the following step to summarize linear model fits:

1. Compute a detailed summary of the fitted model:

   > summary (model2)

   Output:

   Call:

   lm(formula = Salary ~ YearsExperience, data = data2)

   Residuals:

Min	1Q	Median	3Q	Max
–7958.0	–4088.5	–459.9	3372.6	11448.0

   Coefficients:

   Estimate Std. Error *t* value *Pr*(>|*t*|)

   (Intercept) 24848.2 2306.7 10.77 1.82*e*-11 ***

   YearsExperience 9450.0 378.8 24.95 < 2*e*-16 ***

   Signif. codes: 0 '***' 0.001 '**' 0.01 '*' 0.05 '.' 0.1 ' ' 1

   Residual standard error: 5788 on 28 degrees of freedom

   Multiple *R*-squared: 0.957, Adjusted *R*-squared: 0.9554

   F-statistic: 622.5 on 1 and 28 *DF*, *p*-value: < 2.2*e* – 16

3.2.2h How it works

The summary function is a generic function used to produce summary statistics. In this case, it computes and returns a list of the summary statistics of the fitted linear model. Here, it will output information such as residuals, coefficient standard error *R*-squared, *f*-statistic, and a degree of freedom. In the Call section, the function called to generate the fitted model is displayed. In the Residuals section, it provides a quick summary (Min, 1*Q*, Median, 3*Q*, Max) of the distribution.

In the Coefficients section, each coefficient is a Gaussian random variable. Within this section, Estimate represents the mean distribution of the variable; Std. Error displays the standard error of the variable; the *t* value is Estimate divided by Std. Error and the *p* value indicates the probability of getting a value larger than the *t* value. In this sample, the *p* value of intercept (1.82*e* – 11) and prestige (2*e* – 16) have a 95 percent level of confidence. Residual standard error outputs the standard deviation of residuals, while the degree of freedom indicates the differences between the observation in training samples and the number used in the model. Multiple *R*-squared is obtained by dividing the sum of squares. One can use *R*-squared to measure how close the data is to fitting into the regression line. Mostly, the higher the *R*-squared, the better the model fits your data. However, it does not necessarily indicate whether the regression model is adequate. This means you might get a good model with a low *R*-squared or you can have a bad model with a high *R*-squared. Since multiple *R*-squared ignores a degree of freedom, the calculated score is biased. To make the calculation fair, an adjusted *R*-squared (0.9554) uses an unbiased estimate, and will be slightly less than multiple *R*-squared (0.957). *F*-statistic is retrieved by performing an *f*-test on the model. A *p* value equal to 2.2*e* – 16 (< 0.05) rejects the null hypothesis (no linear correlation between variables) and indicates that the observed *F* is greater than the critical *F* value. In other words, the result shows that there is a significant positive linear correlation between the variables.

3.2.2*i* Using Linear Regression to Predict Unknown Values

With a fitted regression model, we can apply the model to predict unknown values. For regression models, we can express the precision of prediction with a prediction interval and a confidence interval. In the following recipe, we will introduce how to predict unknown values under these two measurements.

3.2.2*j* Getting Ready

You need to have completed the previous recipe by computing the linear model of the prestige and income variables from the prestige dataset.

3.2.2*k* How to do it

Perform the following steps to predict values with linear regression:

1. Fit a linear model with the years experience and salary variables:

   ```
   > model2 = lm(Salary~YearsExperience,data2)
   ```

2. Assign values to be predicted into newdata:

   ```
   >newdata = data.frame(YearsExperience = c(3.6,7.5,9.5))
   ```

3. Compute the prediction result using the confidence interval with level set as 0.95:

   ```
   >predict(model2, newdata, interval="confidence", level=0.95)
   ```

   Output:

   ```
   0.91
         fit        lwr        upr
   1   58868.07   56286.32   61449.81
   2   95722.92   93019.76   98426.08
   3  114622.85  110783.71  118461.98
   ```

4. Compute the prediction result using this prediction interval:

   ```
   >predict(model2, newdata, interval="predict")
   ```

   Output:

   ```
         fit        lwr        upr
   1   58868.07   46733.42   71002.72
   2   95722.92   83561.86  107883.98
   3  114622.85  102159.97  127085.72
   ```

3.2.2*l* How it works

We first build a linear fitted model with x and y_1 variables. Next, we assign values to be predicted into a DataFrame, newdata. It is important to note that the generated model is in the form of $y_1 \sim x$.

Next, we compute the prediction result using a confidence interval by specifying confidence in the argument interval. From the output of row 1, we get fitted y_1 of the $x = 3.6$ input, which equals to 58868.07, and a 95 percent confidence interval (set 0.95 in the level argument) of the y_1 mean for $x = 3$ is between 56286.32 and 61449.81. In addition to this, row 2 and 3 give the prediction result of y_1 with an input of $x = 7.5$ and $x = 9.5$.

Next, we compute the prediction result using a prediction interval by specifying prediction in the argument interval. From the output of row 1, we can see fitted y_1 of the $x = 3.6$ input is equal to 58868.07, and a 95 percent prediction interval of y_1 for $x = 3.6$ is between 46733.42 and 71002.72. Row 2 and 3 output the prediction result of y_1 with an input of $x = 7.5$ and $x = 9.5$.

3.2.2*m* Generating a diagnostic Plot of a Fitting Model

Diagnostics are methods to evaluate assumptions of the regression, which can be used to determine whether a fitted model adequately represents the data. In the following recipe, we will introduce how to diagnose a regression model through the use of a diagnostic plot.

3.2.2*n* Getting Ready

You need to have completed the previous recipe by computing a linear model of the x and y_1 variables from the salary, and have the model assigned to the model2 variable.

3.2.2*o* How to do it

Perform the following step to generate a diagnostic plot of the fitted model:

```
> par(mfrow=c(2,2))
> plot(model2)
```

Output:

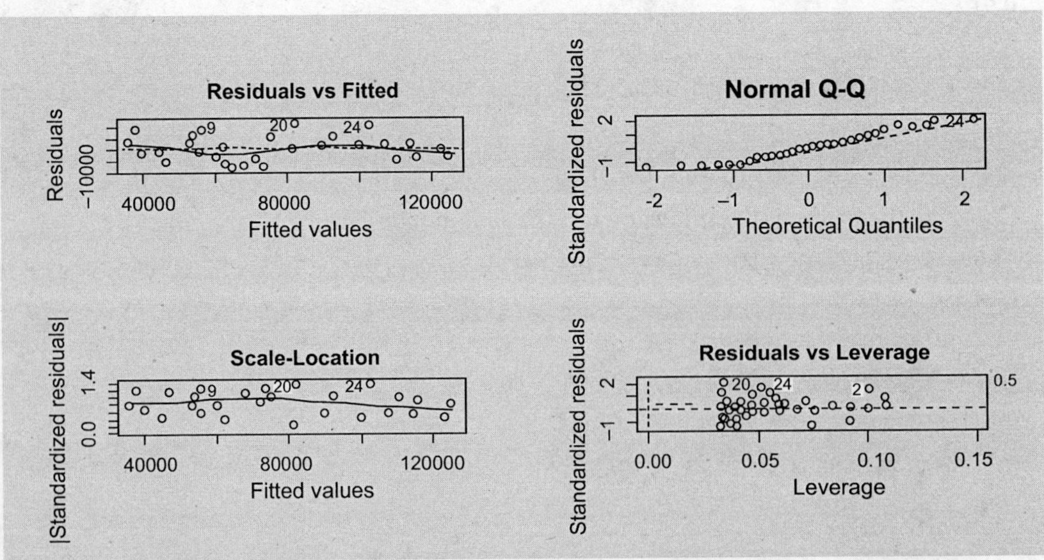

Fig. 3.13: Diagnostic plot of fitted linear regression model

3.2.2*p* How it works

The plot function generates four diagnostic plots of a regression model:

The upper-left plot shows residuals versus fitted values. Within the plot, residuals represent the vertical distance from a point to the regression line. If all points fall exactly on the regression line, all residuals will fall exactly on the dotted gray line. The red line within the plot is a smooth curve with regard to residuals, and if all the dots fall exactly on the regression line, the position of the red line should exactly match the dotted gray line.

The upper-right shows the normal for the residuals. This plot verifies the assumption that residuals were normally distributed. Thus, if the residuals were normally distributed, they should lie exactly on the gray dotted line. The Scale-Location plot on the bottom-left is used to measure the square root of the standardized residuals against the fitted value. Therefore, if all dots lie on the regression line, the value of y should be close to zero. Since it is assumed that the variance of residuals does not change the distribution substantially, if the assumption is correct, the red line should be relatively flat.

The bottom-right plot shows standardized residuals versus leverage. The leverage is a measurement of how each data point influences the regression. It is a measurement of the distance from the centroid of regression and level of isolation (measured by whether it has neighbors). Also, you can find the contour of Cook's distance, which is affected by high leverage and large residuals. You can use this to measure how regression would change if a single point is deleted. The red line is smooth with regard to standardized residuals. For a perfect fit regression, the red line should be close to the dashed line with no points over 0.5 in Cook's distance.

3.2.2*q* There's more

To see more of the diagnostic plot function, you can use the help function to access further information:

```
> ?plot.lm
```

In this case, where the point on index 2 and 24 show greater Cook's distance than other points, one can investigate whether these points might be an outlier. In order to discover whether there are points with large Cook's distance, one can use the cooks.distance function to compute the Cook's distance of each point, and analyze the distribution of distance through visualization:

```
> plot(cooks.distance(model2))
```

Output:

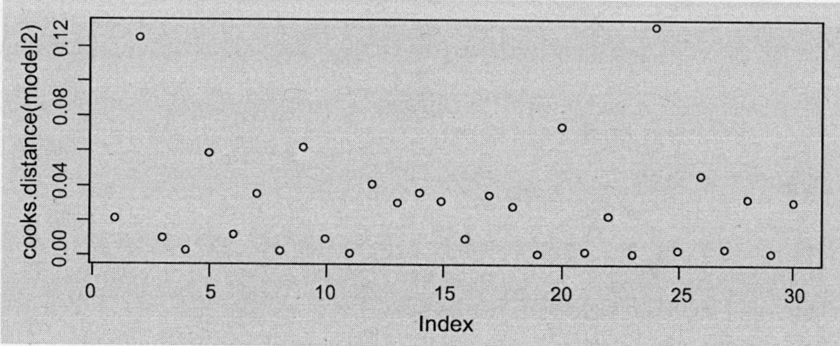

Fig. 3.14: Distribution of Cook's distance from linear regression model

To evaluate residuals of model2, you can use the resid function for obtaining this

```
> res2=resid(model2)
> res2
> plot(res2)
```

Output:

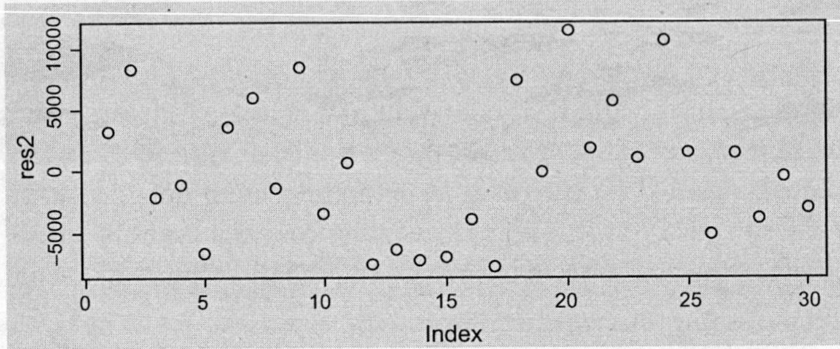

Fig. 3.15: Distribution of residuals of linear regression model

To evaluate the fitted values of the model2, you can use the fitted function for obtaining this:

```
> fmodel2=fitted(model2)
> plot(fmodel2)
```

Output:

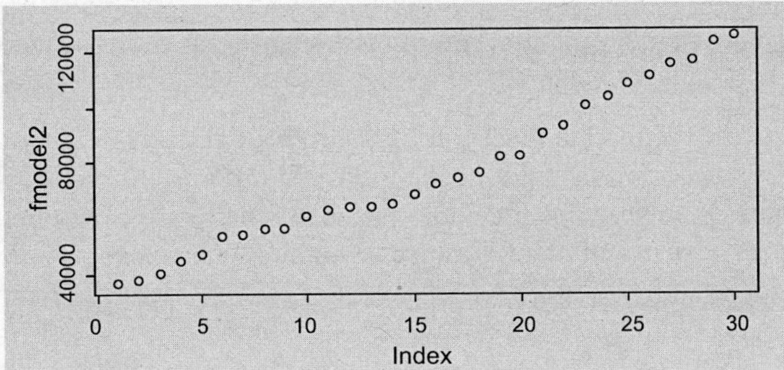

Fig. 3.16: Distribution of predicted values of linear regression model

To evaluate the ANOVA table of model1, you can use the anova function for obtaining this:

```
>anova(model2)
```

Output:

```
Analysis of Variance Table
Response: Salary
Df Sum Sq Mean Sq F valuePr(>F)
YearsExperience 1 2.0857e+10 2.0857e+10 622.51 < 2.2e-16 ***
Residuals 28 9.3813e+08 3.3505e+07
---
```

Signif. codes: 0 '***' 0.001 '**' 0.01 '*' 0.05 '.' 0.1 ' ' 1

From ANOVA table it is concluded that the present regression model is statistically significant.

Table 3.2: Coding of Linear Regression Model

```
>install.packages("car")
> library(car)
>url="https://drive.google.com/file/d/18ssBdfTpFhl1OgWmAjqDKzC6QJfG_oMX/view?usp=sharing"
> data2=read.csv(url)
> str(data2)
> head(data2)
> plot(data2)
> plot(data2$YearsExperience,data2$Salary)
> model2 = lm(Salary~YearsExperience,data2)
>abline(model2, col="red")
> model2
> summary (model2)
>newdata = data.frame(YearsExperience = c(3.6,7.5,9.5))
>predict(model2, newdata, interval="confidence", level=0.95)
>predict(model2, newdata, interval="predict")
> par(mfrow=c(2,2))
> plot(model2)
> plot(cooks.distance(model2))
> res2=resid(model2)
> res2
> plot(res2)
> fmodel2=fitted(model2)
> plot(fmodel2)
>anova(model2)
```

3.3 MULTIPLE LINEAR REGRESSION MODEL

Multiple regression includes multiple predictors and using the same lm function we can create a model. This is the oldest type and most widely known type of regression. In this the dependent variable is continuous and the independent variables can be discrete or continuous and the regression line is linear. Multiple regression model is very sensitive to outliers and cross-correlations.

3.3.1 Case – I: Fitting of Multiple Linear Regression

The simplest model in regression is multiple linear regression, which is best used when there is more than one predictor variables, and the relationship between the response variable and the independent variables is linear. In *R*, we can fit a multiple linear model includes multiple predictors to data with the lm function.

3.3.1*a* Getting Ready

You have completed the previous recipes and have installed the car package. You are also aware of using the lm function. In this recipe, we will use the Prestige dataset from the car package.

3.3.1*b* How to do it

Perform the following steps to perform multiple linear regression with *lm*:

1. You should install the car package and load its library:

   ```
   >install.packages("car")
   > library(car)
   ```

2. From the package, you can load the Prestige dataset:

   ```
   >url="https://drive.google.com/file/d/1zZuozCHlX5nddUVUkBNrGbCJXL55QZPj/view?usp
   =sharing"
   > data1=read.csv(url)
   ```

3. You can use the str function to display the structure of the Prestige dataset:

   ```
   > str(data1)
   ```

   Output:

   ```
   'data.frame' : 102 obs. of 7 variables:
   $ job : chr "gov.administrators" "general.managers" "accountants" "purchasing.officers" ...
   $ education : num 13.1 12.3 12.8 11.4 14.6 ...
   $ income : int 12351 25879 9271 8865 8403 11030 8258 14163 11377 11023 ...
   $ women : num 11.16 4.02 15.7 9.11 11.68 ...
   $ prestige : num 68.8 69.1 63.4 56.8 73.5 77.6 72.6 78.1 73.1 68.8 ...
   $ census : int 1113 1130 1171 1175 2111 2113 2133 2141 2143 2153 ...
   $ type : chr "prof" "prof" "prof" "prof" ...
   >head(data1)
   ```

   Output:

   ```
   job education income women prestige census type
   1. gov.administrators  13.11  12351  11.16  68.8  1113 prof
   2. general.managers    12.26  25879   4.02  69.1  1130 prof
   3. accountants         12.77   9271  15.70  63.4  1171 prof
   ```

4. Draw a scatter plot of the *x* and *y* variables with plot:

   ```
   > plot (data1)
   ```

Output:

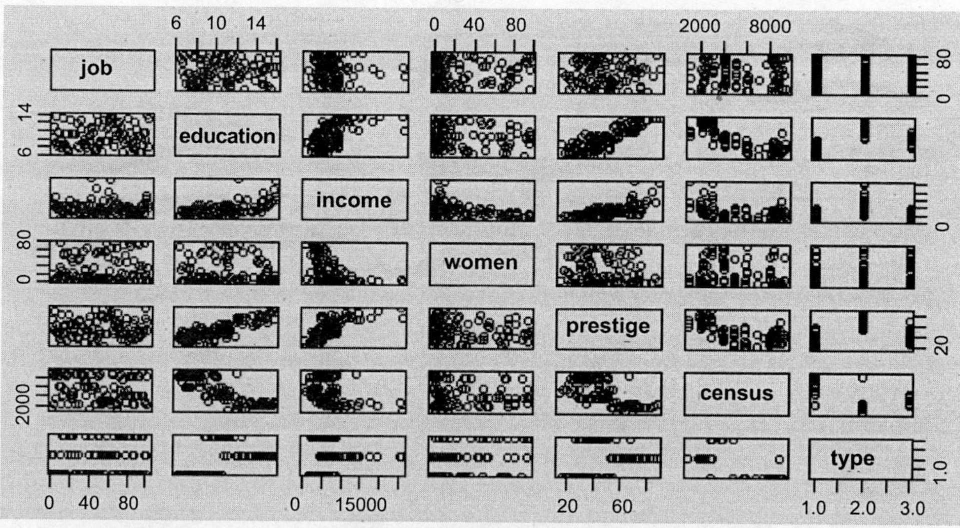

Fig. 3.17: A matrix of scatter plots

5. To view the fit model, execute the following:

   Fit a linear model with the prestige and income variables:

   > model1=lm(formula = income ~ prestige + women)

   >model1

   Output:

   Call:

   lm(formula = income ~ prestige + women, data = data3)

   Coefficients:

(Intercept)	prestige	women
431.57	165.87	−48.38

   > scatter3d(income~prestige+women, data1)

   Output:

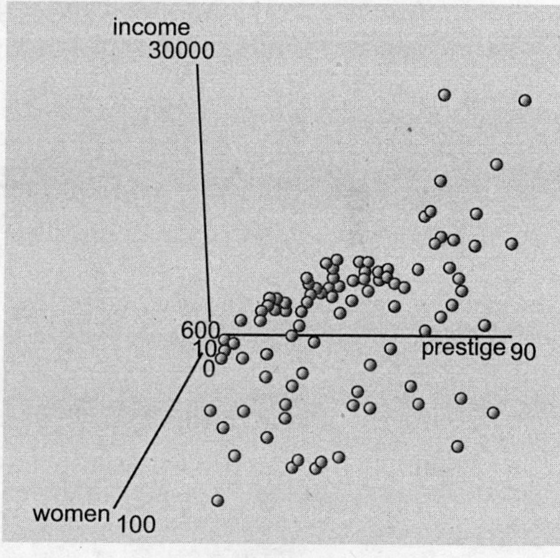

Fig. 3.18: 3D scatter plot

3.3.1c How it works

The regression model has the income ~ prestige + women form, where income is the response vector, and prestige and women specifies a predictor. We can illustrate a simple regression model in the formula $y = \alpha + \beta_1 x_1 + \beta_2 x_2$, where α is the intercept while the slope, β_1 and β_2, describes the change in y when x changes. By using the least squares method, we can estimate and (where indicates the mean value of y and denotes the mean value of x_1 and x_2). In this example, we load the Prestige dataset from the car package. To generate the regression line, we use the *lm* function to generate a model of the three variables. Further, we use scatter 3d to plot a regression line in a 3d plot.

3.3.1*d* Summarizing multiple regression

The summary function can be used to obtain the formatted coefficient, standard errors, degree of freedom, and other summarized information of a fitted model. This recipe introduces how to obtain overall information on a model using the summary function.

3.3.1*e* Getting ready

You need to have completed the previous recipe by computing the linear model of the income, prestige and women variables from the Prestige dataset, and have the fitted model assigned to the model variable.

3.3.1*f* How to do it...

Perform the following step to summarize linear model fits:

1. Compute a detailed summary of the fitted model:

   >summary(model1)

   Output:

   Call:

   lm(formula = income ~ prestige + women, data = data3)

   Residuals:

Min	1Q	Median	3Q	Max
−7620.9	−1008.7	−240.4	873.1	14180.0

   Coefficients:

   Estimate Std. Error *t* value *Pr*(>|*t*|)

(Intercept)	431.574	807.630	0.534	0.594
prestige	165.875	14.988	11.067<	2e-16 ***
women	−48.385	8.128	−5.953	4.02e-08 ***

   Signif. codes: 0 '***' 0.001 '**' 0.01 '*' 0.05 '.' 0.1 ' ' 1

   Residual standard error: 2573 on 99 degrees of freedom

   Multiple *R*-squared: 0.64, Adjusted *R*-squared: 0.6327

   F-statistic: 87.98 on 2 and 99 *DF*, *p*-value: < 2.2e − 16

3.3.1*g* How it works...

The summary function is a generic function used to produce summary statistics. In this case, it computes and returns a list of the summary statistics of the fitted linear model. Here, it will output information such as residuals, coefficient standard error *R*-squared, f-statistic, and a degree of freedom. In the Call section, the function called to generate the fitted model is displayed. In the Residuals section, it provides a quick summary (min, 1Q, median, 3Q, max) of the distribution.

In the Coefficients section, each coefficient is a Gaussian random variable. Within this section, Estimate represents the mean distribution of the variable; Std. Error displays the standard error of the variable; the *t* value is Estimate divided by Std. Error and the *p* value indicates the probability of getting a value larger than the *t* value.

Residual standard error outputs the standard deviation of residuals, while the degree of freedom indicates the differences between the observation in training samples and the number used in the model. Multiple *R*-squared is obtained by dividing the sum of squares. One can use *R*-squared to measure how close the data is to fit into the regression line. Mostly, the higher the *R*-squared, the better the model fits your data. However, it does not necessarily indicate whether the regression model is adequate. This means you might get a good model with a low *R*-squared or you can have a bad model with a high *R*-squared. Since multiple *R*-squared ignores a degree of freedom, the calculated score is biased. To make the calculation fair, an adjusted *R*-squared (0.6327) uses an unbiased estimate, and will be slightly less than multiple *R*-squared (0.64).

3.3.1*h* Using multiple regression to predict unknown values

With a fitted regression model, we can apply the model to predict unknown values. For regression models, we can express the precision of prediction with a prediction interval and a confidence interval. In the following recipe, we will introduce how to predict unknown values under these two measurements.

5.3.1*i* Getting Ready

You need to have completed the previous recipe by computing the linear model of the income, prestige, and women variables from the Prestige dataset.

3.3.1*j* How to do it

Perform the following steps to predict values with multiple regression:

1. Fit a linear model with the income, prestige, and women variables:

   ```
   > model = lm(income ~ prestige + women, Prestige)
   ```

2. Assign values to be predicted into newdata:

   ```
   > newdata1 = data.frame(prestige = c(72,83,92), women=c(12,16,25))
   ```

3. Compute the prediction result using the confidence interval with level set as 0.95:

   ```
   >predict(model1, newdata = newdata1)
   ```

   Output:

   ```
          1          2          3
   11793.94   13425.03   14482.44
   ```

4. Compute the prediction result using this prediction interval:

   ```
   >predict(model1, newdata = newdata1, interval="predict")
   ```

   Output:

   ```
          fit        lwr        upr
   1 11793.94   6606.130   16981.76
   2 13425.03   8183.446   18666.61
   3 14482.44   9180.100   19784.77
   ```

3.3.1*k* How it works

We first build a multiple regression model with income, prestige and women variables. Next, we assign values to be predicted into a DataFrame, newdata. It is important to note that the generated model is in the form of income ~ prestige + women. Next, we compute the prediction result using a confidence interval by specifying confidence in the argument interval.

3.3.1*l* There's more

To perform linear regression, we first prepare the data that has a linear relationship between the predictor variable and response variable. In this example, we load prestige dataset from the package car. Within the dataset, the x_1 and x_2 and y_1 variables have a linear relationship, and we prepare a scatter plot of these variables. As per the previous screenshot, the regression line illustrates the linear relationship of x_1 and x_2 and y_1 variables.

3.3.1*m* Generating a diagnostic Plot of a Fitting Model

Diagnostics are methods to evaluate assumptions of the regression, which can be used to determine whether a fitted model adequately represents the data. In the following recipe, we will introduce how to diagnose a regression model through the use of a diagnostic plot.

3.3.1*n* Getting Ready

You need to have completed the previous recipe by computing a linear model of the x_1 and x_2 and y_1 variables from the prestige and women, and have the model assigned to the model1 variable.

3.3.1*o* How to do it

Perform the following step to generate a diagnostic plot of the fitted model:

1. Plot the diagnostic plot of the regression model:

```
> par(mfrow=c(2,2))
> plot(model1)
```

Output:

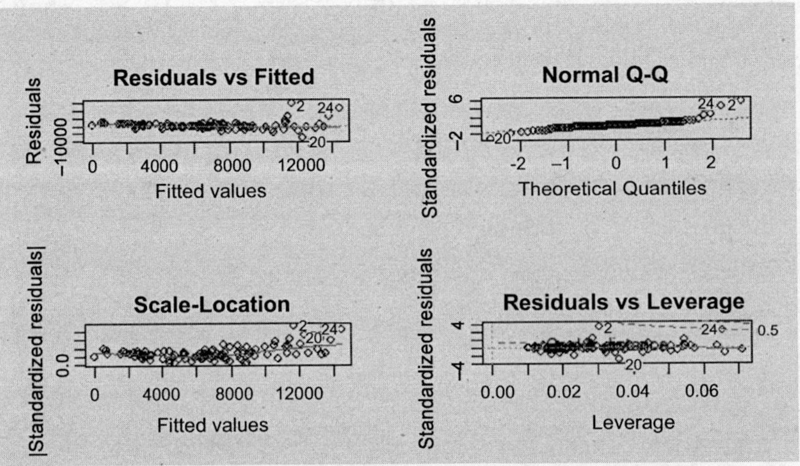

Fig. 3.19: Diagnostic plot of fitted multiple regression model

3.3.1*p* How it works

The plot function generates four diagnostic plots of a regression model:

The upper-left plot shows residuals versus fitted values. Within the plot, residuals represent the vertical distance from a point to the regression line. If all points fall exactly on the regression line, all residuals will fall exactly on the dotted gray line. The red line within the plot is a smooth curve with regard to residuals, and if all the dots fall exactly on the regression line, the position of the red line should exactly match the dotted gray line.

The upper-right shows the normal for the residuals. This plot verifies the assumption that residuals were normally distributed. Thus, if the residuals were normally distributed, they should lie exactly on the gray dotted line. The Scale-Location plot on the bottom-left is used to measure the square root of the standardized residuals against the fitted value. Therefore, if all dots lie on the regression line, the value of y should be close to zero. Since it is assumed that the variance of residuals does not change the distribution substantially, if the assumption is correct, the red line should be relatively flat.

The bottom-right plot shows standardized residuals versus leverage. The leverage is a measurement of how each data point influences the regression. It is a measurement of the distance from the centroid of regression and level of isolation (measured by whether it has neighbors). Also, you can find the contour of Cook's distance, which is affected by high leverage and large residuals. You can use this to measure how regression would change if a single point is deleted. The red line is smooth with regard to standardized residuals. For a perfect fit regression, the red line should be close to the dashed line with no points over 0.5 in Cook's distance.

3.3.1*q* There's more

To see more of the diagnostic plot function, you can use the help function to access further information:

```
> ?plot.lm
```

In this case, where the point on index 2 and 24 show greater Cook's distance than other points, one can investigate whether these points might be an outlier. In order to discover whether there are points with large Cook's distance, one can use the cooks.distance function to compute the Cook's distance of each point, and analyze the distribution of distance through visualization:

```
> plot(cooks.distance(model1))
```

Output:

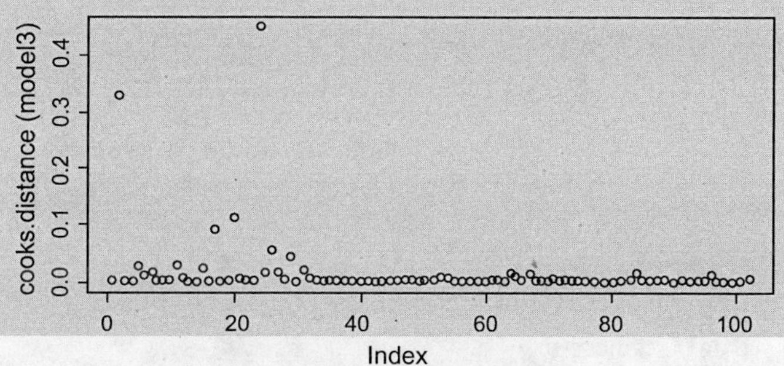

Fig. 3.20: Distribution of Cook's distance from multiple regression model

To evaluate residuals of model1, you can use the resid function for obtaining this:

```
>res1=resid(model1)
>res1
>plot(res1)
```

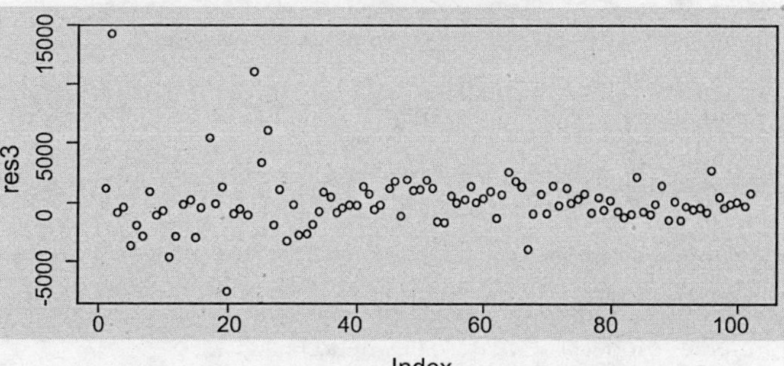

Fig. 3.21: Distribution of residuals of multiple regression model

Output:

To evaluate the fitted values of the model1, you can use the fitted function for obtaining this:

```
>fmodel1=fitted(model1)
>plot(fmodel1)
```

Output:

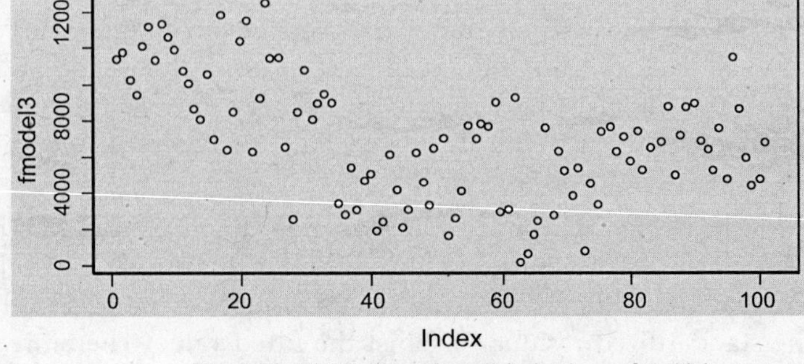

Fig. 3.21: Distribution of predicted values of multiple regression model

To evaluate the ANOVA table of model1, you can use the anova function for obtaining this:

```
>anova(model1)
```

Output:

Analysis of Variance Table

Response: income

Df	Sum	Sq	Mean	Sq	F valuePr(>F)
prestige	1	930599714	930599714	140.534	< 2.2*e* – 16 ***
women	1	234647032	234647032	35.435	4.016e – 08 ***
Residuals	99	655566665	6621886		

Signif. codes: 0 '***' 0.001 '**' 0.01 '*' 0.05 '.' 0.1 ' ' 1

From ANOVA table it is concluded that the present regression model is statistically significant.

Table 3.3: Coding of Multiple Regression Model

```
>install.packages("car")
> library(car)
>url="https://drive.google.com/file/d/1zZuozCHlX5nddUVUkBNrGbCJXL55QZPj/view?usp=sharing"
> data1=read.csv(url)
> str(data1)
> head(data1)
> plot(data1)
> attach(data1)
> model1 = lm(income~prestige+women, data1)
> model1
> scatter3d(income~prestige+women, data1)
> summary(model1)
> newdata1 = data.frame(prestige = c(72,83,92), women=c(12,16,25))
>predict(model1, newdata = newdata1)
```

```
>predict(model1, newdata = newdata1, interval="predict")
> par(mfrow=c(2,2))
> plot(model1)
> plot(cooks.distance(model1))
> res1=resid(model1)
> res1
> plot(res1)
> fmodel1=fitted(model1)
> plot(fmodel1)
>anova(model1)
```

3.3.1*r* Another Multiple Regression Model

```
> model2 = lm(income~prestige+women+education,data2)
> model2
Output:
Call:
lm(formula = income ~ prestige + women + education, data = data3)
Coefficients:
(Intercept)  prestige    women   education
  -253.8      141.4      -50.9     177.2
> summary(model2)
Output:
Call:
lm(formula = income ~ prestige + women + education, data = data3)
Residuals:
   Min        1Q      Median      3Q        Max
 -7715.3   -929.7    -231.2     689.7    14391.8
Coefficients:
              Estimate   Std. Error   t value    Pr(>|t|)
(Intercept)   -253.850   1086.157     -0.234     0.816
 prestige      141.435     29.910      4.729     7.58e - 06 ***
 women         -50.896      8.556     -5.948     4.19e - 08 ***
education      177.199    187.632      0.944     0.347
---
Signif. codes:  0 '***'    0.001 '**'    0.01 '*'    0.05 '.' 0.1 ' ' 1
Residual standard error: 2575 on 98 degrees of freedom
Multiple R-squared: 0.6432, Adjusted R-squared: 0.6323
```

F-statistic: 58.89 on 3 and 98 *DF*, *p*-value: < 2.2*e* – 16

```
>newdata2=data.frame(prestige=c(72,82,92),women=c(12,16,25),education=c(11.2,12.5,12.2))
>predict(model2, newdata = newdata2)
>predict(model2, newdata = newdata2, interval="predict")
```

Output:

1	2	3
11321.10	12885.94	13824.84

	fit	lwr	upr
1	11321.10	6035.563	16606.63
2	12885.94	7519.904	18251.98
3	13824.84	8341.950	19307.73

```
> par(mfrow=c(2,2))
> plot(model2)
```

Output:

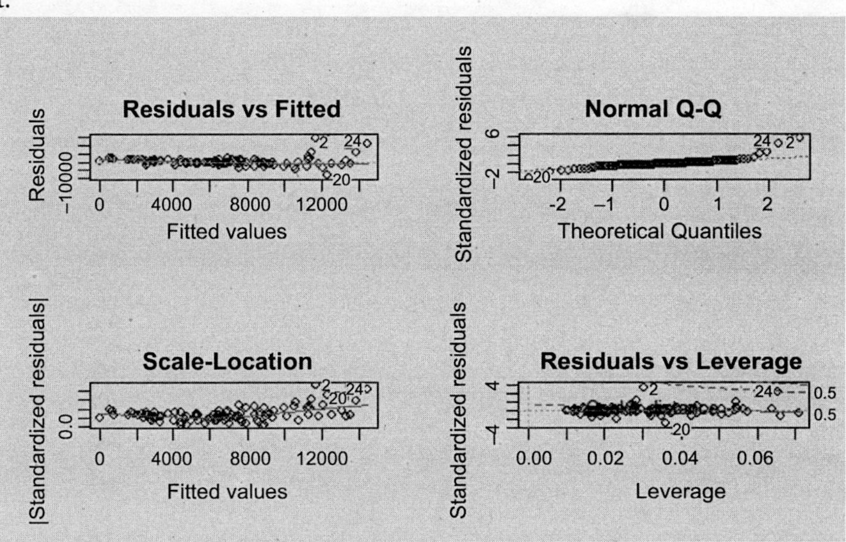

Fig. 3.23: Diagnostic plot of fitted multiple regression model

```
> plot(cooks.distance(model2))
> res2=resid(model2)
> res2
> plot(res2)
```

Output:

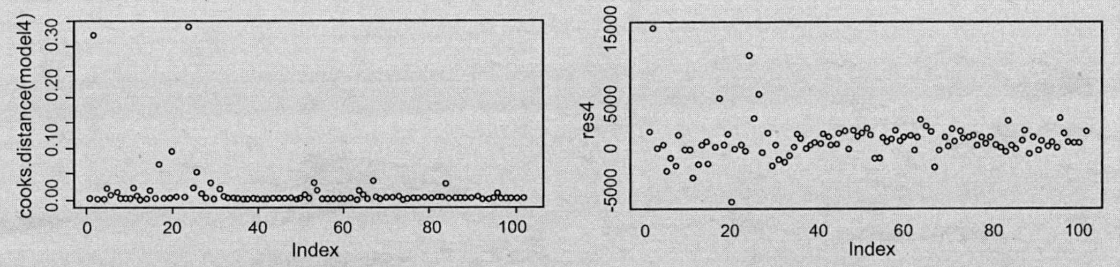

Fig. 3.24: Distribution of Cook's distance from multiple regression model

Fig. 3.25: Distribution of residuals of multiple regression model

```
> fmodel2=fitted(model2)
> plot(fmodel2)
```

Output:

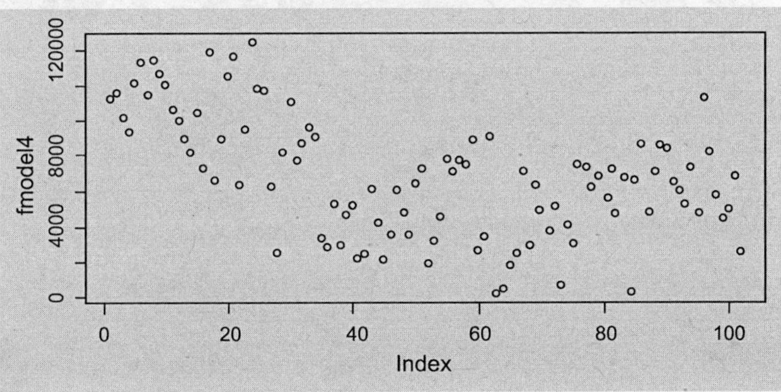

Fig. 3.26: Distribution of predicted values of multiple regression model

```
>anova(model2)
```

Output:

Analysis of Variance Table

Response: income

	Df	Sum *Sq*	Mean *Sq*	*F* value	*Pr*(>*F*)
prestige	1	930599714	930599714	140.3805	< 2.2e-16 ***
women	1	234647032	234647032	35.3964	4.169e-08 ***
education	1	5912400	5912400	0.8919	0.3473
Residuals	98	649654265	6629125		

Signif. codes: 0 '***' 0.001 '**' 0.01 '*' 0.05 '.' 0.1 ' ' 1

Table 3.4: Coding of Multiple Regression Model

```
>install.packages("car")
> library(car)
>url="https://drive.google.com/file/d/1zZuozCHlX5nddUVUkBNrGbCJXL55QZPj/view?usp=sharing"
> data2=read.csv(url)
> str(data2)
> head(data2)
> plot(data2)
> attach(data2)
> model2 = lm(income~prestige+women+education,data2)
> model2
> summary(model2)
> newdata2 = data.frame(prestige = c(72,82,92), women=c(12,16,25),education=c(11.2,12.5,12.2))
>predict(model2, newdata = newdata2)
>predict(model2, newdata = newdata2, interval="predict")
> par(mfrow=c(2,2))
> plot(model2)
> plot(cooks.distance(model2))
> res2=resid(model2)
> res2
> plot(res2)
> fmodel2=fitted(model2)
> plot(fmodel2)
>anova(model2)
```

3.3.2 Case – II: Fitting of Multiple Linear Regression

The simplest model in regression is multiple linear regression, which is best used when there is more than one predictor variables, and the relationship between the response variable and the independent variables is linear. In *R*, we can fit a multiple linear model includes multiple predictors to data with the lm function.

3.3.2*a* Getting Ready

You have completed the previous recipes and have installed the car package. You are also aware of using the lm function. In this recipe, we will use the Student_Marks dataset from the car package.

3.3.2*b* How to do it

Perform the following steps to perform multiple linear regression with *lm*:

1. You should install the car package and load its library:

```
>install.packages("car")
> library(car)
```

2. From the package, you can load the Students_Marksdataset:

   >url="https://drive.google.com/file/d/1YQkALwtc0fdzLKNrM2OoldDETFudg92e/view?usp=sharing"

   > data3=read.csv(url)

3. You can use the str function to display the structure of the Students_Marks dataset:

   > str(data3)

   Output:

   'data.frame': 100 obs. of 3 variables:

   $ number_courses: int 3 4 4 6 8 6 3 5 4 3 ...

   $ time_study: num 4.508 0.096 3.133 7.909 7.811 ...

   $ Marks: num 19.2 7.73 13.81 53.02 55.3 ...

   > head(data3)

   Output:

number	_coursestime	_study	Marks
1	3	4.508	19.202
2	4	0.096	7.734
3	4	3.133	13.811
4	6	7.909	53.018
5	8	7.811	55.299
6	6	3.211	17.822

4. Draw a scatter plot of the *x* and *y* variables with plot:

   > plot(data3)

   Output:

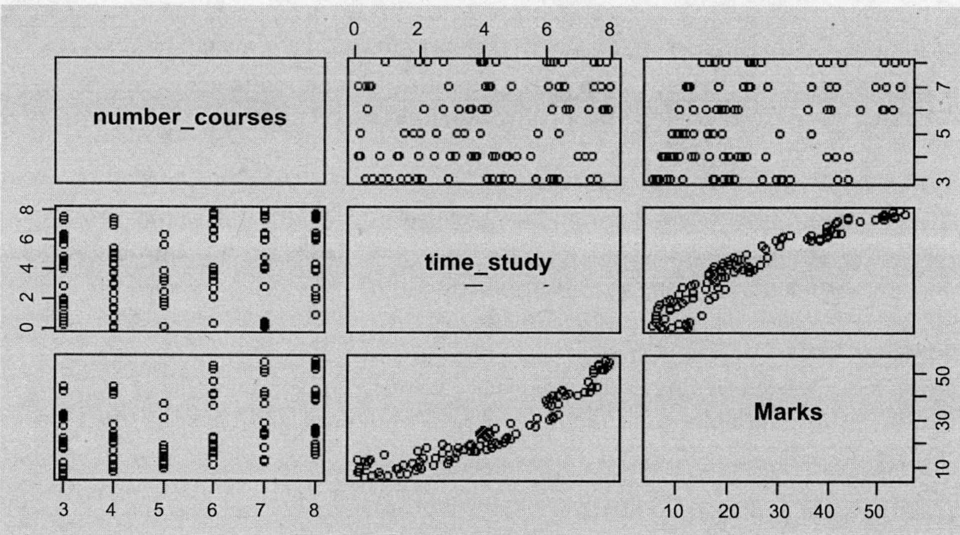

Fig. 3.27: A matrix of scatter plots

5. To view the fit model, execute the following:

Fit a linear model with the prestige and income variables:

```
> attach(data3)
> model3 = lm(Marks~number_courses+time_study, data3)
> model3
```

Output:

Call:

lm(formula = Marks ~ number_courses + time_study, data = data3)

Coefficients:

(Intercept) number_coursestime_study

-7.456 1.864 5.399

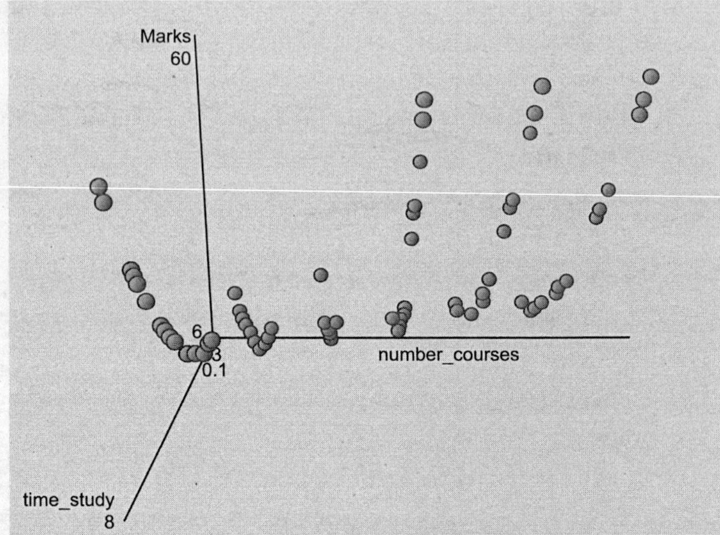

Fig. 3.28: 3D scatter plot

```
> scatter3d(Marks~number_courses+ time_study, data3)
```

Output:

3.3.2*c* How it works

The regression model has the Marks ~ number_courses + time_study form, where marks is the response vector, and prestige and women specifies a predictor. We can illustrate a simple regression model in the formula $y = \alpha + \beta_1 x_1 + \beta_2 x_2$, where α is the intercept while the slope, β_1 and β_2, describes the change in y when x changes. By using the least squares method, we can estimate and (where indicates the mean value of y and denotes the mean value of x_1 and x_2). In this example, we load the Student_Marks dataset from the car package. To generate the regression line, we use the *lm* function to generate a model of the three variables. Further, we use scatter3d to plot a regression line in a 3d plot.

3.3.2*d* Summarizing multiple regression

The summary function can be used to obtain the formatted coefficient, standard errors, degree of freedom, and other summarized information of a fitted model. This recipe introduces how to obtain overall information on a model using the summary function.

3.3.2*e* Getting ready

You need to have completed the previous recipe by computing the linear model of the Marks, number_courses and time_study variables from the Student_Marks dataset, and have the fitted model assigned to the model variable.

3.3.2*f* How to do it...

Perform the following step to summarize linear model fits:

1. Compute a detailed summary of the fitted model:

```
>summary(model3)
Output:
Call:
lm(formula = Marks ~ number_courses + time_study, data = data3)
Residuals:
0.91
    Min       1Q    Median      3Q      Max
-4.5617  -3.1023   -0.8361  3.6051   7.2158
Coefficients:
Estimate Std. Error t value Pr(>|t|)
(Intercept)        -7.4563   1.1745   -6.349 6.98e - 09 ***
number_courses      1.8641   0.2017    9.243 5.78- - 15 ***
time_study          5.3992   0.1529   35.303  < 2e-16 ***
---
Signif. codes: 0 '***'  0.001 '**'  0.01 '*' 0.05 '.' 0.1 ' ' 1
Residual standard error: 3.534 on 97 degrees of freedom
Multiple R-squared: 0.9404, Adjusted R-squared: 0.9391
F-statistic: 764.8 on 2 and 97 DF, p-value: < 2.2e - 16
```

3.3.2g How it works...

The summary function is a generic function used to produce summary statistics. In this case,

it computes and returns a list of the summary statistics of the fitted linear model. Here, it will output information such as residuals, coefficient standard error *R*-squared, *f*-statistic, and a degree of freedom. In the Call section, the function called to generate the fitted model is displayed. In the Residuals section, it provides a quick summary (min, 1Q, median, 3Q, max) of the distribution.

In the Coefficients section, each coefficient is a Gaussian random variable. Within this section, Estimate represents the mean distribution of the variable; Std.Error displays the standard error of the variable; the *t* value is Estimate divided by Std.Error and the pvalue indicates the probability of getting a value larger than the *t* value.

Residual standard error outputs the standard deviation of residuals, while the degree of freedom indicates the differences between the observation in training samples and the number used in the model. Multiple *R*-squared is obtained by dividing the sum of squares. One can use *R*-squared to measure how close the data is to fit into the regression line. Mostly, the higher the *R*-squared, the better the model fits your data. However, it does not necessarily indicate whether the regression model is adequate. This means you might get a good model with a low *R*-squared or you can have a bad model with a high *R*-squared. Since multiple *R*-squared ignores a degree of freedom, the calculated score is biased. To make the calculation fair, an adjusted *R*-squared (0.9391) uses an unbiased estimate, and will be slightly less than multiple *R*-squared (0.9404).

3.3.2*h* Using multiple regression to predict unknown values

With a fitted regression model, we can apply the model to predict unknown values. For regression models, we can express the precision of prediction with a prediction interval and a confidence interval. In the following recipe, we will introduce how to predict unknown values under these two measurements.

3.3.2*i* Getting Ready

You need to have completed the previous recipe by computing the linear model of the marks, number_course, and time_study variables from the Student_Marks dataset.

3.3.2*j* How to do it

Perform the following steps to predict values with multiple regression:

1. Fit a linear model with the marks, number_course, and time_study variables:

   ```
   > model3 = lm(Marks~number_courses+time_study, data3)
   ```

2. Assign values to be predicted into newdata:

   ```
   > newdata3 = data.frame(number_course = c(72,82,92), time_study =c(12,16,22))
   ```

3. Compute the prediction result using the confidence interval with level set as 0.95:

   ```
   >predict(model3, newdata = newdata3)
   ```

   Output:

   ```
          1          2          3
   30.10161   53.86334   40.03877
   ```

4. Compute the prediction result using this prediction interval:

   ```
   >predict(model3, newdata = newdata3, interval="predict")
   ```

   Output:

   ```
          fit        lwr        upr
   1  30.10161   23.04108   37.16214
   2  53.86334   46.60128   61.12539
   3  40.03877   32.93528   47.14226
   ```

3.3.2*k* How it works

We first build a multiple regression model with income, prestige and women variables. Next, we assign values to be predicted into a DataFrame, newdata. It is important to note that the generated model is in the form of Marks~ number_course +time_study. Next, we compute the prediction result using a confidence interval by specifying confidence in the argument interval.

3.3.2*l* There's more

To perform linear regression, we first prepare the data that has a linear relationship between the predictor variable and response variable. In this example, we load prestige dataset from the package car. Within the dataset, the x_1 and x_2 and y_1 variables have a linear relationship, and we prepare a scatter plot of these variables. As per the previous screenshot, the regression line illustrates the linear relationship of x_1 and x_2 and y_1 variables.

3.3.2*m* Generating a diagnostic Plot of a Fitting Model

Diagnostics are methods to evaluate assumptions of the regression, which can be used to determine whether a fitted model adequately represents the data. In the following recipe, we will introduce how to diagnose a regression model through the use of a diagnostic plot.

3.3.2*n* Getting Ready

You need to have completed the previous recipe by computing a linear model of the x_1 and x_2 and y_1 variables from the prestige and women, and have the model assigned to the model1 variable.

3.3.2*o* How to do it

Perform the following step to generate a diagnostic plot of the fitted model:

1. Plot the diagnostic plot of the regression model:

```
> par(mfrow=c(2,2))
> plot(model3)
```

Output:

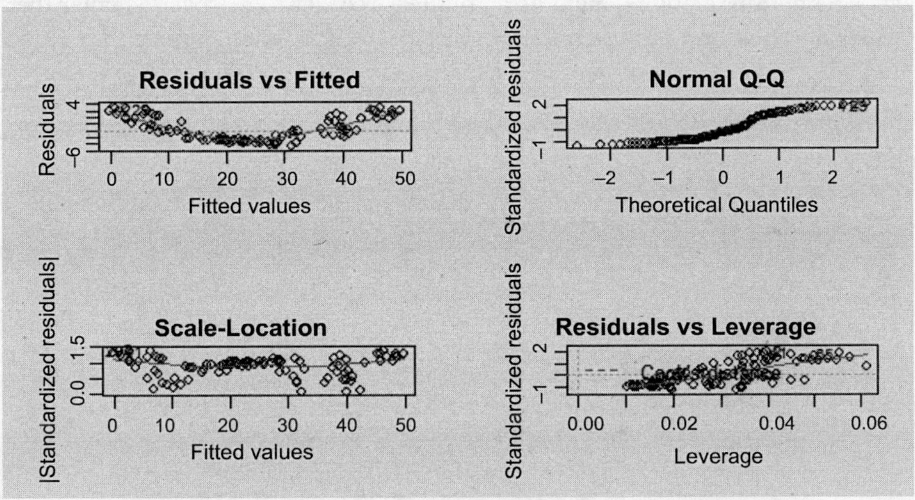

Fig. 3.29: Diagnostic plot of fitted multiple regression model

3.3.2*p* How it works

The plot function generates four diagnostic plots of a regression model:

The upper-left plot shows residuals versus fitted values. Within the plot, residuals represent the vertical distance from a point to the regression line. If all points fall exactly on the regression line, all residuals will fall exactly on the dotted gray line. The red line within the plot is a smooth curve with regard to residuals, and if all the dots fall exactly on the regression line, the position of the red line should exactly match the dotted gray line.

The upper-right shows the normal for the residuals. This plot verifies the assumption that residuals were normally distributed. Thus, if the residuals were normally distributed, they should lie exactly on the gray dotted line. The Scale-Location plot on the bottom-left is used to measure the square root of the standardized residuals against the fitted value. Therefore, if all dots lie on the regression line, the value of y should be close to zero. Since it is assumed that the variance of residuals does not change the distribution substantially, if the assumption is correct, the red line should be relatively flat.

The bottom-right plot shows standardized residuals versus leverage. The leverage is a measurement of how each data point influences the regression. It is a measurement of the distance from the centroid of regression and level of isolation (measured by whether it has neighbors). Also, you can find the contour of Cook's distance, which is affected by high leverage and large residuals. You can use this to measure how regression would change if a single point is deleted. The red line is smooth with regard to standardized residuals. For a perfect fit regression, the red line should be close to the dashed line with no points over 0.5 in Cook's distance.

3.3.2*q* There's more

To see more of the diagnostic plot function, you can use the help function to access further information:

```
> ?plot.lm
```

In this case, where the point on index 2 and 64 show greater Cook's distance than other points, one can investigate whether these points might be an outlier. In order to discover whether there are points with large Cook's distance, one can use the cooks.distance function to compute the Cook's distance of each point, and analyze the distribution of distance through visualization:

```
> plot(cooks.distance(model3))
```

Output:

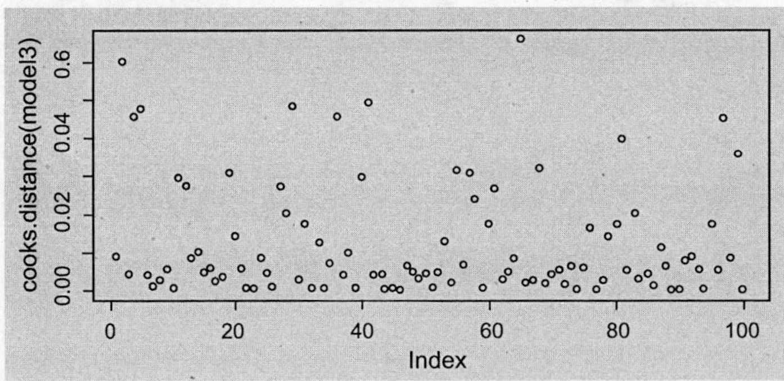

Fig. 3.30: Distribution of Cook's distance from multiple regression model

To evaluate residuals of model3, you can use the resid function for obtaining this:

```
> res3=resid(model3)
> res3
> plot(res3)
```

Output:

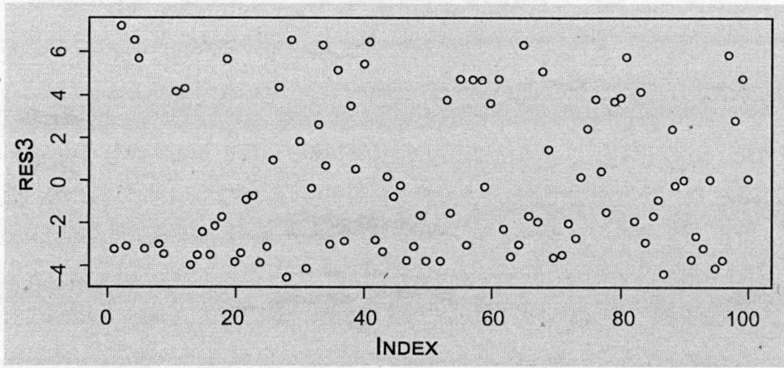

Fig. 3.31: Distribution of residuals of multiple regression model

To evaluate the fitted values of the model3, you can use the fitted function for obtaining this:

```
> fmodel3=fitted(model3)
> plot(fmodel3)
```

Output:

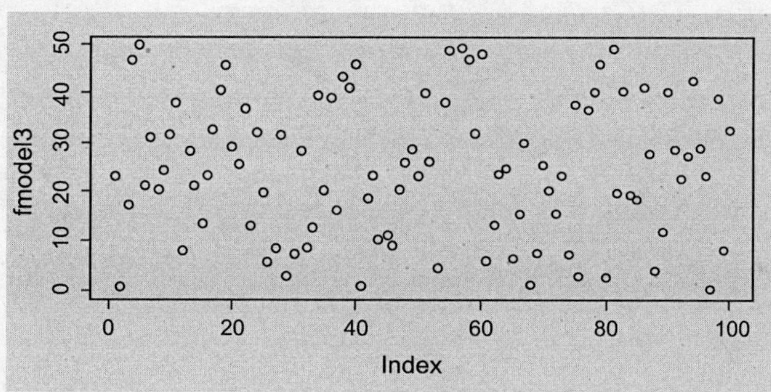

Fig. 3.32: Distribution of predicted values of multiple regression model

To evaluate the ANOVA table of model3, you can use the anova function for obtaining this:

```
>anova(model3)
```

Output:

Response: Marks

	Df	SumSq	Mean Sq	F value	Pr(>F)
number_courses	1	3538.9	3538.9	283.3	< 2.2e-16 ***
time_study	1	15568.2	15568.2	1246.3	< 2.2e-16 ***
Residuals	97	1211.7	12.5		

Signif. codes: 0 '***' 0.001 '**' 0.01 '*' 0.05 '.' 0.1 ' ' 1

From ANOVA table it is concluded that the present regression model is statistically significant.

Table 3.5: Coding of Multiple Regression Model

```
>install.packages("car")
> library(car)
>url="https://drive.google.com/file/d/1YQkALwtc0fdzLKNrM2OoldDETFudg92e/view?usp=sharing"
> data3=read.csv(url)
> str(data3)
> head(data3)
> plot(data3)
> attach(data3)
> model3 = lm(Marks~number_courses+time_study, data3)
> model3
> scatter3d(Marks~number_courses+time_study, data3)
> summary(model3)
> newdata3 = data.frame(number_course = c(72,82,92), time_study =c(12,16,22))
>predict(model3, newdata = newdata3)
>predict(model3, newdata = newdata3, interval="predict")
> par(mfrow=c(2,2))
> plot(model3)
> plot(cooks.distance(model3))
> res3=resid(model3)
> res3
> plot(res3)
> fmodel3=fitted(model3)
> plot(fmodel3)
>anova(model3)
```

Quiz Questions

1. A .... considers the effect of more than one explanatory variable on some outcome of interest and It evaluates the relative effect of these explanatory variables on the dependent variable when holding all the other variables in the model constant.
   (*a*) linear regression (*b*) multiple regression
   (*c*) Multiple correlation (*d*) Partial correlation
2. The case of one explanatory variable is called ....
   (*a*) Simple linear regression model (*b*) Multiple regression model
   (*c*) Multivariate regression model (*d*) None of the above
3. The case of more than one explanatory variable is called ....
   (*a*) Simple linear regression model (*b*) Multiple regression model
   (*c*) Multivariate regression model (*d*) None of the above

4. Linear regression models are often fitted using the .... approach.
   (a) Least square (b) Maximum likelihood
   (c) Bayesian (d) None of the above
5. The .... model provides a sloped straight line representing the relationship between the variables.
   (a) Nonlinear regression (b) Multiple regression
   (c) Linear regression (d) None of the above
6. In regression analysis, the variable that is being predicted is the ....
   (a) response, or dependent, variable (b) independent variable
   (c) intervening variable (d) is usually x
7. If the dependent variable increases on the Y-axis and independent variable increases on X-axis, then such a relationship is termed as a .... linear relationship.
   (a) Positive (b) Negative
   (c) Spurious (d) None of the above
8. If the dependent variable decreases on the Y-axis and independent variable increases on X-axis, then such a relationship is termed as a .... linear relationship.
   (a) Positive (b) Negative
   (c) Spurious (d) None of the above
9. The best fit line will have the .... error.
   (a) Maximum (b) Least
   (c) Mean (d) None of the above
10. If the coefficient of determination is 0.81, the correlation coefficient
   (a) is 0.6561 (b) could be either + 0.9 or – 0.9
   (c) must be positive (d) must be negative

ANSWERS

1.(b)	2.(a)	3.(b)	4.(a)	5.(c)	6.(a)	7.(a)	8.(b)	9.(b)	10. (b)

4 Classification: Decision Tree and Random Forest Models

Objectives

1. Introduce the theoretical foundations of decision tress and random forests, including methods for splitting nodes and handling categorial and numerical features.
2. Explore advanced topic such as feature importance analysis, handling imbalanced datasets, and addressing computational efficiency issues.
3. Illustrate real-world applications of decision tree and random forest techniques to solve classification problems.

Outcomes

1. Interpret decision tree structures to gain insights into feature importance, decision rules and model behaviour.
2. Explain the concept of ensemple learning and understand how random forests combine multiple decision trees to improve classification accuracy and robustness.
3. Communicate effectively about classification results, model interpretations, and recommendations to stakeholders through written reports and presentations.

4.1 INTRODUCTION

Decision tree learners are powerful classifiers, which utilize a tree structure to model the relationships among the features and the potential outcomes. In the case a final decision can be made, the tree is terminated by leaf nodes (also known as terminal nodes) that denote the action to be taken as the result of the series of decisions. In the case of a predictive model, the leaf nodes provide the expected result given the series of events in the tree. A great benefit of decision tree algorithms is that the flowchart-like tree structure is not necessarily exclusively for the learner's internal use. After the model is created, many decision tree algorithms output the resulting structure in a human-readable format. This provides tremendous insight into how and why the model works or doesn't work well for a particular task. This also makes decision trees particularly appropriate for applications in which the classification mechanism needs to be transparent for legal reasons, or in case the results need to be shared with others in order to inform future business practices. With this in mind, some potential uses include:

- Credit scoring models in which the criteria that causes an applicant to be rejected need to be clearly documented and free from bias

- Marketing studies of customer behavior such as satisfaction or churn, which will be shared with management or advertising agencies
- Diagnosis of medical conditions based on laboratory measurements, symptoms, or the rate of disease progression

Although the previous applications illustrate the value of trees in informing decision processes, this is not to suggest that their utility ends here. In fact, decision trees are perhaps the single most widely used machine learning technique, and can be applied to model almost any type of data—often with excellent out-of-the-box applications. This said, in spite of their wide applicability, it is worth noting some scenarios where trees may not be an ideal fit. One such case might be a task where the data has a large number of nominal features with many levels or it has a large number of numeric features. These cases may result in a very large number of decisions and an overly complex tree. They may also contribute to the tendency of decision trees to overfit data, though as we will soon see, even this weakness can be overcome by adjusting some simple parameters. Random forest is another useful ensemble learning method that grows multiple decision trees during the training process. Each decision tree will output its own prediction results corresponding to the input. The forest will use the voting mechanism to select the most voted class as the prediction result. In this recipe, we will illustrate how to classify data using the randomForest package.

4.2 Decision Tree Model

Decision trees are very popular tools for classification and prediction problems. A decision tree is a classifier which recursively partitions the instance space or the variable set. Decision trees are represented as a tree structure where each node can be classified as either a leaf node or a decision node. A leaf node holds the value of the target attribute, while a decision node specifies the rule to be implemented on a single attribute-value. Each decision node splits the instance space into two or more sub-spaces according to a certain discrete function of the input attributes-values. Each test considers a single attribute, such that the instance space is partitioned according to the attribute's value. In the case of numeric attributes, the condition refers to a range. After implementing the rule on the decision node, a sub-tree is an outcome. Each of the leaf nodes holds a probability vector indicating the probability of the target attribute having a certain value. Instances are classified by navigating them from the root of the tree down to a leaf, according to the outcome of the tests along the path.

4.2.1 Case – I: Fitting of Decision Tree Model

Decision trees are very popular tools for classification and prediction problems. A decision tree is a classifier which recursively partitions the instance space or the variable set. In *R*, we can classify using a decision tree model to data with the rpart function.

4.2.1*a* Getting Ready

We need to prepare data with many predictors and one response variable, and with a classification of many variables.

4.2.1*b* How to do it

Perform the following steps to perform decision tree model with *r* part:

1. You should install all the following packages and load its library:

```
>install.packages("rpart.plot")
>install.packages("rpart")
>install.packages("RColorBrewer")
>install.packages("rattle")
>install.packages("caret")
>install.packages("vip")
>library(vip)
>library(rpart)
>library(rpart.plot)
>library(RColorBrewer)
>library(rattle)
>library(caret)
```

2. From the package, you can load the churn dataset:

```
>url="https://drive.google.com/file/d/1PmsZsiKck64FyQcvOf3vZdfnA06C64Np/view?usp=sharing
"
>data1=read.csv(url)
```

3. You can use the str function to display the structure of the churn dataset:

```
>str(data1)
```

Output:

```
'data.frame': 2666 obs. of 17 variables:
$ International.plan: int 0 0 0 1 1 1 0 1 1 0 ...
$ Voice.mail.plan: int 1 1 0 0 0 0 1 0 1 0 ...
$ Number.vmail.messages: int 25 26 0 0 0 0 24 0 37 0 ...
$ Total.day.minutes: num 265 162 243 299 167 ...
$ Total.day.calls: int 110 123 114 71 113 98 88 79 84 127 ...
$ Total.day.charge: num 45.1 27.5 41.4 50.9 28.3 ...
$ Total.eve.minutes: num 197.4 195.5 121.2 61.9 148.3 ...
$ Total.eve.calls: int 99 103 110 88 122 101 108 94 111 148 ...
$ Total.eve.charge: num 16.78 16.62 10.3 5.26 12.61 ...
$ Total.night.minutes: num 245 254 163 197 187 ...
$ Total.night.calls: int 91 103 104 89 121 118 118 96 97 94 ...
$ Total.night.charge: num 11.01 11.45 7.32 8.86 8.41 ...
$ Total.intl.minutes: num 10 13.7 12.2 6.6 10.1 6.3 7.5 7.1 11.2 9.1 ...
$ Total.intl.calls: int 3 3 5 7 3 6 7 6 5 5 ...
$ Total.intl.charge: num 2.7 3.7 3.29 1.78 2.73 1.7 2.03 1.92 3.02 2.46 ...
```

```
$ Customer.service.calls: int 1 1 0 2 3 0 3 0 0 0 ...
$ Churn: int 0 0 0 0 0 0 0 0 0 0 ...
```

4. You can use the summary function to display the summary of the churn dataset:

```
> summary(data1)
```

Output:

```
International.planVoice.mail.planNumber.vmail.messagesTotal.day.minutes
Min. :0.0000 Min. :0.0000 Min. : 0.000 Min. : 0.0
1st Qu.:0.0000 1st Qu.:0.0000 1st Qu.: 0.000 1st Qu.:143.4
Median :0.0000 Median :0.0000 Median : 0.000 Median :179.9
Mean :0.1013 Mean :0.2749 Mean : 8.022 Mean :179.5
3rd Qu.:0.0000 3rd Qu.:1.0000 3rd Qu.:19.000 3rd Qu.:215.9
Max. :1.0000 Max. :1.0000 Max. :50.000 Max. :350.8
Total.day.callsTotal.day.chargeTotal.eve.minutesTotal.eve.callsTotal.eve.charge
Min. : 0.0 Min. : 0.00 Min. : 0.0 Min. : 0 Min. : 0.00
1st Qu.: 87.0 1st Qu.:24.38 1st Qu.:165.3 1st Qu.: 87 1st Qu.:14.05
Median :101.0 Median :30.59 Median :200.9 Median :100 Median :17.08
Mean :100.3 Mean :30.51 Mean :200.4 Mean :100 Mean :17.03
3rd Qu.:114.0 3rd Qu.:36.70 3rd Qu.:235.1 3rd Qu.:114 3rd Qu.:19.98
Max. :160.0 Max. :59.64 Max. :363.7 Max. :170 Max. :30.91
Total.night.minutesTotal.night.callsTotal.night.chargeTotal.intl.minutes
Min. : 43.7 Min. : 33.0 Min. : 1.970 Min. : 0.00
1st Qu.:166.9 1st Qu.: 87.0 1st Qu.: 7.513 1st Qu.: 8.50
Median :201.2 Median :100.0 Median : 9.050 Median :10.20
Mean :201.2 Mean :100.1 Mean : 9.053 Mean :10.24
3rd Qu.:236.5 3rd Qu.:113.0 3rd Qu.:10.640 3rd Qu.:12.10
Max. :395.0 Max. :166.0 Max. :17.770 Max. :20.00
Total.intl.callsTotal.intl.chargeCustomer.service.calls Churn
Min. : 0.000 Min. :0.000 Min. :0.000 Min. :0.0000
1st Qu.: 3.000 1st Qu.:2.300 1st Qu.:1.000 1st Qu.:0.0000
Median : 4.000 Median :2.750 Median :1.000 Median :0.0000
Mean : 4.467 Mean :2.764 Mean :1.563 Mean :0.1455
3rd Qu.: 6.000 3rd Qu.:3.270 3rd Qu.:2.000 3rd Qu.:0.0000
Max. :20.000 Max. :5.400 Max. :9.000 Max. :1.0000
```

5. You can use the sapply function to take a list, vector, or data frame as input and give output in the form of an array or matrix object of the churn dataset:

```
>sapply(data1, var, na.rm=TRUE)
```

Output:

```
International.planVoice.mail.planNumber.vmail.messages
  9.105278e - 02        1.994245e - 01        1.852941e + 02
 Total.day.minutes       Total.day.calls       Total.day.charge
  2.938762e + 03        3.995266e + 02        8.492973e + 01
Total.eve.minutes        Total.eve.calls       Total.eve.charge
  2.596057e + 03        4.064839e + 02        1.875638e + 01
Total.night.minutes      Total.night.calls     Total.night.charge
  2.578641e + 03        3.770765e + 02        5.221771e + 00
 Total.intl.minutes      Total.intl.calls      Total.intl.charge
  7.774888e + 00        6.032893e + 00        5.667260e - 01
Customer.service.calls       Churn
  1.719339e + 00        1.244022e - 01
>sapply(data1, sd, na.rm=TRUE)
International.plan      Voice.mail.plan    Number.vmail.messages
     0.3017495             0.4465697            13.6122770
 Total.day.minutes       Total.day.calls       Total.day.charge
    54.2103502            19.9881622             9.2157329
 Total.eve.minutes       Total.eve.calls       Total.eve.charge
    50.9515151            20.1614451             4.3308642
Total.night.minutes     Total.night.calls     Total.night.charge
    50.7803234            19.4184586             2.2851195
 Total.intl.minutes      Total.intl.calls      Total.intl.charge
     2.7883486             2.4561949             0.7528121
Customer.service.calls       Churn
     1.3112358             0.3527070
```

6. We now then use churn as a label to generate the prediction model in use. After that, we assign the classification tree model into the churn variable:

```
>mydt = rpart(Churn~., method = "anova", data=data1, minsplit=5)
>summary(mydt)
```

Output:

```
Call:
rpart(formula = Churn ~ ., data = data1, method = "anova", minsplit = 5)
n = 2666
  CP       nsplitrel        error        xerrorx        std
  1   0.10443378 0   1.0000000     1.0007179     0.03896178
  2   0.07231950 2   0.7911324     0.8016536     0.03476223
```

```
3  0.07191178 3  0.7188129  0.7072042  0.03230450
4  0.04944420 5  0.5749894  0.5857106  0.02995099
5  0.03167745 6  0.5255452  0.5510143  0.03122623
6  0.02439067 7  0.4938677  0.5524490  0.03187509
7  0.02232482 9  0.4450864  0.5368267  0.03223373
8  0.01729585 10 0.4227616  0.5015803  0.03070841
9  0.01352243 11 0.4054657  0.4825907  0.03052938
10 0.01345237 13 0.3784209  0.4771937  0.03082656
11 0.01240239 14 0.3649685  0.4669912  0.03090991
12 0.01057156 15 0.3525661  0.4561390  0.03091085
13 0.01000000 16 0.3419946  0.4560860  0.03120069
Variable importance
  Total.day.charge        Total.day.minutes  Customer.service.calls
        17                      17                  9
  Total.eve.charge        Total.eve.minutes     Total.intl.charge
        8                       8                   7
 Total.intl.minutes       International.plan     Total.intl.calls
        7                       6                   6
Number.vmail.messages       Voice.mail.plan     Total.night.charge
        5                       4                   1
Total.night.minutes         Total.day.calls     Total.night.calls
        1                       1                   1
   Total.eve.calls
        1
Node number 1: 2666 observations, complexity param = 0.1044338
mean = 0.1455364, MSE = 0.1243555
left son = 2 (2506 obs) right son = 3 (160 obs)
Primary splits:
Total.day.minutes<264.4 to the left, improve=0.10314400, (0 missing)
Total.day.charge<44.95 to the left, improve=0.10314400, (0 missing)
Customer.service.calls< 3.5 to the left, improve=0.10087950, (0 missing)
International.plan< 0.5 to the left, improve=0.07700002, (0 missing)
Total.intl.minutes< 13.25 to the left, improve=0.01454845, (0 missing)
Surrogate splits:
Total.day.charge<44.95 to the left, agree=1, adj=1, (0 split)
Node number 2: 2506 observations, complexity param=0.1044338
mean=0.1169194, MSE=0.1032492
```

left son=4 (2305 obs) right son=5 (201 obs)
Primary splits:
Customer.service.calls< 3.5 to the left, improve=0.13546570, (0 missing).
International.plan< 0.5 to the left, improve=0.09408122, (0 missing)
Total.day.minutes< 223.25 to the left, improve=0.02036688, (0 missing)
Total.day.charge<37.95 to the left, improve=0.02036688, (0 missing)
Total.intl.minutes< 13.25 to the left, improve=0.01612651, (0 missing)
Surrogate splits:
Total.day.calls< 38 to the right, agree=0.92, adj=0.005, (0 split)
Node number 3: 160 observations, complexity param=0.03167745
mean=0.59375, MSE=0.2412109
left son=6 (40 obs) right son=7 (120 obs)
Primary splits:
Voice.mail.plan< 0.5 to the right, improve=0.27211880, (0 missing)
Number.vmail.messages< 6.5 to the right, improve=0.27211880, (0 missing)
Total.eve.minutes<167.3 to the left, improve=0.16448980, (0 missing)
Total.eve.charge<14.22 to the left, improve=0.16448980, (0 missing)
Total.day.minutes< 313.95 to the left, improve=0.07602339, (0 missing)
Surrogate splits:
Number.vmail.messages< 6.5 to the right, agree=1.000, adj=1.000, (0 split)
Total.night.calls< 50 to the left, agree=0.762, adj=0.050, (0 split)
Total.night.minutes< 298.75 to the right, agree=0.756, adj=0.025, (0 split)
Total.night.charge< 13.445 to the right, agree=0.756, adj=0.025, (0 split)
Node number 4: 2305 observations, complexity param=0.0723195
mean=0.08199566, MSE=0.07527237
left son=8 (2081 obs) right son=9 (224 obs)
Primary splits:
International.plan< 0.5 to the left, improve=0.13818920, (0 missing)
Total.day.minutes< 221.85 to the left, improve=0.04762550, (0 missing)
Total.day.charge< 37.715 to the left, improve=0.04762550, (0 missing)
Total.intl.minutes< 13.15 to the left, improve=0.02313642, (0 missing)
Total.intl.charge< 3.55 to the left, improve=0.02313642, (0 missing)
Node number 5: 201 observations, complexity param=0.0494442
mean=0.5174129, MSE=0.2496968
left son=10 (96 obs) right son=11 (105 obs)
Primary splits:
Total.day.minutes< 173.55 to the right, improve=0.32661160, (0 missing)

Total.day.charge< 29.505 to the right, improve=0.32661160, (0 missing)
Total.eve.minutes<190.8 to the right, improve=0.11893690, (0 missing)
Total.eve.charge<16.22 to the right, improve=0.11893690, (0 missing)
Total.intl.calls< 4.5 to the right, improve=0.04092089, (0 missing)
Surrogate splits:
Total.day.charge< 29.505 to the right, agree=1.000, adj=1.000, (0 split)
Total.day.calls<105.5 to the right, agree=0.577, adj=0.115, (0 split)
Total.eve.minutes< 222.65 to the right, agree=0.567, adj=0.094, (0 split)
Total.eve.calls< 66.5 to the left, agree=0.567, adj=0.094, (0 split)
Total.eve.charge<18.93 to the right, agree=0.567, adj=0.094, (0 split)
Node number 6: 40 observations
mean=0.15, MSE=0.1275
Node number 7: 120 observations, complexity param=0.02232482
mean=0.7416667, MSE=0.1915972
left son=14 (48 obs) right son=15 (72 obs)
Primary splits:
Total.eve.minutes< 187.75 to the left, improve=0.3219162, (0 missing)
Total.eve.charge<15.96 to the left, improve=0.3219162, (0 missing)
Total.night.minutes< 212.45 to the left, improve=0.1173057, (0 missing)
Total.night.charge< 9.56 to the left, improve=0.1173057, (0 missing)
Total.day.minutes<277.7 to the left, improve=0.1014584, (0 missing)
Surrogate splits:
Total.eve.charge<15.96 to the left, agree=1.000, adj=1.000, (0 split)
Total.night.minutes< 284.9 to the right, agree=0.633, adj=0.083, (0 split)
Total.night.charge< 12.82 to the right, agree=0.633, adj=0.083, (0 split)
Total.day.calls< 68 to the left, agree=0.625, adj=0.063, (0 split)
Total.night.calls< 75 to the left, agree=0.625, adj=0.063, (0 split)
Node number 8: 2081 observations, complexity param=0.02439067
mean=0.04853436, MSE=0.04617877
left son=16 (1783 obs) right son=17 (298 obs)
Primary splits:
Total.day.minutes< 223.25 to the left, improve=0.05742534, (0 missing)
Total.day.charge<37.95 to the left, improve=0.05742534, (0 missing)
Total.eve.minutes< 244.95 to the left, improve=0.02732784, (0 missing)
Total.eve.charge< 20.825 to the left, improve=0.02732784, (0 missing)
Total.night.minutes< 163.85 to the left, improve=0.00708362, (0 missing)

Surrogate splits:
Total.day.charge<37.95 to the left, agree=1, adj=1, (0 split)
Node number 9: 224 observations, complexity param=0.07191178
mean=0.3928571, MSE=0.2385204
left son=18 (179 obs) right son=19 (45 obs)
Primary splits:
Total.intl.calls< 2.5 to the right, improve=0.38852210, (0 missing)
Total.intl.minutes< 13.1 to the left, improve=0.34624940, (0 missing)
Total.intl.charge< 3.535 to the left, improve=0.34624940, (0 missing)
Total.day.minutes< 236.65 to the left, improve=0.03236453, (0 missing)
Total.day.charge< 40.235 to the left, improve=0.03236453, (0 missing)
Surrogate splits:
Total.day.calls< 48 to the right, agree=0.808, adj=0.044, (0 split)
Total.night.calls< 58.5 to the right, agree=0.804, adj=0.022, (0 split)
Node number 10: 96 observations, complexity param=0.01345237
mean=0.21875, MSE=0.1708984
left son=20 (87 obs) right son=21 (9 obs)
Primary splits:
Total.eve.minutes<135.1 to the right, improve=0.27184090, (0 missing)
Total.eve.charge< 11.485 to the right, improve=0.27184090, (0 missing)
Total.day.calls< 97.5 to the left, improve=0.11228330, (0 missing)
Customer.service.calls< 8 to the left, improve=0.07598784, (0 missing)
Total.night.calls< 106.5 to the left, improve=0.07142857, (0 missing)
Surrogate splits:
Total.eve.charge< 11.485 to the right, agree=1, adj=1, (0 split)
Node number 11: 105 observations, complexity param=0.01352243
mean=0.7904762, MSE=0.1656236
left son=22 (39 obs) right son=23 (66 obs)
Primary splits:
Total.eve.minutes< 212.35 to the right, improve=0.22659490, (0 missing)
Total.eve.charge<18.05 to the right, improve=0.22659490, (0 missing)
Total.day.minutes<135.8 to the right, improve=0.15886270, (0 missing)
Total.day.charge< 23.085 to the right, improve=0.15886270, (0 missing)
Total.night.minutes< 194.9 to the right, improve=0.08641058, (0 missing)
Surrogate splits:
Total.eve.charge<18.05 to the right, agree=1.000, adj=1.000, (0 split)

Total.night.minutes< 285.6 to the right, agree=0.657, adj=0.077, (0 split)
Total.night.charge< 12.855 to the right, agree=0.657, adj=0.077, (0 split)
Total.eve.calls< 76.5 to the left, agree=0.648, adj=0.051, (0 split)
Total.day.calls< 76 to the left, agree=0.638, adj=0.026, (0 split)
Node number 14: 48 observations, complexity param=0.01057156
mean=0.4375, MSE=0.2460938
left son=28 (39 obs) right son=29 (9 obs)
Primary splits:
Total.day.minutes< 302.45 to the left, improve=0.2967033, (0 missing)
Total.day.charge< 51.415 to the left, improve=0.2967033, (0 missing)
Total.night.minutes< 212.65 to the left, improve=0.2385562, (0 missing)
Total.night.charge< 9.57 to the left, improve=0.2385562, (0 missing)
Total.eve.minutes< 144.25 to the left, improve=0.1962323, (0 missing)
Surrogate splits:
Total.day.charge< 51.415 to the left, agree=1.000, adj=1.000, (0 split)
Total.day.calls<131.5 to the left, agree=0.833, adj=0.111, (0 split)
Node number 15: 72 observations
mean=0.9444444, MSE=0.05246914
Node number 16: 1783 observations
mean=0.02748177, MSE=0.02672652
Node number 17: 298 observations, complexity param=0.02439067
mean=0.1744966, MSE=0.1440476
left son=34 (235 obs) right son=35 (63 obs)
Primary splits:
Total.eve.minutes<244.9 to the left, improve=0.24819600, (0 missing)
Total.eve.charge<20.82 to the left, improve=0.24819600, (0 missing)
Number.vmail.messages< 7.5 to the right, improve=0.06570566, (0 missing)
Voice.mail.plan< 0.5 to the right, improve=0.06570566, (0 missing)
Total.night.minutes< 166.05 to the left, improve=0.04428944, (0 missing)
Surrogate splits:
Total.eve.charge<20.82 to the left, agree=1, adj=1, (0 split)
Node number 18: 179 observations, complexity param=0.07191178
mean=0.2402235, MSE=0.1825162
left son=36 (142 obs) right son=37 (37 obs)
Primary splits:
Total.intl.minutes< 13.1 to the left, improve=0.82410740, (0 missing)
Total.intl.charge< 3.535 to the left, improve=0.82410740, (0 missing)

Total.day.minutes<237.2 to the left, improve=0.04650840, (0 missing)

Total.day.charge< 40.325 to the left, improve=0.04650840, (0 missing)

Total.day.calls<122.5 to the right, improve=0.02283338, (0 missing)

Surrogate splits:

Total.intl.charge< 3.535 to the left, agree=1.000, adj=1.000, (0 split)

Number.vmail.messages< 40.5 to the left, agree=0.799, adj=0.027, (0 split)

Total.day.minutes<52.45 to the right, agree=0.799, adj=0.027, (0 split)

Total.day.charge< 8.92 to the right, agree=0.799, adj=0.027, (0 split)

Total.night.calls< 141.5 to the left, agree=0.799, adj=0.027, (0 split)

Node number 19: 45 observations

mean=1, MSE=0

Node number 20: 87 observations

mean=0.1494253, MSE=0.1270974

Node number 21: 9 observations

mean=0.8888889, MSE=0.09876543

Node number 22: 39 observations, complexity param=0.01352243

mean=0.5384615, MSE=0.2485207

left son=44 (12 obs) right son=45 (27 obs)

Primary splits:

Total.day.minutes< 151.65 to the right, improve=0.51851850, (0 missing)

Total.day.charge<25.78 to the right, improve=0.51851850, (0 missing)

Total.intl.calls< 4.5 to the right, improve=0.18563790, (0 missing)

Total.night.calls< 129 to the right, improve=0.09722222, (0 missing)

Total.eve.minutes< 250 to the right, improve=0.07524985, (0 missing)

Surrogate splits:

Total.day.charge<25.78 to the right, agree=1.000, adj=1.000, (0 split)

Total.eve.minutes< 219.45 to the left, agree=0.769, adj=0.250, (0 split)

Total.eve.charge<18.65 to the left, agree=0.769, adj=0.250, (0 split)

Total.night.calls< 129 to the right, agree=0.769, adj=0.250, (0 split)

Customer.service.calls< 6.5 to the right, agree=0.718, adj=0.083, (0 split)

Node number 23: 66 observations

mean=0.9393939, MSE=0.05693297

Node number 28: 39 observations

mean=0.3076923, MSE=0.2130178

Node number 29: 9 observations

mean=1, MSE=0

Node number 34: 235 observations

mean=0.07659574, MSE=0.07072884
Node number 35: 63 observations, complexity param=0.01729585
mean=0.5396825, MSE=0.2484253
left son=70 (15 obs) right son=71 (48 obs)
Primary splits:
Voice.mail.plan< 0.5 to the right, improve=0.3663793, (0 missing)
Number.vmail.messages< 8.5 to the right, improve=0.3663793, (0 missing)
Total.night.minutes< 181.15 to the left, improve=0.1830629, (0 missing)
Total.night.charge< 7.84 to the left, improve=0.1699660, (0 missing)
Total.intl.minutes< 12.15 to the left, improve=0.1388438, (0 missing)
Surrogate splits:
Number.vmail.messages< 8.5 to the right, agree=1.000, adj=1.000, (0 split)
Total.eve.calls< 66.5 to the left, agree=0.778, adj=0.067, (0 split)
Node number 36: 142 observations
mean=0.04225352, MSE=0.04046816
Node number 37: 37 observations
mean=1, MSE=0
Node number 44: 12 observations
mean=0, MSE=0
Node number 45: 27 observations
mean=0.7777778, MSE=0.1728395
Node number 70: 15 observations
mean=0, MSE=0
Node number 71: 48 observations, complexity param=0.01240239
mean=0.7083333, MSE=0.2065972
left son=142 (7 obs) right son=143 (41 obs)
Primary splits:
Total.night.minutes< 147.15 to the left, improve=0.4146341, (0 missing)
Total.night.charge< 6.625 to the left, improve=0.4146341, (0 missing)
Total.intl.minutes< 7.45 to the left, improve=0.2028812, (0 missing)
Total.intl.charge< 2.015 to the left, improve=0.2028812, (0 missing)
Total.eve.minutes< 269 to the left, improve=0.1811984, (0 missing)
Surrogate splits:
Total.night.charge< 6.625 to the left, agree=1, adj=1, (0 split)
Node number 142: 7 observations
mean=0, MSE=0
Node number 143: 41 observations
mean=0.8292683, MSE=0.1415824

6. We use a plot function and a rpart.plot function to plot the tree:

   > plot(mydt)

   >text(mydt, use.n=TRUE, all=TRUE, cex=0.7)

   Output:

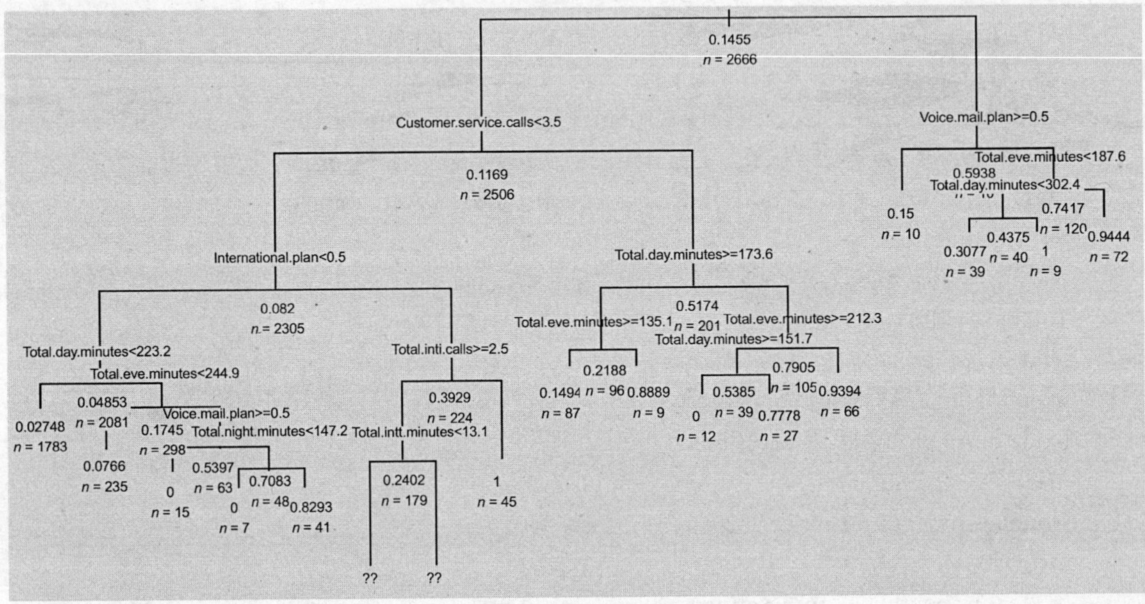

Fig. 4.1: Decision tree model

>rpart.plot(mydt)

>mydt

Output:

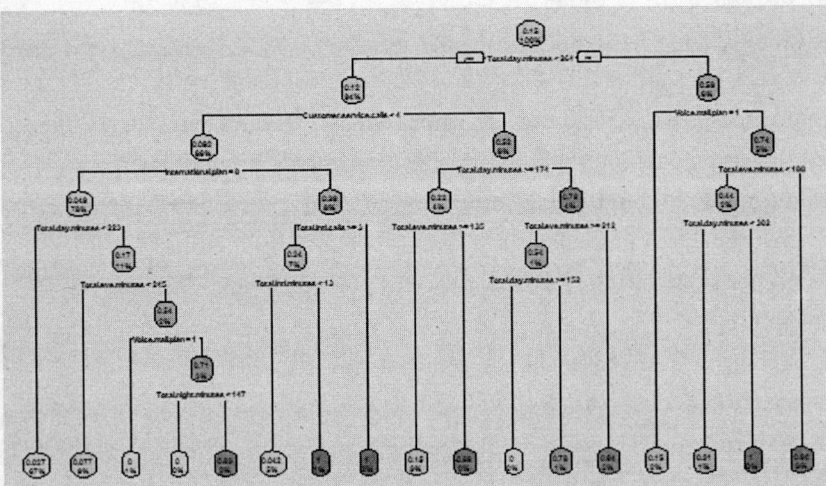

Fig. 4.2: Decision tree model

7. We use a variable importance function to know the variable importance of the dataset according to the fitting of decision tree model:

```
> dt=mydt$variable.importance
> dt
```

Output:

```
    Total.day.charge         Total.day.minutes    Customer.service.calls
       65.364428                65.364428               35.469546
    Total.eve.charge         Total.eve.minutes       Total.intl.charge
       29.249167                29.249167               26.923912
   Total.intl.minutes       International.plan       Total.intl.calls
       26.923912                23.976219               20.758180
 Number.vmail.messages       Voice.mail.plan        Total.night.charge
       16.963884                16.236210                5.294246
  Total.night.minutes        Total.day.calls        Total.night.calls
        5.294246                 3.928306                3.433067
     Total.eve.calls
        2.121138
```

```
>barplot(dt,horiz=TRUE,las=1)
```

Output:

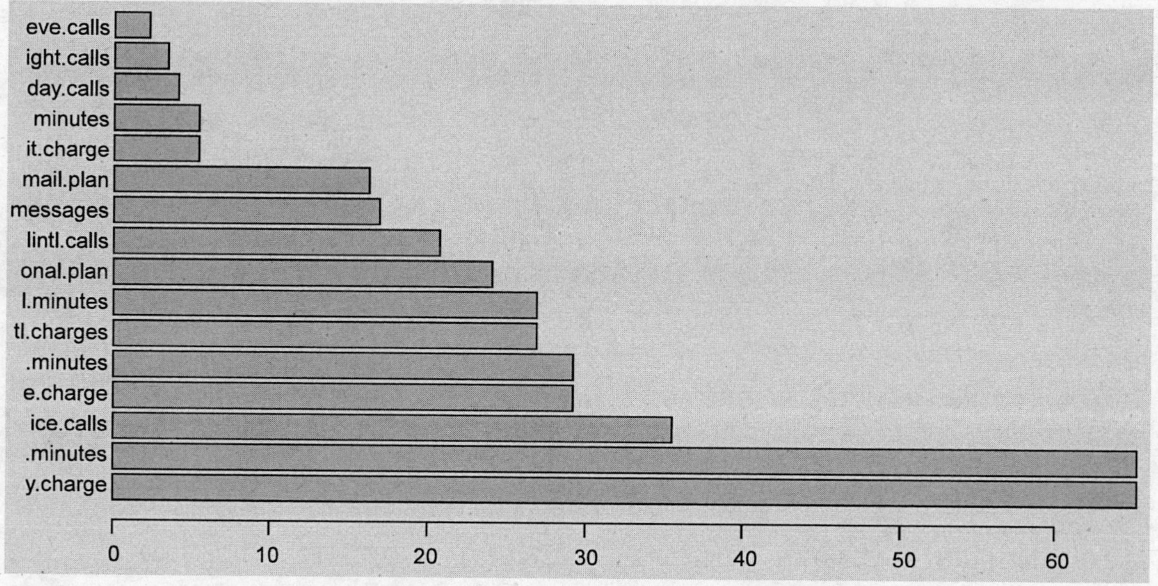

Fig. 4.3: Relative influence plot of fitted model

```
>varImp(mydt)
```

Output:

Overall

```
Customer.service.calls    0.3123330
International.plan        0.3092705
Number.vmail.messages     0.7042037
Total.day.calls           0.1351167
Total.day.charge          1.6081308
Total.day.minutes         1.7856126
Total.eve.charge          1.3793025
Total.eve.minutes         1.8319831
Total.intl.calls          0.6150809
Total.intl.charge         1.3963744
Total.intl.minutes        1.5658932
Total.night.calls         0.1686508
Total.night.charge        0.9404620
Total.night.minutes       1.0913425
Voice.mail.plan           0.7042037
Total.eve.calls           0.0000000
```

8. While the plotting is not great, you can follow the decision points to arrive at a valuation fairly easily.

   Let's generate the predicted values using the test data, as follows:

   ```
   >mydt= predict(mydt)
   >predicted_mydt
   ```

   Output:

   ```
        1          2          3          4          5          6
   0.15000000 0.02748177 0.07659574 0.30769231 0.04225352 0.04225352
        7          8          9         10         11         12
   0.02748177 0.04225352 0.04225352 0.02748177 0.02748177 0.02748177
       13         14         15         16         17         18
   0.77777778 0.02748177 0.02748177 0.02748177 0.07659574 0.02748177
       19         20         21         22         23         24
   0.93939394 0.02748177 0.02748177 0.02748177 0.02748177 0.02748177
       25         26         27         28         29         30
   0.02748177 0.02748177 0.07659574 0.02748177 0.82926829 0.02748177
       31         32         33         34         35         36
   0.02748177 0.02748177 0.04225352 0.02748177 0.02748177 1.00000000
       37         38         39         40         41         42
   0.02748177 0.02748177 0.02748177 0.02748177 0.02748177 0.02748177
       43         44         45         46         47         48
   0.02748177 0.02748177 0.02748177 0.77777778 0.02748177 0.02748177
       49         50         51         52         53         54
   ```

```
0.02748177  0.07659574  0.02748177  0.15000000  0.02748177  0.02748177
        55          56          57          58          59          60
0.02748177  0.04225352  0.04225352  0.02748177  0.14942529  0.07659574
        61          62          63          64          65          66
0.07659574  0.07659574  0.02748177
        67          68          69
[ reached getOption("max.print") -- omitted 1666 entries ]
> write.csv(predicted_mydt,file='predmydt.csv')
```

9. Plot the complexity parameter plot to see how the tree performs at different values of CP:

   >plotcp(mydt)

   Output:

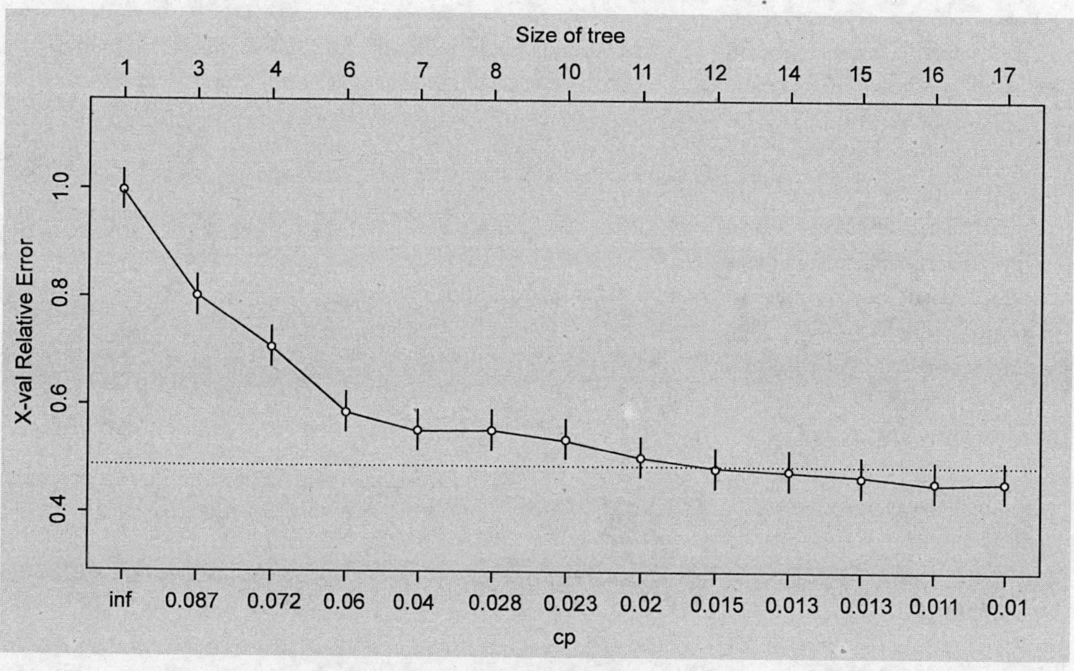

Fig. 4.4: Complexity parameter plot

1. We will verify the correctness of the model (using the sum of squares defined in the previous section), as follows:

   > diff = predicted_mydt - data1$Churn

   >sumofsquares = function(x) {return(sum(x^2))}

   >sumofsquares(diff)

   Output:

   [1] 113.3821

   From the above result it maybe concluded that this model gives the better result as the sum of square of difference is very low and this would be a better modeling technique.

Table 4.1: Coding of Decision Tree Model

```
>install.packages("rpart.plot")
>install.packages("rpart")
>install.packages("RColorBrewer")
>install.packages("rattle")
>install.packages("caret")
>install.packages("vip")
> library(vip)
> library(rpart)
> library(rpart.plot)
>library(RColorBrewer)
> library(rattle)
> library(caret)
>url="https://drive.google.com/file/d/1PmsZsiKck64FyQcvOf3vZdfnA06C64Np/view?usp=sharing
"
> data1=read.csv(url)
> str(data1)
> summary(data1)
>sapply(data1, var, na.rm=TRUE)
>sapply(data1, sd, na.rm=TRUE)
>mydt = rpart(Churn~., method = "anova", data=data1, minsplit=5)
> summary(mydt)
> plot(mydt)
>text(mydt, use.n=TRUE, all=TRUE, cex=0.7)
>rpart.plot(mydt)
>mydt
> dt=mydt$variable.importance
> dt
>barplot(dt,horiz=TRUE,las=1)
>varImp(mydt)
>predicted_mydt= predict(mydt)
>predicted_mydt
> write.csv(predicted_mydt,file='predmydt.csv')
>plotcp(mydt)
> diff = predicted_mydt - data1$Churn
>sumofsquares = function(x) {return(sum(x^2))}
>sumofsquares(diff)
```

4.2.2 Case – II: Fitting of Decision Tree Model

Decision trees are very popular tools for classification and prediction problems. A decision tree is a classifier which recursively partitions the instance space or the variable set. In *R*, we can classify a decision tree model to data with the rpart function.

4.2.2*a* Getting Ready

We need to prepare data with many predictors and one response variable, and with a classification of many variables.

4.2.2*b* How to do it

Perform the following steps to perform decision tree model with rpart:

1. You should install all the following packages and load its library:

```
>install.packages("rpart.plot")
>install.packages("rpart")
>install.packages("RColorBrewer")
>install.packages("rattle")
>install.packages("caret")
>install.packages("vip")
>library(vip)
>library(rpart)
>library(rpart.plot)
>library(RColorBrewer)
>library(rattle)
>library(caret)
```

2. From the package, you can load the breast cancer dataset:

```
>url="https://drive.google.com/file/d/1p82HUfZwhvYtrJM3OB_-gpG6vJbdq-PX/view?usp=sharing"
>data2=read.csv(url)
```

3. You can use the str function to display the structure of the breast cancer dataset:

```
>str(data2)
```

Output:

```
'data.frame': 569 obs. of 31 variables:
$ radius_mean :num 18 20.6 19.7 11.4 20.3 ...
$ texture_mean :num 10.4 17.8 21.2 20.4 14.3 ...
$ perimeter_mean :num 122.8 132.9 130 77.6 135.1 ...
$ area_mean :num 1001 1326 1203 386 1297 ...
$ smoothness_mean :num 0.1184 0.0847 0.1096 0.1425 0.1003 ...
$ compactness_mean :num 0.2776 0.0786 0.1599 0.2839 0.1328 ...
$ concavity_mean :num 0.3001 0.0869 0.1974 0.2414 0.198 ...
$ concave.points_mean : num 0.1471 0.0702 0.1279 0.1052 0.1043 ...
$ symmetry_mean :num 0.242 0.181 0.207 0.26 0.181 ...
$ fractal_dimension_mean :num 0.0787 0.0567 0.06 0.0974 0.0588 ...
```

```
$ radius_se :num 1.095 0.543 0.746 0.496 0.757 ...
$ texture_se :num 0.905 0.734 0.787 1.156 0.781 ...
$ perimeter_se :num 8.59 3.4 4.58 3.44 5.44 ...
$ area_se :num 153.4 74.1 94 27.2 94.4 ...
$ smoothness_se :num 0.0064 0.00522 0.00615 0.00911 0.01149 ...
$ compactness_se :num 0.049 0.0131 0.0401 0.0746 0.0246 ...
$ concavity_se :num 0.0537 0.0186 0.0383 0.0566 0.0569 ...
$ concave.points_se : num 0.0159 0.0134 0.0206 0.0187 0.0188 ...
$ symmetry_se :num 0.03 0.0139 0.0225 0.0596 0.0176 ...
$ fractal_dimension_se :num 0.00619 0.00353 0.00457 0.00921 0.00511 ...
$ radius_worst :num 25.4 25 23.6 14.9 22.5 ...
$ texture_worst :num 17.3 23.4 25.5 26.5 16.7 ...
$ perimeter_worst :num 184.6 158.8 152.5 98.9 152.2 ...
$ area_worst :num 2019 1956 1709 568 1575 ...
$ smoothness_worst :num 0.162 0.124 0.144 0.21 0.137 ...
$ compactness_worst :num 0.666 0.187 0.424 0.866 0.205 ...
$ concavity_worst :num 0.712 0.242 0.45 0.687 0.4 ...
$ concave.points_worst : num 0.265 0.186 0.243 0.258 0.163 ...
$ symmetry_worst :num 0.46 0.275 0.361 0.664 0.236 ...
$ fractal_dimension_worst: num 0.1189 0.089 0.0876 0.173 0.0768 ...
$ diagnosis : int 1 1 1 1 1 1 1 1 1 1 ...
```

4. You can use the summary function to display the summary of the breast cancer dataset:

```
> summary(data2)
```

Output:

```
radius_meantexture_meanperimeter_meanarea_meansmoothness_mean
Min. : 6.981 Min. : 9.71 Min. : 43.79 Min. : 143.5 Min. :0.05263
1st Qu.:11.700 1st Qu.:16.17 1st Qu.: 75.17 1st Qu.: 420.3 1st Qu.:0.08637
Median :13.370 Median :18.84 Median : 86.24 Median : 551.1 Median :0.09587
Mean :14.127 Mean :19.29 Mean : 91.97 Mean : 654.9 Mean :0.09636
3rd Qu.:15.780 3rd Qu.:21.80 3rd Qu.:104.10 3rd Qu.: 782.7 3rd Qu.:0.10530
Max. :28.110 Max. :39.28 Max. :188.50 Max. :2501.0 Max. :0.16340
compactness_meanconcavity_meanconcave.points_meansymmetry_mean
Min. :0.01938 Min. :0.00000 Min. :0.00000 Min. :0.1060
1st Qu.:0.06492 1st Qu.:0.02956 1st Qu.:0.02031 1st Qu.:0.1619
Median :0.09263 Median :0.06154 Median :0.03350 Median :0.1792
Mean :0.10434 Mean :0.08880 Mean :0.04892 Mean :0.1812
3rd Qu.:0.13040 3rd Qu.:0.13070 3rd Qu.:0.07400 3rd Qu.:0.1957
```

Max. :0.34540 Max. :0.42680 Max. :0.20120 Max. :0.3040

fractal_dimension_meanradius_setexture_seperimeter_se

Min. :0.04996 Min. :0.1115 Min. :0.3602 Min. : 0.757

1st Qu.:0.05770 1st Qu.:0.2324 1st Qu.:0.8339 1st Qu.: 1.606

Median :0.06154 Median :0.3242 Median :1.1080 Median : 2.287

Mean :0.06280 Mean :0.4052 Mean :1.2169 Mean : 2.866

3rd Qu.:0.06612 3rd Qu.:0.4789 3rd Qu.:1.4740 3rd Qu.: 3.357

Max. :0.09744 Max. :2.8730 Max. :4.8850 Max. :21.980

area_sesmoothness_secompactness_seconcavity_se

Min. : 6.802 Min. :0.001713 Min. :0.002252 Min. :0.00000

1st Qu.: 17.850 1st Qu.:0.005169 1st Qu.:0.013080 1st Qu.:0.01509

Median : 24.530 Median :0.006380 Median :0.020450 Median :0.02589

Mean : 40.337 Mean :0.007041 Mean :0.025478 Mean :0.03189

3rd Qu.: 45.190 3rd Qu.:0.008146 3rd Qu.:0.032450 3rd Qu.:0.04205

Max. :542.200 Max. :0.031130 Max. :0.135400 Max. :0.39600

concave.points_sesymmetry_sefractal_dimension_seradius_worst

Min. :0.000000 Min. :0.007882 Min. :0.0008948 Min. : 7.93

1st Qu.:0.007638 1st Qu.:0.015160 1st Qu.:0.0022480 1st Qu.:13.01

Median :0.010930 Median :0.018730 Median :0.0031870 Median :14.97

Mean :0.011796 Mean :0.020542 Mean :0.0037949 Mean :16.27

3rd Qu.:0.014710 3rd Qu.:0.023480 3rd Qu.:0.0045580 3rd Qu.:18.79

Max. :0.052790 Max. :0.078950 Max. :0.0298400 Max. :36.04

texture_worstperimeter_worstarea_worstsmoothness_worstcompactness_worst

Min. :12.02 Min. : 50.41 Min. : 185.2 Min. :0.07117 Min. :0.02729

1st Qu.:21.08 1st Qu.: 84.11 1st Qu.: 515.3 1st Qu.:0.11660 1st Qu.:0.14720

Median :25.41 Median : 97.66 Median : 686.5 Median :0.13130 Median :0.21190

Mean :25.68 Mean :107.26 Mean : 880.6 Mean :0.13237 Mean :0.25427

3rd Qu.:29.72 3rd Qu.:125.40 3rd Qu.:1084.0 3rd Qu.:0.14600 3rd Qu.:0.33910

Max. :49.54 Max. :251.20 Max. :4254.0 Max. :0.22260 Max. :1.05800

concavity_worstconcave.points_worstsymmetry_worstfractal_dimension_worst

Min. :0.0000 Min. :0.00000 Min. :0.1565 Min. :0.05504

1st Qu.:0.1145 1st Qu.:0.06493 1st Qu.:0.2504 1st Qu.:0.07146

Median :0.2267 Median :0.09993 Median :0.2822 Median :0.08004

Mean :0.2722 Mean :0.11461 Mean :0.2901 Mean :0.08395

3rd Qu.:0.3829 3rd Qu.:0.16140 3rd Qu.:0.3179 3rd Qu.:0.09208

Max. :1.2520 Max. :0.29100 Max. :0.6638 Max. :0.20750

```
diagnosis
Min. :0.0000
1st Qu.:0.0000
Median :0.0000
Mean :0.3726
3rd Qu.:1.0000
Max. :1.0000
```

5. You can use the sapply function to take a list, vector, or data frame as input and give output in the form of an array or matrix object of the breast cancer dataset:

```
>sapply(data2, var, na.rm=TRUE)
Output:
radius_meantexture_meanperimeter_mean
    1.241892e+01    1.849891e+01    5.904405e+02
area_meansmoothness_meancompactness_mean
    1.238436e+05    1.977997e-04    2.789187e-03
concavity_meanconcave.points_meansymmetry_mean
    6.355248e-03    1.505661e-03    7.515428e-04
fractal_dimension_meanradius_setexture_se
    4.984872e-05    7.690235e-02    3.043159e-01
perimeter_searea_sesmoothness_se
    4.087896e+00    2.069432e+03    9.015114e-06
compactness_seconcavity_seconcave.points_se
    3.207029e-04    9.111982e-04    3.807242e-05
symmetry_sefractal_dimension_seradius_worst
6.833290e-05        7.001692e-06    2.336022e+01
texture_worstperimeter_worstarea_worst
    3.777648e+01    1.129131e+03    3.241674e+05
smoothness_worstcompactness_worstconcavity_worst
    5.213198e-04    2.475477e-02    4.352409e-02
concave.points_worstsymmetry_worstfractal_dimension_worst
    4.320741e-03    3.827584e-03    3.262094e-04
      diagnosis
    2.341766e-01
>sapply(data2, sd, na.rm=TRUE)
radius_meantexture_meanperimeter_mean
    3.524049e+00    4.301036e+00    2.429898e+01
```

```
area_meansmoothness_meancompactness_mean
   3.519141e+02    1.406413e-02    5.281276e-02
concavity_meanconcave.points_meansymmetry_mean
   7.971981e-02    3.880284e-02    2.741428e-02
fractal_dimension_meanradius_setexture_se
   7.060363e-03    2.773127e-01    5.516484e-01
perimeter_searea_sesmoothness_se
   2.021855e+00    4.549101e+01    3.002518e-03
compactness_seconcavity_seconcave.points_se
   1.790818e-02    3.018606e-02    6.170285e-03
symmetry_sefractal_dimension_seradius_worst
   8.266372e-03    2.646071e-03    4.833242e+00
texture_worstperimeter_worstarea_worst
6.146258e+00       3.360254e+01    5.693570e+02
smoothness_worstcompactness_worstconcavity_worst
   2.283243e-02    1.573365e-01    2.086243e-01
concave.points_worstsymmetry_worstfractal_dimension_worst
   6.573234e-02    6.186747e-02    1.806127e-02
     diagnosis
   4.839180e-01
```

6. We now then use churn as a label to generate the prediction model in use. After that, we assign the classification tree model into the diagnosis variable:

```
>mydt1 = rpart(diagnosis~., method = "anova", data=data2, minsplit=5)
>summary(mydt1)
```

Output:

```
Call:
rpart(formula = diagnosis ~ ., data = data2, method = "anova",
minsplit = 5)
n = 569
CP nsplitrel error xerrorxstd
1  0.69559352 0  1.00000000   1.0042807   0.02222635
2  0.10709688  1 0.30440648   0.4193716   0.04710992
3  0.03858260  2 0.19730960   0.3359450   0.04291781
4  0.03152445  3 0.15872700   0.2938249   0.04011470
5  0.01108590  5 0.09567810   0.2827151   0.04096659
6  0.01002414  6 0.08459220   0.2447467   0.03904136
```

```
7   0.01000000   8 0.06454393   0.2408372   0.03897168
Variable importance
radius_worstarea_worstperimeter_worstarea_mean
      15          15          14          13
radius_meanperimeter_meanconcave.points_worstconcave.points_mean
      13          13           3           2
concavity_meantexture_worsttexture_meanconcavity_worst
       2           2           1           1
compactness_worstcompactness_meanarea_secompactness_se
       1           1           1           1
concavity_setexture_se
       1           1
Node number 1: 569 observations, complexity param=0.6955935
mean=0.3725835, MSE=0.233765
left son=2 (379 obs) right son=3 (190 obs)
Primary splits:
radius_worst< 16.795 to the left, improve=0.6955935, (0 missing)
area_worst< 884.55 to the left, improve=0.6909787, (0 missing)
perimeter_worst< 105.95 to the left, improve=0.6886915, (0 missing)
concave.points_worst< 0.14235 to the left, improve=0.6827965, (0 missing)
concave.points_mean< 0.05142 to the left, improve=0.6745396, (0 missing)
Surrogate splits:
area_worst< 868.2 to the left, agree=0.991, adj=0.974, (0 split)
perimeter_worst< 111.7 to the left, agree=0.977, adj=0.932, (0 split)
area_mean< 700.35 to the left, agree=0.960, adj=0.879, (0 split)
radius_mean< 15.045 to the left, agree=0.958, adj=0.874, (0 split)
perimeter_mean< 96.405 to the left, agree=0.954, adj=0.863, (0 split)
Node number 2: 379 observations, complexity param=0.1070969
mean=0.08707124, MSE=0.07948984
left son=4 (333 obs) right son=5 (46 obs)
Primary splits:
concave.points_worst< 0.1358 to the left, improve=0.4728439, (0 missing)
concave.points_mean< 0.04923 to the left, improve=0.3718983, (0 missing)
compactness_worst< 0.3849 to the left, improve=0.3357055, (0 missing)
concavity_mean< 0.1037 to the left, improve=0.3228568, (0 missing)
concavity_worst< 0.3695 to the left, improve=0.3181098, (0 missing)
Surrogate splits:
```

concave.points_mean< 0.0501 to the left, agree=0.931, adj=0.435, (0 split)
concavity_worst< 0.35585 to the left, agree=0.931, adj=0.435, (0 split)
compactness_worst< 0.3795 to the left, agree=0.929, adj=0.413, (0 split)
concavity_mean< 0.11185 to the left, agree=0.923, adj=0.370, (0 split)
compactness_mean< 0.1332 to the left, agree=0.918, adj=0.326, (0 split)
Node number 3: 190 observations, complexity param=0.03152445
mean=0.9421053, MSE=0.05454294
left son=6 (17 obs) right son=7 (173 obs)
Primary splits:
texture_mean< 16.11 to the left, improve=0.4005521, (0 missing)
texture_worst< 19.91 to the left, improve=0.4005521, (0 missing)
texture_se< 0.4923 to the left, improve=0.3860330, (0 missing)
concavity_mean< 0.07214 to the left, improve=0.3777386, (0 missing)
concavity_worst< 0.21805 to the left, improve=0.3412453, (0 missing)
Surrogate splits:
texture_worst< 19.91 to the left, agree=0.979, adj=0.765, (0 split)
texture_se< 0.47315 to the left, agree=0.932, adj=0.235, (0 split)
radius_se< 0.18995 to the left, agree=0.921, adj=0.118, (0 split)
perimeter_se< 1.245 to the left, agree=0.921, adj=0.118, (0 split)
area_se< 16.88 to the left, agree=0.921, adj=0.118, (0 split)
Node number 4: 333 observations
mean=0.01501502, MSE=0.01478956
Node number 5: 46 observations, complexity param=0.0385826
mean=0.6086957, MSE=0.2381853
left son=10 (19 obs) right son=11 (27 obs)
Primary splits:
texture_worst< 25.67 to the left, improve=0.4683932, (0 missing)
texture_mean< 20.3 to the left, improve=0.4523810, (0 missing)
concave.points_worst< 0.1603 to the left, improve=0.2740537, (0 missing)
concave.points_mean< 0.04944 to the left, improve=0.2528481, (0 missing)
smoothness_worst< 0.1303 to the left, improve=0.2528481, (0 missing)
Surrogate splits:
texture_mean< 18.42 to the left, agree=0.848, adj=0.632, (0 split)
texture_se< 0.82555 to the left, agree=0.739, adj=0.368, (0 split)
smoothness_worst< 0.1303 to the left, agree=0.739, adj=0.368, (0 split)
concave.points_worst< 0.14235 to the left, agree=0.739, adj=0.368, (0 split)
concave.points_mean< 0.05249 to the left, agree=0.717, adj=0.316, (0 split)

Node number 6: 17 observations, complexity param=0.03152445
mean=0.4705882, MSE=0.2491349
left son=12 (9 obs) right son=13 (8 obs)
Primary splits:
concave.points_mean< 0.06626 to the left, improve=1.0000000, (0 missing)
compactness_se<0.020705 to the left, improve=1.0000000, (0 missing)
concavity_se<0.033715 to the left, improve=1.0000000, (0 missing)
concave.points_worst< 0.1454 to the left, improve=1.0000000, (0 missing)
concavity_mean< 0.08505 to the left, improve=0.7901235, (0 missing)
Surrogate splits:
compactness_se<0.020705 to the left, agree=1.000, adj=1.000, (0 split)
concavity_se<0.033715 to the left, agree=1.000, adj=1.000, (0 split)
concave.points_worst< 0.1454 to the left, agree=1.000, adj=1.000, (0 split)
concavity_mean< 0.08505 to the left, agree=0.941, adj=0.875, (0 split)
area_se< 31.165 to the left, agree=0.941, adj=0.875, (0 split)
Node number 7: 173 observations
mean=0.9884393, MSE=0.01142704
Node number 10: 19 observations, complexity param=0.0110859
mean=0.2105263, MSE=0.166205
left son=20 (15 obs) right son=21 (4 obs)
Primary splits:
area_worst< 810.3 to the left, improve=0.4669444, (0 missing)
smoothness_mean< 0.12265 to the left, improve=0.4411765, (0 missing)
smoothness_worst< 0.17855 to the left, improve=0.4411765, (0 missing)
area_se< 22.275 to the left, improve=0.2400000, (0 missing)
radius_worst< 15.41 to the left, improve=0.2400000, (0 missing)
Surrogate splits:
radius_worst< 16.21 to the left, agree=0.895, adj=0.50, (0 split)
perimeter_worst< 109.85 to the left, agree=0.842, adj=0.25, (0 split)
concave.points_worst< 0.139 to the right, agree=0.842, adj=0.25, (0 split)
Node number 11: 27 observations, complexity param=0.01002414
mean=0.8888889, MSE=0.09876543
left son=22 (6 obs) right son=23 (21 obs)
Primary splits:
concavity_mean< 0.09679 to the left, improve=0.4375000, (0 missing)
concave.points_mean< 0.0541 to the left, improve=0.4375000, (0 missing)
smoothness_mean< 0.09096 to the left, improve=0.3906250, (0 missing)

texture_mean< 19.435 to the left, improve=0.3571429, (0 missing)
compactness_mean< 0.11505 to the left, improve=0.2968750, (0 missing)
Surrogate splits:
smoothness_mean<0.097875 to the left, agree=0.926, adj=0.667, (0 split)
compactness_mean< 0.11505 to the left, agree=0.926, adj=0.667, (0 split)
concave.points_mean< 0.0541 to the left, agree=0.926, adj=0.667, (0 split)
compactness_se< 0.02177 to the left, agree=0.889, adj=0.500, (0 split)
fractal_dimension_se< 0.0029555 to the left, agree=0.889, adj=0.500, (0 split)
Node number 12: 9 observations
mean=0, MSE=0
Node number 13: 8 observations
mean=1, MSE=0
Node number 20: 15 observations
mean=0.06666667, MSE=0.06222222
Node number 21: 4 observations
mean=0.75, MSE=0.1875
Node number 22: 6 observations, complexity param=0.01002414
mean=0.5, MSE=0.25
left son=44 (3 obs) right son=45 (3 obs)
Primary splits:
texture_mean< 19.435 to the left, improve=1.0, (0 missing)
texture_worst< 28.545 to the left, improve=1.0, (0 missing)
concave.points_mean< 0.050355 to the left, improve=0.5, (0 missing)
radius_se< 0.2886 to the left, improve=0.5, (0 missing)
texture_se< 1.5015 to the left, improve=0.5, (0 missing)
Surrogate splits:
texture_worst< 28.545 to the left, agree=1.000, adj=1.000, (0 split)
concave.points_mean< 0.050355 to the left, agree=0.833, adj=0.667, (0 split)
radius_se< 0.2886 to the left, agree=0.833, adj=0.667, (0 split)
texture_se< 1.5015 to the left, agree=0.833, adj=0.667, (0 split)
area_se< 25.86 to the left, agree=0.833, adj=0.667, (0 split)
Node number 23: 21 observations
mean=1, MSE=0
Node number 44: 3 observations
mean=0, MSE=0
Node number 45: 3 observations
mean=1, MSE=0

6. We use a plot function and a rpart.plot function to plot the tree:

```
> plot(mydt1)
>text(mydt1, use.n=TRUE, all=TRUE, cex=0.8)
```

Output:

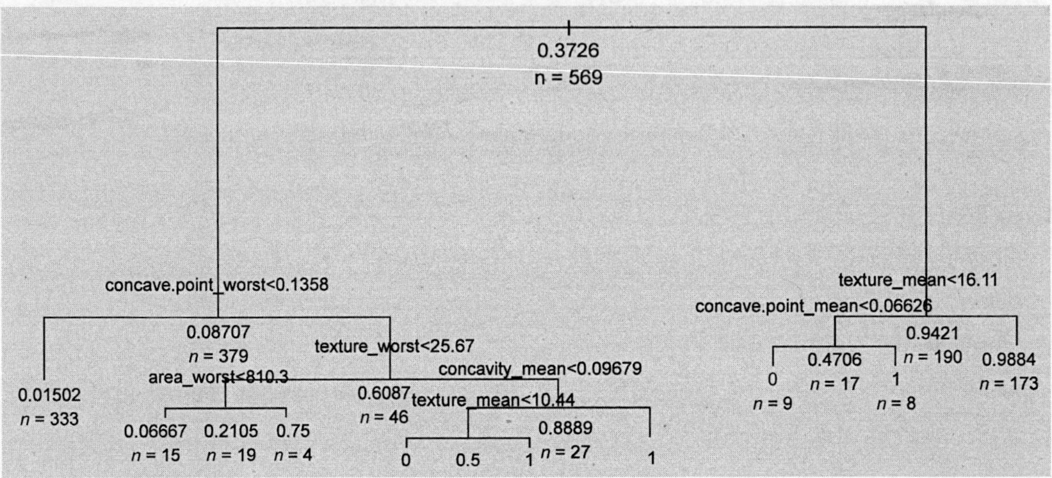

Fig. 4.5: Decision tree model

```
>rpart.plot(mydt1)
```

Output:

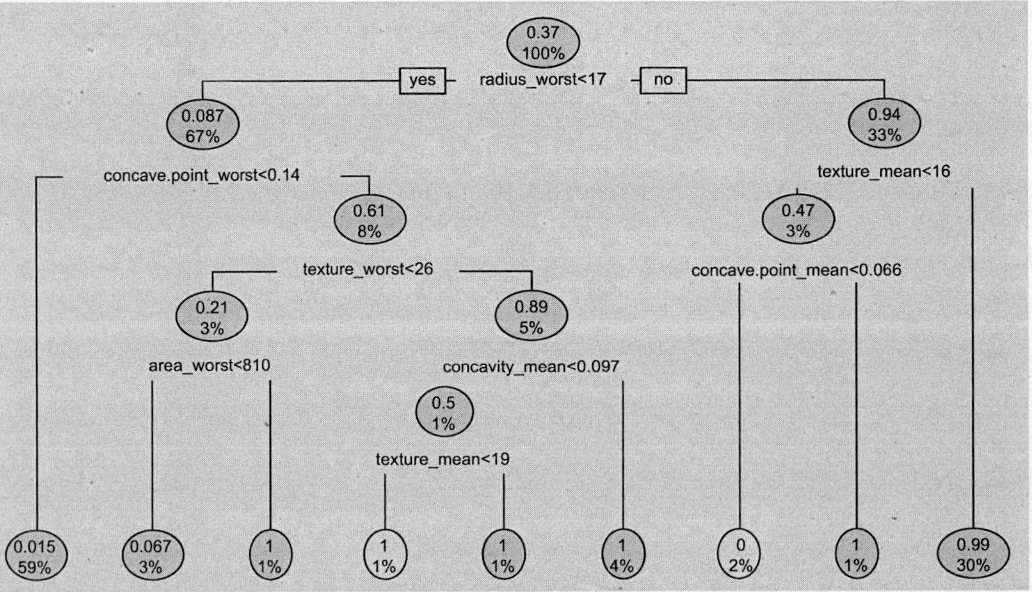

Fig. 4.6: Decision tree model

7. We use a variable importance function to know the variable importance of the dataset according to the fitting of decision tree model:

   >mydt1

   Output:

   n= 569

   node), split, n, deviance, yval

   * denotes terminal node

   1. root 569 133.0123000 0.37258350
   2. radius_worst< 16.795 379 30.1266500 0.08707124
   4. concave.points_worst< 0.1358 333 4.9249250 0.01501502 *
   5. concave.points_worst>=0.1358 46 10.9565200 0.60869570
   10. texture_worst< 25.67 19 3.1578950 0.21052630
   20. area_worst< 810.3 15 0.9333333 0.06666667 *
   21. area_worst>=810.3 4 0.7500000 0.75000000 *
   11. texture_worst>=25.67 27 2.6666670 0.88888890
   22. concavity_mean< 0.09679 6 1.5000000 0.50000000
   44. texture_mean< 19.435 3 0.0000000 0.00000000 *
   45. texture_mean>=19.435 3 0.0000000 1.00000000 *
   23. concavity_mean>=0.09679 21 0.0000000 1.00000000 *
   3. radius_worst>=16.795 190 10.3631600 0.94210530
   6. texture_mean< 16.11 17 4.2352940 0.47058820
   12. concave.points_mean< 0.06626 9 0.0000000 0.00000000 *
   13. concave.points_mean>=0.06626 8 0.0000000 1.00000000 *
   7. texture_mean>=16.11 173 1.9768790 0.98843930 *

   >dt=mydt1$variable.importance

   >dt

   Output:

   radius_worstarea_worstperimeter_worstarea_mean

   93.2597760 91.5622542 86.5606491 81.3224038

   radius_meanperimeter_meanconcave.points_worstconcave.points_mean

   80.8354433 79.8615223 20.7398591 13.8272572

   concavity_meantexture_worsttexture_meanconcavity_worst

   10.1370803 9.8062431 8.8922233 6.1935663

   compactness_worstcompactness_meanarea_secompactness_se

   5.8838880 5.4229525 5.1942335 4.8186275

   concavity_setexture_sesmoothness_worstradius_se

   4.2352941 3.8674246 1.8907222 1.4883512

smoothness_meanfractal_dimension_seperimeter_se

0.7777778 0.5833333 0.4883512

```
>barplot(dt,horiz=TRUE,las=1)
```

Output:

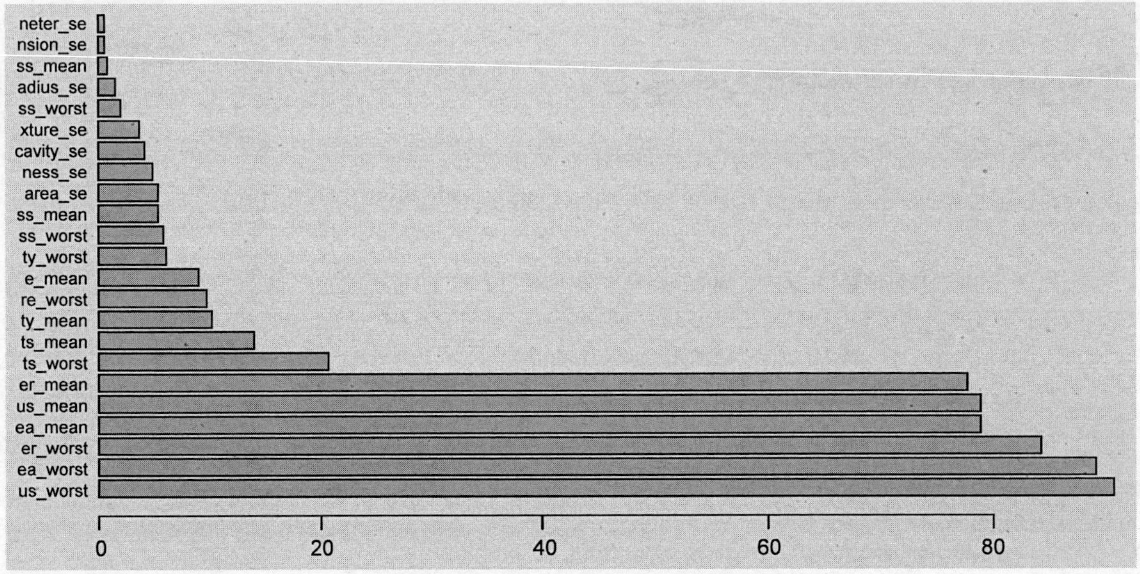

Fig. 4.7: Relative influence plot of fitted model

```
>varImp(mydt1)
```

Output:

	Overall
area_se	0.2400000
area_worst	1.1579231
compactness_mean	0.2968750
compactness_se	1.0000000
compactness_worst	0.3357055
concave.points_mean	3.2367860
concave.points_worst	2.4296941
concavity_mean	1.9282189
concavity_se	1.0000000
concavity_worst	0.6593551
perimeter_worst	0.6886915
radius_se	0.5000000
radius_worst	0.9355935

```
smoothness_mean              0.8318015
smoothness_worst             0.6940246
texture_mean                 2.2100760
texture_se                   0.8860330
texture_worst                1.8689454
radius_mean                  0.0000000
perimeter_mean               0.0000000
area_mean                    0.0000000
symmetry_mean                0.0000000
fractal_dimension_mean       0.0000000
perimeter_se                 0.0000000
smoothness_se                0.0000000
concave.points_se            0.0000000
symmetry_se                  0.0000000
fractal_dimension_se         0.0000000
symmetry_worst               0.0000000
fractal_dimension_worst      0.0000000
varImp(mydt1)
```

8. While the plotting is not great, you can follow the decision points to arrive at a valuation fairly easily.

   Let's generate the predicted values using the test data, as follows:

   ```
   predicted_mydt1= predict(mydt1)
   predicted_mydt1
   ```

   Output:

   ```
        1           2           3           4           5           6
   1.00000000  0.98843931  0.98843931  1.00000000  1.00000000  0.06666667
        7           8           9          10          11          12
   0.98843931  0.98843931  1.00000000  1.00000000  0.98843931  0.98843931
       13          14          15          16          17          18
   0.98843931  0.98843931  1.00000000  0.98843931  0.98843931  0.98843931
       19          20          21          22          23          24
   0.98843931  0.01501502  0.01501502  0.01501502  1.00000000  0.98843931
       25          26          27          28          29          30
   0.98843931  0.98843931  0.98843931  0.98843931  0.98843931  1.00000000
   ```

```
        31          32          33          34          35          36
0.98843931  0.98843931  0.98843931  0.98843931  0.98843931
        37          38          39          40          41          42
```

write.csv(predicted_mydt1,file='predmydt1.csv')

9. Plot the complexity parameter plot to see how the tree performs at different values of CP:

   >plotcp(mydt1)

   Output:

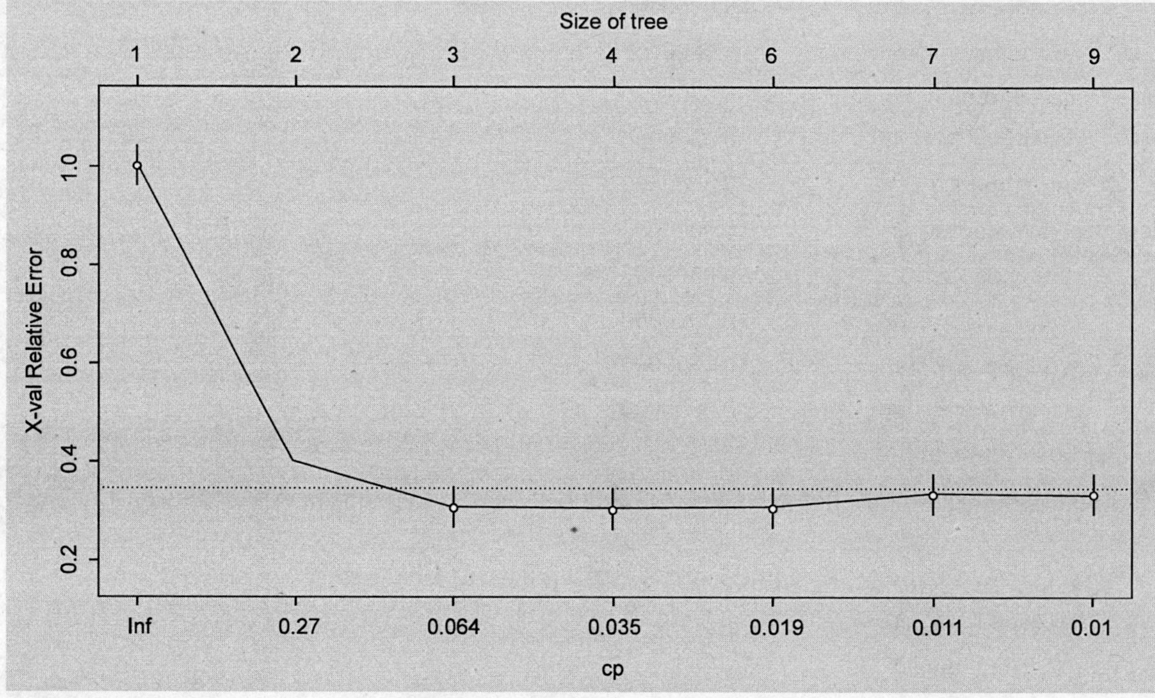

Fig. 4.8: Complexity parameter plot

10. We will verify the correctness of the model (using the sum of squares defined in the previous section), as follows:

    >diff = predicted_mydt1 - data2$diagnosis

    >sumofsquares = function(x) {return(sum(x^2))}

    >sumofsquares(diff)

    Output:

    [1] 8.585137

    From the above result it maybe concluded that this model gives the better result as the sum of square of difference is very low and this would be a better modeling technique.

Table 4.2: Coding of Decision Tree Model

```
>install.packages("rpart.plot")
>install.packages("rpart")
>install.packages("RColorBrewer")
>install.packages("rattle")
>install.packages("caret")
>install.packages("vip")
> library(vip)
> library(rpart)
> library(rpart.plot)
>library(RColorBrewer)
> library(rattle)
> library(caret)
>url="https://drive.google.com/file/d/1p82HUfZwhvYtrJM3OB_-gpG6vJbdq-PX/view?usp=sharing"
> data2=read.csv(url)
> str(data2)
> summary(data2)
>sapply(data2, var, na.rm=TRUE)
>sapply(data2, sd, na.rm=TRUE)
> mydt1 = rpart(diagnosis~., method = "anova", data=data2, minsplit=5)
> summary(mydt1)
> plot(mydt1)
>text(mydt1, use.n=TRUE, all=TRUE, cex=0.8)
>rpart.plot(mydt1)
> mydt1
> dt=mydt1$variable.importance
> dt
>barplot(dt,horiz=TRUE,las=1)
>varImp(mydt1)
> predicted_mydt1= predict(mydt1)
> predicted_mydt1
> write.csv(predicted_mydt1,file='predmydt1.csv')
>plotcp(mydt1)
>diff = predicted_mydt1 - data2$diagnosis
>sumofsquares = function(x) {return(sum(x^2))}
>sumofsquares(diff)
```

4.3 RANDOM FOREST

Random forests are collections of decision trees that provide predictions into the structure of data. They are a tool that pulls the power of multiple decision trees in judicious randomization, and ensemble learning to produce predictive models. They provide variable rankings, missing values, segmentations, and reporting for each record to ensure deep data understanding. After each tree is built, all the data is run down the tree. For each of the pairs of cases, vicinities are computed. If two cases occupy the same terminal node, their vicinities are increased by one. At the end of the run, normalization is carried out by dividing by the number of trees. Proximities are used in replacing missing data, locating outliers, and producing to reveal low-dimensional understandings of the data. The training data, which is out-of-bag data, is used to estimate classification error and to calculate the importance of variables. Random forests run very efficiently on large databases, producing accurate results.

They handle multiple variables without deletion, giving estimates of the importance of the variables to solve the classification problems. They generate an internal unbiased estimate of the generalization error as the forest building progresses. A random forest is an effective method for estimating missing data, and maintains accuracy when a large proportion of the data is missing.

4.3.1 Case – I: Fitting of Random Forest Model

Random forests run very efficiently on large databases, producing accurate results. They handle multiple variables without deletion, giving estimates of the importance of the variables to solve the classification problems. In *R*, we can classify using a random forest model to data with the randomForest function.

4.3.1*a* Getting Ready

We need to prepare data with many predictors and one response variable, and with a classification of many variables.

4.3.1*b* How to do it

Perform the following steps to perform random forest model with randomForest:

1. You should install all the following packages and load its library:

```
>install.packages("randomForest")
> library(randomForest)
>install.packages("C50")
>install.packages("caret")
>install.packages("e1071")
> library(caret)
> library(e1071)
> library(C50)
```

2. From the package, you can load the outcome dataset:

```
>url="https://drive.google.com/file/d/1epnX2w3aImgJ7u35VNl0Zp99Rlw6Ndfm/
view?usp=sharing"
> data1=read.csv(url)
```

3. You can use the str function to display the structure of the outcome dataset:

```
> str(data1)
```

Output:

```
'data.frame': 980 obs. of 4 variables:
$ Ind_Exp_Act_Score: num 6.2 2.6 9.5 2.6 10 0.2 2.5 0.4 0.2 8.9 ...
$ Tran_Speed_Score : num 9.3 2.2 1.5 5 7.7 2.3 2.8 1.6 9.8 6.1 ...
$ Peer_Comb_Score : num 7.4 8.7 8.2 0.4 7.2 3.4 4.6 5.3 0.8 9.2 ...
$ Outcome : int 1 1 1 0 1 0 0 0 0 1 ...
>set.seed(2)
```

4. Use 70% of dataset as training set and remaining 30% as testing set

```
> sample = sample(c(TRUE, FALSE), nrow(data1), replace=TRUE, prob=c(0.7,0.3))
>train = data1[sample, ]
> test = data1[!sample, ]
```

5. View dimensions of training set

```
> dim(train)
```

Output:

```
[1]   687   4
> dim(test)
```

Output:

```
[1]   293   4
```

6. We now then use churn as a label to generate the prediction model in use. After that, we assign the classification tree model into the Outcome variable:

```
> data1.rf = randomForest(Outcome ~ ., data = train, importance = T)
> data1.rf
```

Output:

```
Call:
randomForest(formula = Outcome ~ ., data = train, importance = T)
Type of random forest: regression
Number of trees: 500
No. of variables tried at each split: 1
Mean of squared residuals: 0.04050645
% Var explained: 80.01
```

7. Perform the following steps to predict values with random forest model:

```
> data1.prediction = predict(data1.rf, test)
> tab=table(data1.prediction, test$Outcome)
> tab
```

Output:

	0	1
0.00329999999999957	1	0
0.00559999999999958	1	0
0.0137092691622099	1	0
0.0149833333333329	1	0
0.0170666666666662	1	0
0.0197142857142854	1	0
0.0242666666666664	1	0
0.0245999999999997	1	0
0.0272999999999998	1	0
0.0302333333333331	1	0
0.0311666666666663	1	0
0.0336714285714284	1	0
0.0350999999999999	1	0
0.0364999999999999	1	0
0.0414809523809523	1	0
0.0447999999999999	1	0
0.0506333333333332	1	0
0.0526380952380951	1	0
0.0552003663003662	1	0
0.0575333333333333	1	0
0.0583476190476189	1	0
0.0595357142857141	1	0
0.06185	1	0
0.0618999999999999	1	0
0.0662999999999999	1	0
0.0690333333333331	1	0
0.0696666666666666	1	0
0.0729428571428571	1	0
0.0765008658008658	1	0
0.0799999999999999	1	0
0.0803666666666666	1	0

4. Draw an error plot of random forest model using plot function:

```
>plot(data1.rf)
```

Output:

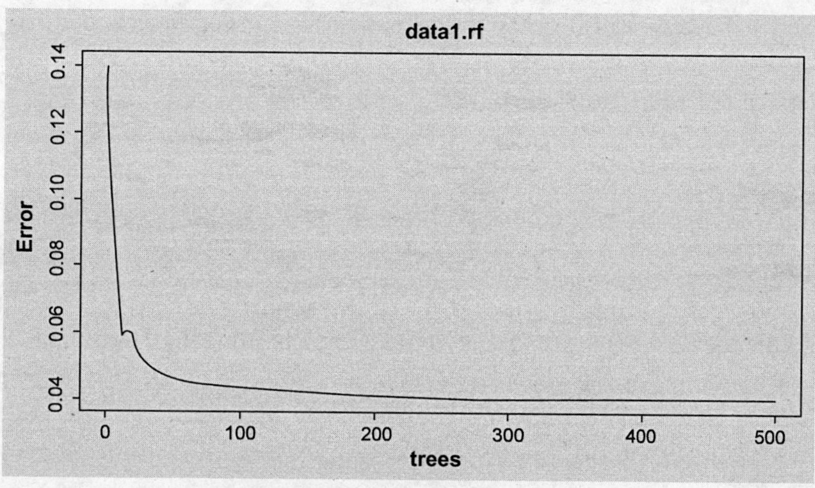

Fig. 4.9: Error plot of random forest model

7. We use a variable importance function to know the variable importance of the dataset according to the fitting of random forest model:

   >importance(data1.rf)

   Output:

   %IncMSEIncNodePurity

Ind_Exp_Act_Score	88.72334	38.44835
Tran_Speed_Score	92.85605	37.92132
Peer_Comb_Score	121.57420	55.46990

   >varImpPlot(data1.rf)

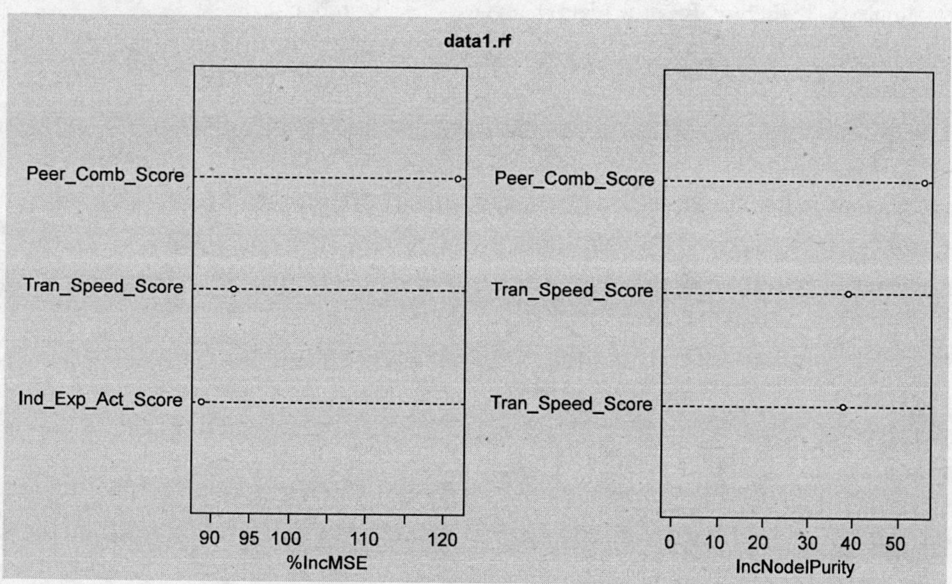

Fig. 4.10: Variable importance plot using random forest model

8. We will verify the correctness of the model (using the sum of squares defined in the previous section), as follows:

   > diff= data1.prediction - test$Outcome

   > value= sum((diff)^2)

   > value

   Output:

   [1] 11.87474

   From the above result it maybe concluded that this model gives the better result as the sum of square of difference is very low and this would be a better modeling technique.

Table 4.3: Coding of Random Forest Model

```
>install.packages("randomForest")
> library(randomForest)
>install.packages("C50")
>install.packages("caret")
>install.packages("e1071")
> library(caret)
> library(e1071)
> library(C50)
>url="https://drive.google.com/file/d/1epnX2w3aImgJ7u35VNl0Zp99Rlw6Ndfm/view?usp=sharing"
> data1=read.csv(url)
> str(data1)
>set.seed(2)
> sample = sample(c(TRUE, FALSE), nrow(data1), replace=TRUE, prob=c(0.7,0.3))
>train = data1[sample, ]
> test = data1[!sample, ]
> dim(train)
> dim(test)
> data1.rf = randomForest(Outcome ~ ., data = train, importance = T)
> data1.rf
> data1.prediction = predict(data1.rf, test)
> tab=table(data1.prediction, test$Outcome)
> tab
>plot(data1.rf)
>importance(data1.rf)
>varImpPlot(data1.rf)
> diff= data1.prediction – test$Outcome
> value= sum((diff)^2)
> value
```

4.3.2 Case – II: Fitting of Random Forest Model

Random forests run very efficiently on large databases, producing accurate results. They handle multiple variables without deletion, giving estimates of the importance of the variables to solve the classification problems. In *R*, we can classify using a random forest model to data with the randomForest function.

4.3.2*a* Getting Ready

We need to prepare data with many predictors and one response variable, and with a classification of many variables.

4.3.2*b* How to do it

Perform the following steps to perform random forest model with randomForest:

1. You should install all the following packages and load its library:

```
>install.packages("randomForest")
>library(randomForest)
>install.packages("C50")
>install.packages("caret")
>install.packages("e1071")
>library(caret)
>library(e1071)
>library(C50)
```

2. From the package, you can load the outcome dataset:

```
>url="https://drive.google.com/file/d/1PmsZsiKck64FyQcvOf3vZdfnA06C64Np/
view?usp=sharing"
>data2=read.csv(url)
```

3. You can use the str function to display the structure of the churn dataset:

```
>str(data2)
```

Output:

```
'data.frame': 2666 obs. of 17 variables:
$ International.plan : int 0 0 0 1 1 1 0 1 1 0 ...
$ Voice.mail.plan : int 1 1 0 0 0 0 1 0 1 0 ...
$ Number.vmail.messages : int 25 26 0 0 0 0 24 0 37 0 ...
$ Total.day.minutes : num 265 162 243 299 167 ...
$ Total.day.calls : int 110 123 114 71 113 98 88 79 84 127 ...
$ Total.day.charge : num 45.1 27.5 41.4 50.9 28.3 ...
$ Total.eve.minutes : num 197.4 195.5 121.2 61.9 148.3 ...
$ Total.eve.calls : int 99 103 110 88 122 101 108 94 111 148 ...
$ Total.eve.charge : num 16.78 16.62 10.3 5.26 12.61 ...
$ Total.night.minutes : num 245 254 163 197 187 ...
```

```
$ Total.night.calls : int 91 103 104 89 121 118 118 96 97 94 ...
$ Total.night.charge : num 11.01 11.45 7.32 8.86 8.41 ...
$ Total.intl.minutes : num 10 13.7 12.2 6.6 10.1 6.3 7.5 7.1 11.2 9.1 ...
$ Total.intl.calls : int 3 3 5 7 3 6 7 6 5 5 ...
$ Total.intl.charge : num 2.7 3.7 3.29 1.78 2.73 1.7 2.03 1.92 3.02 2.46 ...
$ Customer.service.calls: int 1 1 0 2 3 0 3 0 0 0 ...
$ Churn : int 0 0 0 0 0 0 0 0 0 0 ...
>set.seed(1)
```

4. Use 70% of dataset as training set and remaining 30% as testing set

```
>sample = sample(c(TRUE, FALSE), nrow(data2), replace=TRUE, prob=c(0.7,0.3))
>train = data2[sample, ]
>test = data2[!sample, ]
```

5. view dimensions of training set

```
>dim(train)
Output:
[1]  1866   17
> dim(test)
Output:
[1]  800   17
```

6. We now then use churn as a label to generate the prediction model in use. After that, we assign the classification tree model into the Churn variable:

```
> rf = randomForest(Churn~ ., data = train, importance = T)
> rf
Output:
Call:
randomForest(formula = Churn ~ ., data = train, importance = T)
Type of random forest: regression
Number of trees: 500
No. of variables tried at each split: 5
Mean of squared residuals: 0.04563779
% Var explained: 63.35
```

7. Perform the following steps to predict values with random forest model:

```
>pred = predict(rf, test)
>tab=table(pred, test$Churn)
>tab
Output:
         pred              0    1
-3.56437102055907e-16      1    0
```

```
-3.00481861614799e-16   1   0
-2.37143638059933e-16   1   0
-2.19824158875781e-16   1   0
0.000399999999999644    1   0
0.000666666666666312    1   0
0.00066666666666639     1   0
0.000999999999999651    1   0
0.000999999999999684    1   0
0.00149999999999966     1   0
0.00179999999999972     1   0
0.00189999999999973     1   0
0.0019999999999997      1   0
0.00199999999999971     1   0
0.00209999999999978     1   0
0.00226666666666636     1   0
[ reached getOption("max.print") -- omitted 263 rows ]
```

8. Draw an error plot of random forest model using plot function:

   >plot(rf)

   Output:

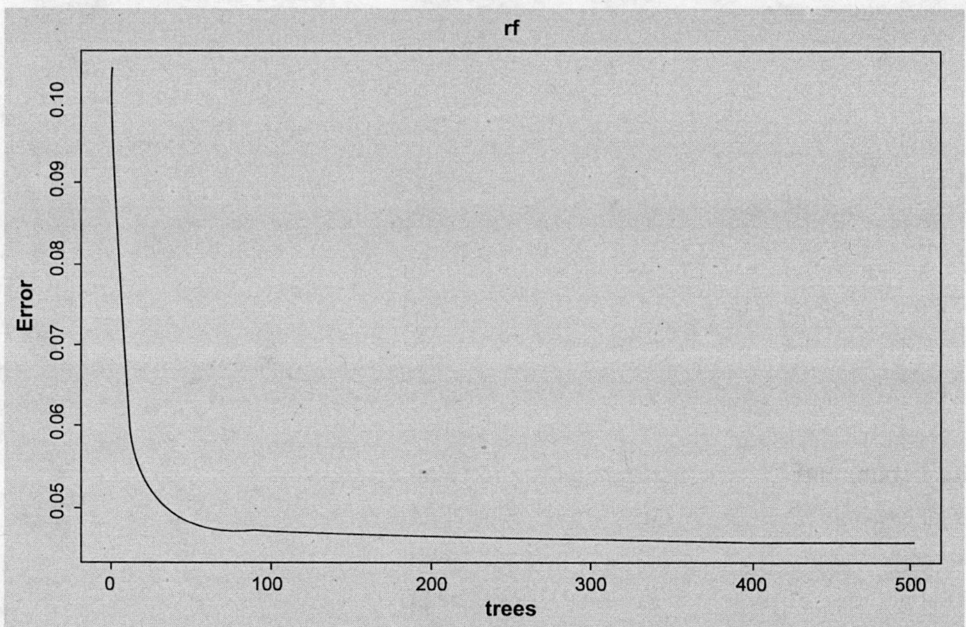

Fig. 4.11: Error plot of random forest model

9. We use a variable importance function to know the variable importance of the dataset according to the fitting of random forest model:

   >importance(rf)

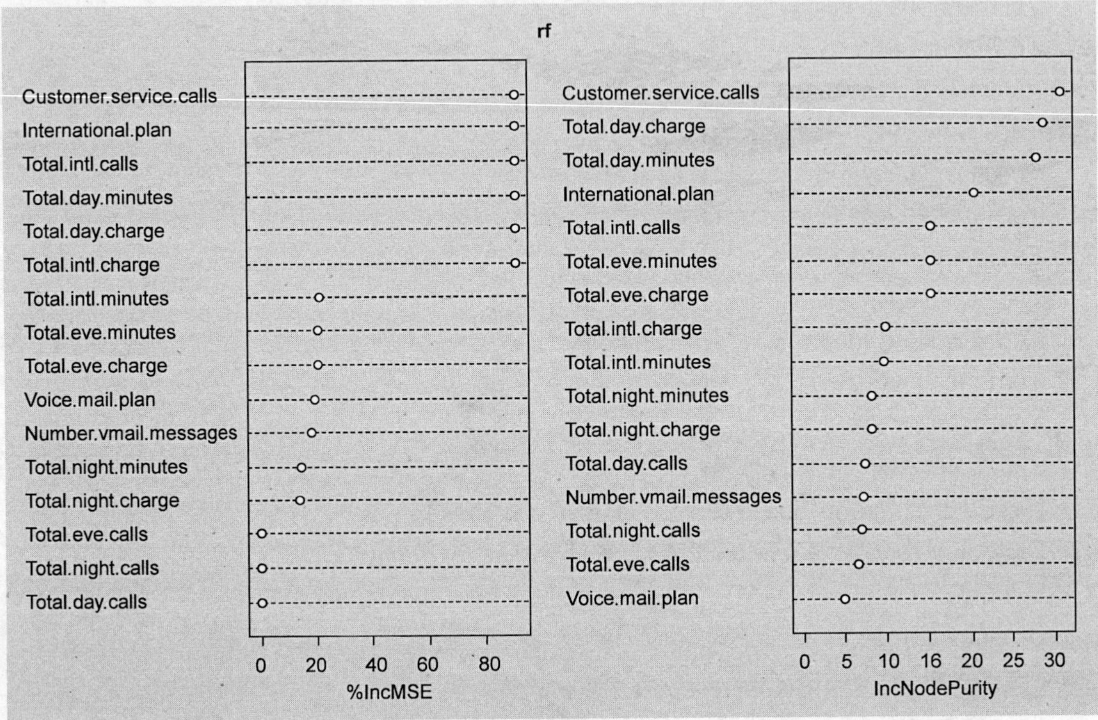

Fig. 4.12: Variable importance plot using random forest model

Output:

%IncMSE	IncNode	Purity
International.plan	76.4741368	20.489046
Voice.mail.plan	1.3925264	4.773063
Number.vmail.messages	18.2769198	6.841028
Total.day.minutes	33.8861990	28.040392
Total.day.calls	–0.3774793	7.055742
Total.day.charge	33.7877103	28.800660
Total.eve.minutes	20.6212309	15.167668
Total.eve.calls	0.3394839	6.127141
Total.eve.charge	20.5162568	15.044390
Total.night.minutes	14.3098931	8.209231
Total.night.calls	0.1765291	6.691366
Total.night.charge	14.1827244	7.927698

Output:

```
Total.intl.minutes        21.3944733    9.408411
Total.intl.calls          45.1435878   15.393827
Total.intl.charge         23.3925271    9.656039
Customer.service.calls    91.1995352   31.018694
>varImpPlot(rf)
```

10. We will verify the correctness of the model (using the sum of squares defined in the previous section), as follows:

```
>diff= pred - test$Churn
>value= sum((diff)^2)
>value
```

Output:

```
[1]   34.90532
```

From the above result it maybe concluded that this model gives the better result as the sum of square of difference is very low and this would be a better modeling technique.

Table 4.4: Coding of Random Forest Model

```
>install.packages("randomForest")
> library(randomForest)
>install.packages("C50")
>install.packages("caret")
>install.packages("e1071")
> library(caret)
> library(e1071)
> library(C50)
>url="https://drive.google.com/file/d/1PmsZsiKck64FyQcvOf3vZdfnA06C64Np/view?usp=sharing"
> data2=read.csv(url)
> str(data2)
>set.seed(1)
> sample = sample(c(TRUE, FALSE), nrow(data2), replace=TRUE, prob=c(0.7,0.3))
>train = data2[sample, ]
> test = data2[!sample, ]
> dim(train)
> dim(test)
> rf = randomForest(Churn~ ., data = train, importance = T)
> rf
> pred = predict(rf, test)
> tab=table(pred, test$Churn)
```

```
> tab
> plot(rf)
> importance(rf)
>varImpPlot(rf)
> diff= pred - test$Churn
> value= sum((diff)^2)
> value
```

Quiz Questions

1. .... are a popular machine learning algorithm that can be used for both regression and classification tasks.
   (*a*) Decision trees (*b*) Random forest
   (*c*) Linear regression (*d*) None of the above
2. Random forest is known as the forest of .... trees.
   (*a*) Regression (*b*) Decision
   (*c*) Classification (*d*) None of the above
3. There is a direct relationship between the number of trees in the .... and the results.
   (*a*) Decision tree (*b*) Classification
   (*c*) Random forest (*d*) None of the above
4. A supervised learning method used for classification and regression is
   (*a*) Decision tree (*b*) Regression analysis
   (*c*) Logistic regression analysis (*d*) Random forest
5. A decision tree is a tree where – non-leaf nodes have ....
   (*a*) an attribute (*b*) a data
   (*c*) a constant (*d*) none of the above
6. A decision tree is a tree where – leaf nodes have a ....
   (*a*) classification (*b*) non classification
   (*c*) regression (*d*) none of the above
7. A decision tree is a tree where each arc has a possible value of its
   (*a*) Attribute (*b*) Constant
   (*c*) Classification (*d*) None of the above
8. .... is a commonly-used machine learning algorithm, trademarked by Leo Breiman and Adele Cutler, that combines the output of multiple decision trees to reach a single result.
   (*a*) Random forest (*b*) Decision trees
   (*c*) Regression trees (*d*) None of the above
9. .... handles both classification and regression problems.
   (*a*) Random forest (*b*) Linear regression
   (*c*) Multiple regression (*d*) None of the above

10. Random forest has nearly the same hyperparameters as a .... or a bagging classifier.

(*a*) Regression tree
(*b*) Classification and regression tree
(*c*) Decision tree
(*d*) None of the above

ANSWERS

1.(*a*)	2.(*b*)	3.(*c*)	4.(*a*)	5.(*a*)	6.(*a*)	7.(*a*)	8.(*a*)	9.(*a*)	10.(*a*)

5 Decision Tree

Objectives:

1. Explain the usage of decision trees in real-time applications.
2. Describe the process of avoiding overfitting.
3. Elucidate the usage of ensemble methods.

Outcomes:

1. The decisions can be made by using decision trees.
2. Techniques of Pruning can be applied to avoid overfitting.
3. Ensemble methods can be implemented for decision making.

5.1 WHAT IS A DECISION TREE?

A decision tree is a type of Supervised Machine Learning Algorithm used to categorize or make predictions based on how previous set of questions were answered. This model is trained and tested on a set of data that contains the desired categorization. This algorithm is used for both regression and classification tasks. Decision tree is a hierarchical tree structure which consists of root node, internal nodes, leaf nodes and branches.

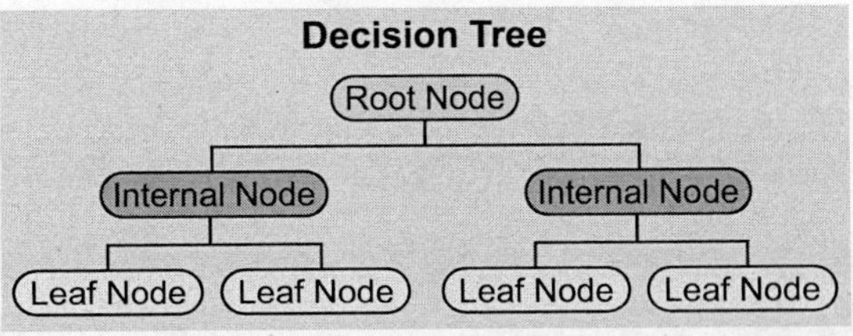

Fig 5.1: Decision Tree

The above figure 5.1 depicts the decision tree which consists of the Root Node which does not has any incoming branches. The outgoing branches from the Root Node are fed as the input branches to the Internal Nodes which are also called as Decision Nodes. Based on the decision nodes the leaf nodes or the terminal nodes are derived to predict the final outcome.

5.1.1 Terminologies in a Decision Tree

1. **Root Node:** This is the starting node of a decision tree, where the entire dataset starts dividing based on various features or conditions.
2. **Decision Nodes:** These nodes are derived after splitting the root node. These nodes represent the conditions or decisions within the tree and are known as decision nodes.

3. **Leaf Nodes:** These nodes are referred to as terminal nodes because it indicates the final outcome and these nodes are not further divided.
4. **Branch/Sub-Tree:** A subsection of the entire decision tree is referred to as a branch or sub-tree. It represents a specific path of decisions and outcomes within the tree.
5. **Pruning:** The process of cutting down or removing specific nodes in a decision tree to prevent overfitting and simplify the model.
6. **Parent and Child Node:** In a decision tree, a node that is divided into sub-nodes is known as a parent node, and the sub-nodes derived from it are referred to as child nodes. The parent node represents a decision or condition, while the child nodes represent the potential outcomes or further decisions based on that condition.

5.1.2 Decision Tree Construction

In a decision tree, the algorithm begins at the root node and works its way up to predict the class of a given dataset. This algorithm checks the values of the root property with the values of the record (actual dataset) attribute and then follows the branch and jumps to the next node depending on the comparison.

This algorithm checks the attribute value with the other sub-nodes and moves on to the next node. It repeats the procedure until it reaches the tree's leaf node. The steps for the algorithm are as follows:

Step 1: Begin the tree with the root node *S*, which includes the whole dataset.

Step 2: Using the Attribute Selection Measure, find the best attribute in the dataset.

Step 3: Subdivide the *S* into subsets containing potential values for the best qualities.

Step 4: Create the decision tree node with the best attribute.

Step 5: Create new decision trees recursively using the subsets of the dataset obtained in Step 3. Continue this procedure until you reach a point where you can no longer categorize the nodes and refer to the last node as a leaf node.

5.1.3 Attribute Selection Measures

The biggest challenge that emerges while developing a decision tree is how to choose the optimal attribute for the root node and sub-nodes. To tackle such challenges, a technique known as Attribute Selection Measure(ASM), is used. We can simply determine the best characteristic for the tree's nodes using this measurement. ASM is commonly performed using three techniques:

1. Information Gain
2. Entropy
3. Gini Index

5.1.3.1 Information Gain

Information gain is the assessment of changes in entropy following attribute-based segmentation of a dataset. It computes the amount of information a feature offers about a class. We divided the node and build the decision tree based on the importance of information obtained. A decision tree algorithm will always try to maximise the value of information gain, and the node/attribute with the most information gain will be split first. It may be computed using the formula below:

*Information Gain = Entropy(S)-[(Weighted Average) * Entropy(each feature)]*

5.1.3.2 Entropy

Entropy is a metric to measure the impurity in a given attribute. It specifies randomness in data. Entropy can be calculated as:

$$Entropy(S) = -P(yes)\ log2\ P(yes) - P(no)\ log2\ P(no)$$

Where,

- S = Total Number of Samples
- P(yes) = Probability of yes
- P(no) = Probability of no

5.1.3.3 Gini Index

The Gini index is a measure of impurity or purity utilised in the CART (Classification and Regression Tree) technique for generating a decision tree. A low Gini index attribute should be favoured over a high Gini index attribute. It only generates binary splits, whereas the CART method generates binary splits using the Gini index. The Gini index may be computed using the formula below:

$$Gini\ Index = 1 - \Sigma\ jPj2$$

Example: To approve a loan on the basis of the age, salary, and no. of children the person has.

The figure 5.2 depicts a simple decision tree in which a person's age is over 30 years and the number of children are less than two will get a loan and also if a person's age is below 30 years and salary is over \$2500 will get a loan. In simple terms, the decision tree is helping us to take a decision regarding to sanction a loan or not to a person.

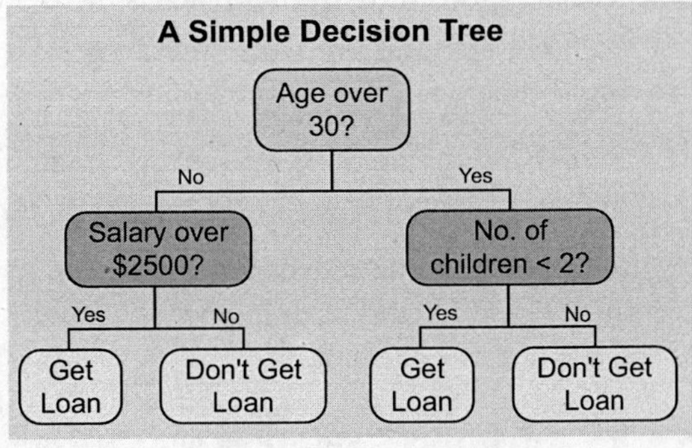

Fig 5.2: A Sample Decision Tree

5.1.4 What is Overfitting?

Overfitting occurs when a model fits too closely to the training data and may become less accurate when encountering new data or predicting future outcomes. In an overfit condition, the model concentrates on the noise of the training data and misses the important patterns.

5.1.4.1 Overfitting in Decision Trees

In decision trees, to fit the data, the model generates new nodes and ultimately the tree becomes more complex to interpret. The decision tree predicts well for the training data but may be inaccurate for new data. If a decision tree model is allowed to train to its fully potential, it can overfit the training data.

5.1.4.2 Avoiding Overfitting

Pruning is a technique to avoid overfitting that removes parts of the decision tree and prevents it from growing to its full extent. Pruning removes those parts of the decision tree that do not have the power to classify instances. Pruning can be of two types i.e., Pre-Pruning and Post-Pruning.

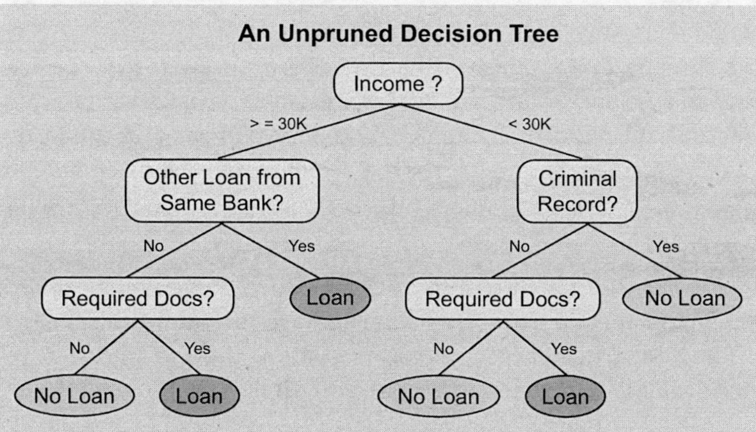

Fig 5.3: An Unpruned Decision Tree

The above figure 5.3 represents an unpruned decision tree which is more complex, denser and resulting in variance. The figure 5.4 represents a pruned decision tree where the unessential parts have been removed which is avoiding overfitting.

5.1.4.3 Pre-Pruning

This process is used to stop the growth of non-significant branches in a decision tree. This is also called as Forward Pruning or Early Stopping because it stops the growth of branches in a decision tree i.e., to prevent it from reaching to the full depth. Pruning involves the tuning of hyperparameters prior to training the model. Hyperparameters are the parameters whose values control the learning process and determine the value of the model parameters.

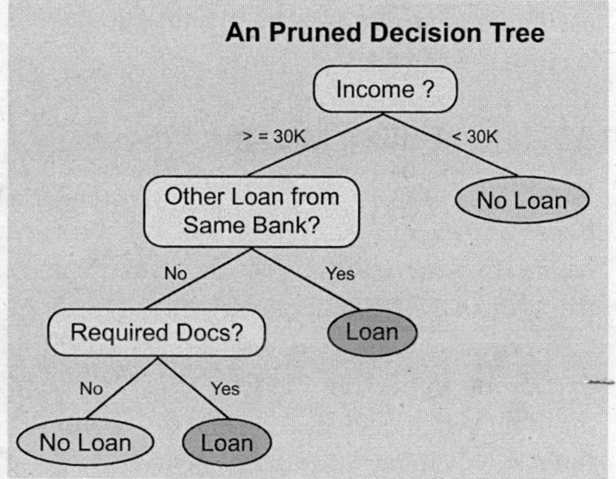

Fig 5.4: An Pruned Decision Tree

Hyperparameter Tuning For Pre-Pruning Decision Trees:

The hyperparameters that can be tuned for pre-pruning or early stopping are **max_depth, min_samples_leaf, and min_samples_split**.

- ***max_depth*:** Specifies the **maximum depth of the tree**. If None, then nodes are expanded until all leaves are pure or until all leaves contain less than min_samples_split samples.

The more the value of *max_depth*, the more complex the tree will be. On increasing the *max_depth* value, the training error will decrease but it can result in inaccurate predictions on the test data (overfitting). Hence, the correct *max_depth* value is the one that results in the **best-fit decision tree** - neither underfits nor overfits the data.

- ***min_samples_leaf*:** Specifies the minimum number of samples required at a leaf node.
- ***min_samples_split*:** Specifies the minimum number of samples required to split an internal node.

5.1.4.4 Post-Pruning

Post-Pruning is a technique that eliminates the branches from fully grown decision tree model to reduce its complexity and variance. This technique is also called as 'Backward Pruning' which allows the decision tree to grow to its full depth, then removes branches to prevent the model from overfitting. This technique can slightly increase the training error but decreasing in testing error.

In Post-Pruning, non-significant branches of the model are removed using the **Cost Complexity Pruning (CCP)** technique.

This algorithm is parameterized by **α (≥ 0) or alpha** known as the complexity parameter. The **cost_complexity_pruning_path** function of the sklearn package in Python calculates the effective alphas and their corresponding impurities at each step of the pruning process. In cost complexity pruning, the *ccp_alpha or the alpha value* **can be tuned to get the best-fit decision tree model.**

5.2 HANDLING CONTINUOUS VALUED ATTRIBUTES

Binning is a technique used to handle continuous valued attributes in a decision tree construction. It works by dividing the range of values for a given attribute into intervals, or bins. Each bin is then converted into a single categorical value, allowing the attribute to be used in the decision tree. Regression is another technique used to handle continuous attributes in decision tree construction. It works by fitting a regression line to the data and then using the regression line to estimate the values for a given attribute. The estimated values are then used in the decision tree. Both binning and regression can be used to handle continuous attributes in decision tree construction, and both can be used to improve the accuracy of the tree.

5.2.1 Handling Missing Values

Missing Values can have a negative impact on the performance of a decision tree and to handle them, there are several techniques that can be used. One of the most common techniques is imputation, which involves replacing missing values with estimates derived from the existing data. This can be done using various methods, such as mean, median, or mode imputation. Another option is to use advanced techniques such as *k*-nearest neighbors or multiple imputation. *K*-nearest neighbors looks for similar data points in the training set and uses those to estimate the missing values. Multiple imputation creates multiple versions of the dataset, each with different versions of the missing values, and then averages the results. Finally, one can also choose to simply ignore the missing values, though this should be done with caution.

5.3 RANDOM FOREST

A Random Forest Algorithm is a supervised machine learning algorithm that is extremely popular and is used for Classification and Regression problems in Machine Learning. We know that a forest comprises numerous trees, and the more trees more it will be robust. Similarly, the greater the number of trees in a Random Forest Algorithm, the higher its accuracy and problem-solving ability. Random Forest is a classifier that contains several decision trees on various subsets of the given dataset and takes the average to improve the predictive accuracy of that dataset. It is based on the concept of ensemble learning which is a process of combining multiple classifiers to solve a complex problem and improve the performance of the model.

Ensemble simply means combining multiple models. Thus a collection of models is used to make predictions rather than an individual model.

5.3.1 Ensemble uses two Types of Methods

5.3.1.1 Bagging

It creates a different training subset from sample training data with replacement and the final output is based on majority voting. For example, Random Forest.

Steps involved in Bagging:

1. **Selection of Subset:** Bagging starts by choosing a random sample, or subset, from the entire dataset.
2. **Bootstrap Sampling:** Each model is then created from these samples, called Bootstrap Samples, which are taken from the original data with replacement. This process is known as row sampling.
3. **Bootstrapping:** The step of row sampling with replacement is referred to as bootstrapping.
4. **Independent Model Training:** Each model is trained independently on its corresponding Bootstrap Sample. This training process generates results for each model.
5. **Majority Voting:** The final output is determined by combining the results of all models through majority voting. The most commonly predicted outcome among the models is selected.
6. **Aggregation:** This step, which involves combining all the results and generating the final output based on majority voting, is known as aggregation.

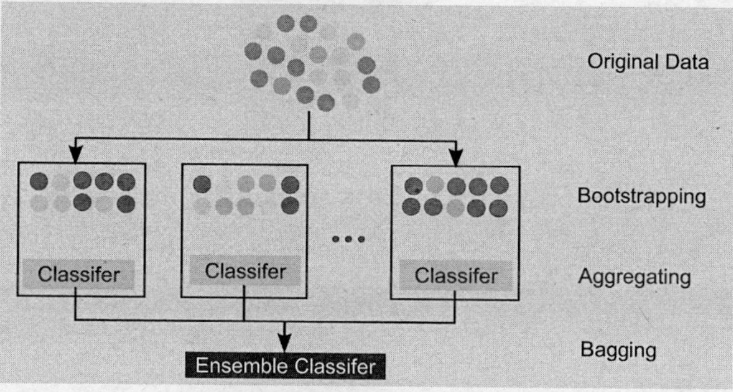

Fig 5.5: Bagging

The above figure 5.5 depicts the process of Bagging in the random forest algorithm wherein the original data is bootstrapped into different decision trees and then aggregating the individual results from the respective decision trees and produces the final result.

5.3.1.2 Boosting

Boosting is one of the techniques that use the concept of ensemble learning. A boosting algorithm combines multiple simple models (also known as weak learners or base estimators) to generate the final output. It is done by building a model by using weak models in series.

There are several boosting algorithms; AdaBoost was the first really successful boosting algorithm that was developed for the purpose of binary classification. AdaBoost is an abbreviation for Adaptive

Boosting and is a prevalent boosting technique that combines multiple "weak classifiers" into a single "strong classifier."

Steps involved in Boosting:

- **Step 1:** In the Random Forest Model, a subset of data points and a subset of features is selected for constructing each decision tree. Simply put, '*n*' random records and '*m*' features are taken from the dataset having '*k*' number of records.
- **Step 2:** Individual decision trees are constructed for each sample.
- **Step 3:** Each decision tree will generate an output.
- **Step 4:** Final output is considered based on Majority Voting or Averaging for Classification and regression, respectively.

For example:

Consider the fruit basket as the data shown in the figure below. Now 'n' number of samples are taken from the fruit basket, and an individual decision tree is constructed for each sample. Each decision tree will generate an output, as shown in the figure 5.6. The final output is considered based on majority voting. In the below figure, you can see that the majority decision tree gives output as an apple when compared to a banana, so the final output is taken as an apple.

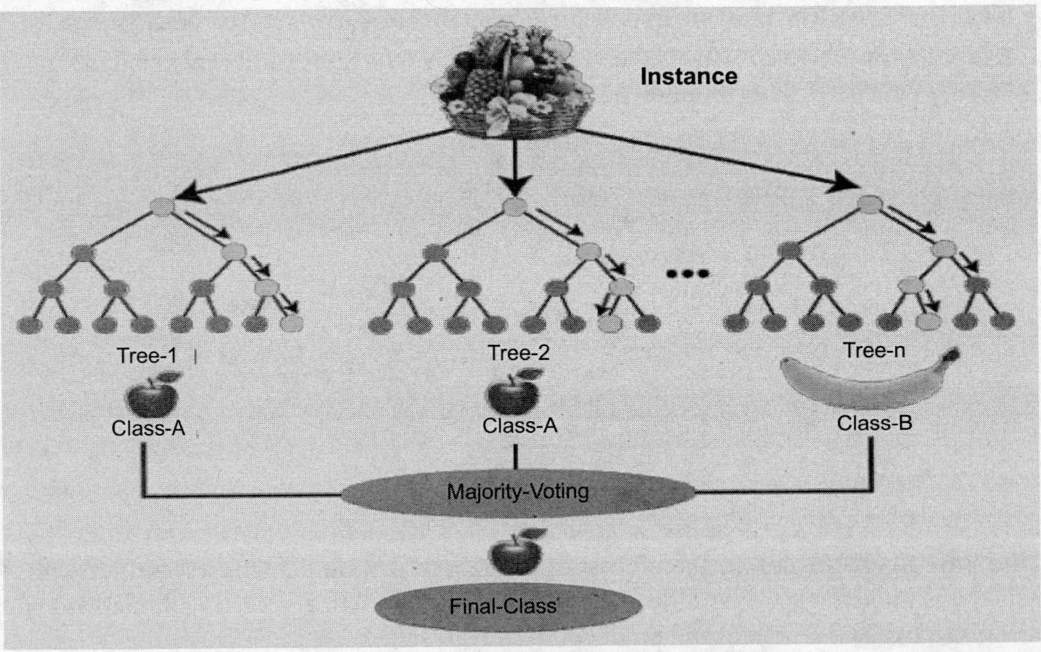

Fig 5.6: Boosting

5.3.1.3 Features of Random Forest

- **Diversity:** Not all attributes/variables/features are considered while making an individual tree; each tree is different.
- **Immune to the curse of dimensionality:** Since each tree does not consider all the features, the feature space is reduced.

- **Parallelization:** Each tree is created independently out of different data and attributes. This means we can fully use the CPU to build random forests.
- **Train-Test split:** In a random forest, we don't have to segregate the data for train and test as there will always be 30% of the data which is not seen by the decision tree.
- **Stability:** Stability arises because the result is based on majority voting/averaging.

5.3.1.4 Advantages and Disadvantages of Random Forest

Advantages:

- It can be used in classification and regression problems.
- It solves the problem of overfitting as output is based on majority voting or averaging.
- It performs well even if the data contains null/missing values.
- Each decision tree created is independent of the other; thus, it shows the property of parallelization.
- It is highly stable as the average answers given by a large number of trees are taken.
- It maintains diversity as all the attributes are not considered while making each decision tree though it is not true in all cases.
- It is immune to the curse of dimensionality. Since each tree does not consider all the attributes, feature space is reduced.
- We don't have to segregate data into train and test as there will always be 30% of the data, which is not seen by the decision tree made out of bootstrap.

Disadvantages:

- Random forest is highly complex compared to decision trees, where decisions can be made by following the path of the tree.
- Training time is more than other models due to its complexity. Whenever it has to make a prediction, each decision tree has to generate output for the given input data.

5.3.1.5 Applications of Random Forest

- **Banking Industry**
  - Credit Card Fraud Detection
  - Customer Segmentation
  - Predicting Loan Defaults on LendingClub.com
- **Healthcare and Medicine**
  - Cardiovascular Disease Prediction
  - Diabetes Prediction
  - Breast Cancer Prediction
- **Stock Market**
  - Stock Market Prediction
  - Stock Market Sentiment Analysis
  - Bitcoin Price Detection

- **E-Commerce**
  - Product Recommendation
  - Price Optimization
  - Search Ranking

Objective Type Questions

1. Which of the following is used to categorize or make predictions based on how previous set of questions were answered?
   (*a*) KNN (*b*) *K*-Means
   (c) Decision Tree (*d*) None of the above
2. Which of the following nodes are derived after splitting the root node in a decision tree?
   (*a*) Root Node (*b*) Decision Nodes
   (*c*) Leaf Nodes (*d*) Terminal Nodes
3. What is the fullform of ASM?
   (*a*) Attribute Selection Method (*b*) Attribute Selection Methodology
   (*c*) Attribute Selection Measure (*d*) Attribute Selection Merger
4. The assessment of changes in entropy following attribute-based segmentation of a dataset is known as
   (*a*) Information Gain (*b*) Entropy
   (*c*) Gini Index (*d*) None of the above
5. Which of the following is a metric to measure the impurity in a given attribute?
   (*a*) Information Gain (*b*) Entropy
   (*c*) Gini Index (*d*) None of the above
6. Which of the following is a measure of impurity or purity utilised in the CART (Classification and Regression Tree) technique for generating a decision tree?
   (*a*) Information Gain (*b*) Entropy
   (*c*) Gini Index (*d*) None of the above
7. Which of the following occurs when a model fits too closely to the training data and may become less accurate when encountering new data or predicting future outcomes?
   (*a*) Pruning (*b*) Un-Pruning
   (*c*) Underfitting (*d*) Overfitting
8. Which of the following technique is used to avoid overfitting that removes parts of the decision tree and prevents it from growing to its full extent?
   (*a*) Pruning (*b*) Un-Pruning
   (*c*) Underfitting (*d*) Overfitting
9. Which of the following process is used to stop the growth of non-significant branches in a decision tree?
   (*a*) Overfitting (*b*) Underfitting
   (*c*) Pre-Pruning (*d*) Post-Pruning

10. Which of the following technique is called as 'Backward Pruning'?

(*a*) Overfitting
(*b*) Underfitting
(*c*) Pre-Pruning
(*d*) Post-Pruning

11. What is the fullform of CCP?

(*a*) Cost Complexity Pruning
(*b*) Cost Complexity Proving
(*c*) Cost Compiling Pruning
(*d*) Cost Compiling Proving

12. Which of the following contains several decision trees on various subsets of the given dataset and takes the average to improve the predictive accuracy of that dataset?

(*a*) Random Forest
(*b*) Decision Tree
(*c*) KNN
(*d*) K-Means

13. Which of the following creates a different training subset from sample training data with replacement and the final output is based on majority voting?

(*a*) Boosting
(*b*) Bagging
(*c*) Aggregating
(*d*) None of the above

14. Which of the following combines multiple simple models to generate the final output?

(*a*) Boosting
(*b*) Bagging
(*c*) Aggregating
(*d*) None of the above

15. Which of the following was the first really successful boosting algorithm that was developed for the purpose of binary classification?

(*a*) XGBoost
(*b*) CatBoost
(*c*) LightGBM
(*d*) AdaBoost

ANSWERS

1.(*c*)	2.(*b*)	3.(*c*)	4.(*a*)	5.(*b*)	6.(*c*)	7.(*d*)	8.(*a*)	9.(*c*)	10. (*d*)
11.(*a*)	12.(*a*)	13.(*b*)	14.(*a*)	15.(*d*)					

6 Neural Networks

Objectives

1. Inculcate knowledge on perceptron and neural networks.
2. Describe the usage of backpropagation networks.
3. Elucidate the usage convolutional neural networks and recurrent neural networks.

Outcomes

1. Design neural networks.
2. Design the model with Backpropagation networks.
3. Implement convolutional neural networks and design the process using recurrent neural networks.

6.1 INTRODUCTION TO PERCEPTRON

The domain of artificial neural networks and machine learning often utilizes the term "Perceptron" to address binary classification challenges. Originating in 1957 by Frank Rosenblatt, the Perceptron algorithm has garnered substantial recognition and found extensive application across various fields. These fields include speech recognition, image recognition, and natural language processing.

The Perceptron algorithm consists of a single layer of neurons that process inputs, compute a weighted total, and then apply an activation function to get an output. Based on a set of features or input variables, the **algorithm** learns to classify input data into one of two potential groups. To reduce the discrepancy between the expected output and the actual output, the weights of the neurons are changed.

One of the major advantages of the Perceptron algorithm is its simplicity. It is user-friendly and can be effectively trained on large datasets. Furthermore, it can be applied to resource-constrained devices, and it incurs minimal computational overhead.

The formula for a perceptron can be expressed as follows:

$$z = w_1x_1 + w_2x_2 + ... + w_nx_n + b$$

In this formula:

- z represents the weighted sum of the input features and bias term.
- $x_1, x_2, ..., x_n$ represent the input features.

- $w_1, w_2, ..., w_n$ represent the corresponding weights assigned to each input feature.
- b represents the bias term.

6.1.1 History of Perceptron

1957: The perceptron was introduced by Frank Rosenblatt, an American psychologist and computer scientist. He proposed a mathematical model inspired by the functioning of neurons in the human brain.

1958: Rosenblatt developed the "Mark I Perceptron," a hardware implementation of the perceptron. It consisted of a network of interconnected electronic circuits that could learn from input data and adjust its weights accordingly.

1959: The perceptron gained attention when Rosenblatt published his book titled "Principles of Neurodynamics: Perceptrons and the Theory of Brain Mechanisms." This book provided a comprehensive introduction to the perceptron model.

1969: The limits of single-layer perceptrons were examined in the book "Perceptrons," written by Marvin Minsky and Seymour Papert. They demonstrated that single-layer perceptrons were unable to learn certain classes of functions, which caused interest in perceptron research to wane.

1986: The perceptron model was revitalized by the introduction of multilayer perceptrons (MLPs). These neural networks with multiple layers of interconnected nodes were capable of learning complex patterns and functions.

2006: Deep learning, characterized by the utilization of multi-layered neural networks, witnessed notable progress, with perceptrons playing a pivotal role within these advanced models. This integration of perceptrons proved instrumental in facilitating groundbreaking achievements in domains like image recognition and natural language processing.

2012: Deep learning gained widespread attention when a deep neural network called AlexNet won the ImageNet Large Scale Visual Recognition Challenge, significantly surpassing previous state-of-the-art performance.

Present: Perceptrons continue to be extensively used in various machine learning applications, including computer vision, speech recognition, and autonomous systems. They serve as the building blocks for more sophisticated neural network architectures, driving advancements in artificial intelligence.

6.1.2 The Need for Perceptron

- **Binary Classification:** Perceptrons are primarily used for binary classification tasks, where the goal is to classify input data into one of two classes. It is particularly useful when the data is linearly separable.
- **Simplicity:** Perceptrons are simple and computationally efficient models compared to more complex neural network architectures. They have a straightforward structure consisting of an input layer, weights, a bias term, and an activation function.
- **Linear Decision Boundary:** Perceptrons are designed to learn linear decision boundaries. This means they can effectively separate data points by a straight line (in 2D) or a hyperplane (in higher dimensions). They work well when the underlying problem can be solved with a linear classifier.

- **Training Algorithm:** The perceptron learning algorithm, also known as the delta rule or the stochastic gradient descent algorithm, is used to train perceptrons. It adjusts the weights and bias iteratively based on the classification errors made by the perceptron, aiming to minimize the overall error.

6.1.3 Working of Perceptron

The Perceptron model is based on a single layer of neurons that generate an output by applying an activation function to a weighted sum of inputs. During training, the weights of the neurons are modified to reduce the discrepancy between the expected and actual output.

In order to reduce the difference between the projected and the actual outputs, the Perceptron algorithm iteratively goes through the training data and changes the weights of the neurons.

The weights are modified in a way that minimizes the error, which is determined as the difference between the output that was predicted and the output that really occurred. Up until the weights converge to a stable solution, this process is repeated.

6.1.3.1 Basic Components of Perceptron:

- **Input:** The perceptron takes input signals, which can be real numbers or binary values, representing features or attributes of the data being processed. These inputs are typically represented as a vector. The perceptron receives input signals, denoted as $x_1, x_2, ..., x_n$.
- **Weights:** Each input has an associated weight, which represents its importance in the overall computation. The weights determine the contribution of each input to the output of the perceptron. Initially, these weights are assigned random values and are updated during the learning process. Each input has an associated weight, represented as $w_1, w_2, ..., w_n$.
- **Summation Function:** The inputs are multiplied by the appropriate weights before being added together to get a weighted sum. Taking the dot product of the input vector and the weight vector is what is required in this phase. This process is represented by the weighted sum formula: $z = w_1x_1 + w_2x_2 + ... + w_nx_n$.
- **Activation Function:** The weighted sum is passed through an activation function, which introduces non-linearity into the perceptron's output. Common activation functions include the step function, sigmoid function, or Rectified Linear Unit (*ReLU*) function. The activation function determines whether the perceptron will fire or remain inactive based on the computed value. It is denoted as $f(z)$.
- **Bias:** A bias term is often included in the perceptron to adjust the output based on a predefined threshold. It allows the perceptron to learn patterns even when all the inputs are zero. Therefore, Bias is denoted as b.
- **Output:** The output of the perceptron denoted as 'y', is the result of the activation function applied to the weighted sum of inputs. It represents the perceptron's decision or prediction based on the input data. $y = f(z + b)$
- **Learning Rule:** During the training of perceptrons, they employ a learning rule, such as the perceptron learning rule or the delta rule, to modify the weights and biases. This adjustment is based on the disparity between the predicted output and the desired output. By repetitively repeating this learning process, the perceptron progressively enhances its performance, according to the following formulas:

$$\Delta w_i = \alpha\ (y^T - t)\ x_i$$
$$\Delta b = \alpha\ (y^T - t)$$

Where:

- Δw_i represents the change in weight for input *i*.
- α is the learning rate, determining the step size of the weight update.
- y^T is the predicted output of the perceptron.
- *t* is the target or expected output.

These basic components work together to enable the perceptron to learn and make predictions based on input data. Multiple perceptrons can be interconnected to form more complex neural network architectures for handling more complex tasks.

6.1.4 Types of Perceptron

Single-Layer Perceptron: A Single-Layer Perceptron as depicted in figure 6.1 consists of a solitary layer of neurons that calculates the weighted sum of inputs and applies an activation function to produce an output. It is particularly suitable for addressing linearly separable problems where the input data can be divided into two categories using a straight line.

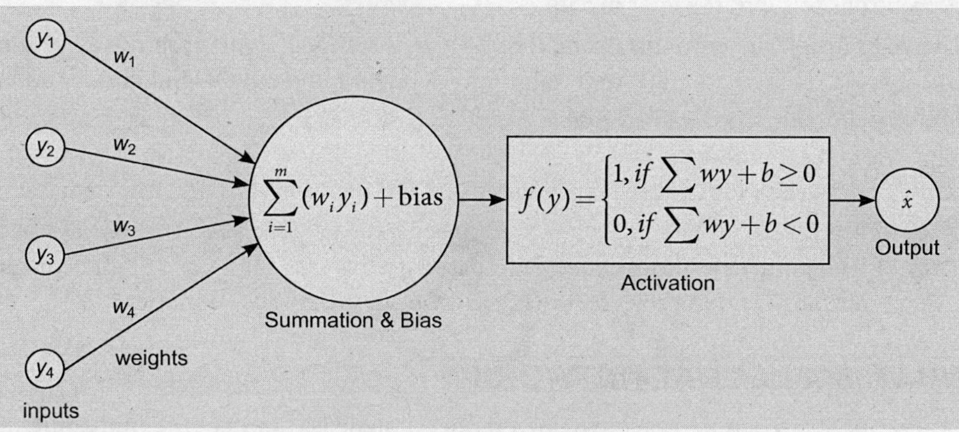

Fig. 6.1: Single-Layer Perceptron

Multi-Layer Perceptron: A Multi-Layer Perceptron as shown in the below figure 6.2 has several layers of neurons, including one or more hidden layers in between the input and output layers. Due to the hidden layers, the model can recognize more complex patterns in the input data, making it appropriate for dealing with nonlinearly separable issues.

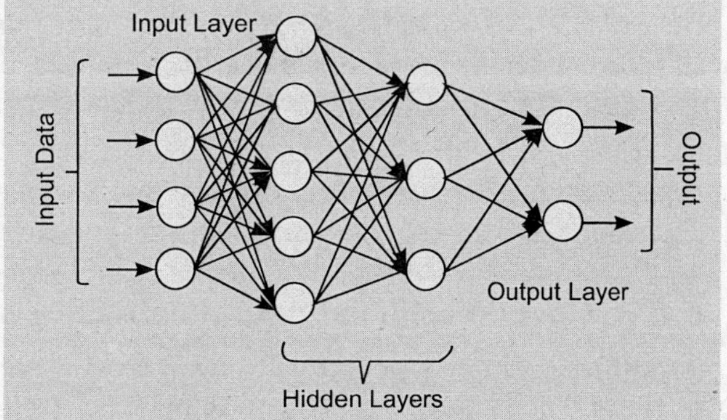

Fig. 6.2: A Multi-Layer Perceptron

6.1.5 Characteristics of Perceptron

- **Linear Separability:** The Perceptron Model assumes that the data is linearly separable, meaning there exists a hyperplane that can accurately separate the data points of different classes.

- **Supervised Learning:** The Perceptron Model employs supervised learning, where labelled data is used to train the model. In order to reduce the error between the expected and actual outputs, the weights of the neurons are changed during training.
- **Threshold Activation Function:** This type of algorithm establishes a threshold activation function, which generates a binary value depending on whether or not the weighted total of the inputs exceeds a threshold value.
- **Online Learning:** Following the processing of each input, the Perceptron Model employs an online learning approach to adjust the weights of its neurons. This characteristic makes the model highly effective and capable of handling large datasets with ease.

6.1.6 Limitations of Perceptron

- **Linear Separability:** The Perceptron algorithm can only solve problems that are linearly separable, which means that the input data can be divided into two groups using a straight line. Nonlinearly separable issues can only be handled by more sophisticated models like multi-layer Perceptrons or support vector machines.
- **Convergence:** If the input data cannot be linearly separated, the Perceptron algorithm may fail to converge. This could result in the algorithm updating the weights indefinitely and the model failing to provide reliable predictions.
- **Bias-Variance Trade-off:** The Perceptron algorithm has a bias-variance trade-off in which adding complexity to the model may lower bias but increase variance. This may cause the data to be over- or under-fitted.
- **Lack of Probabilistic Outputs:** Decisions based on the probability of a prediction can be made using probabilistic outputs, which the Perceptron algorithm does not offer.

6.2 WHAT IS A NEURAL NETWORK?

A neural network is a Machine Learning (*ML*) model designed to imitate the function and structure of the human brain. Neural networks are complex networks of interconnected nodes, or neurons, that collaborate to tackle complicated problems, also referred to as Artificial Neural Networks (*ANNs*) or Deep Neural Networks (*DNN*). Neural Networks represent a type of deep learning technology that's classified under the broader field of artificial intelligence (*AI*).

Neural networks are widely used in a variety of applications, including Image Recognition, Predictive Modeling and Natural Language Processing (*NLP*). Examples of significant commercial applications since 2000 include handwriting recognition for check processing, speech-to-text transcription, oil exploration data analysis, weather prediction and facial recognition.

6.2.1 How do artificial neural networks work?

An artificial neural network usually involves many processors operating in parallel and arranged in tiers or layers. The first tier -- analogous to optic nerves in human visual processing receives the raw input information. Each successive tier receives the output from the tier preceding it rather than the raw input

-- the same way neurons further from the optic nerve receive signals from those closer to it. The last tier produces the output of the system.

Each processing node has its own small sphere of knowledge, including what it has seen and any rules it was originally programmed with or developed for itself. The tiers are highly interconnected, which means each node in Tier N will be connected to many nodes in Tier $N - 1$ -- its inputs -- and in Tier $N + 1$, which provides input data for those nodes. There could be one or more nodes in the output layer, from which the answer it produces can be read.

Artificial Neural Networks (*ANN*) are noted for being adaptive, which means they modify themselves as they learn from initial training and subsequent runs provide more information about the world. The most basic learning model is centered on weighting the input streams, which is how each node measures the importance of input data from each of its predecessors. Inputs that contribute to getting the right answers are weighted higher.

6.2.2 How do Neural Networks Learn?

Typically, an *ANN* is initially trained or fed large amounts of data. Training consists of providing input and telling the network what the output should be. For example, to build a network that identifies the faces of actors, the initial training might be a series of pictures, including actors, non-actors, masks, statues and animal faces. Each input is accompanied by matching identification, such as actors' names or "not actor" or "not human" information. Providing the answers allows the model to adjust its internal weightings to do its job better.

For example, if nodes David, Dianne and Dakota tell node Ernie the current input image is a picture of Brad Pitt, but node Durango says it's George Clooney, and the training program confirms it's Pitt, Ernie decreases the weight it assigns to Durango's input and increase the weight it gives to David, Dianne and Dakota.

In defining the rules and making determinations -- the decisions of each node on what to send to the next tier based on inputs from the previous tier -- neural networks use several principles. These include gradient-based training, fuzzy logic, genetic algorithms and bayesian methods. They might be given some basic rules about object relationships in the data being modelled.

For example, a facial recognition system might be instructed, “Eyebrows are found above eyes”, or “Moustaches are below a nose”. Moustaches are above and/or beside a mouth. Preloading rules can make training faster. But it also includes assumptions about the nature of the problem, which could prove to be either irrelevant and unhelpful or incorrect and counterproductive, making the decision about what, if any, rules to build in important.

Further, the assumptions people make when training algorithms cause neural networks to amplify cultural biases. Biased datasets are an ongoing challenge in training systems that find answers on their own through pattern recognition in data. If the data feeding the algorithm isn't neutral -- and almost no data is -- the machine propagates bias.

6.2.3 Types of Neural Networks

Neural Networks are sometimes described in terms of their depth, including how many layers they have between input and output, or the model's so-called hidden layers. They can also be described by the number of hidden nodes the model has or in terms of how many input layers and output layers each node has. Variations on the classic neural network design enable various forms of forward and backward propagation of information among tiers.

Specific types of artificial neural networks include the following:

6.2.3.1 Feed-Forward Neural Networks:

One of the simplest variants of neural networks, these pass information in one direction, through various input nodes, until it makes it to the output node. The network might or might not have hidden node layers, making their functioning more interpretable. It is prepared to process large amounts of noise.

This type of ANN computational model is used in technologies such as facial recognition and computer vision.

6.2.3.2 Recurrent Neural Networks (RNNs)

RNNs are more complex in nature and save the output of processing nodes and feed the result back into the model. This is how the model learns to predict the outcome of a layer. Each node in the *RNN* model acts as a memory cell, continuing the computation and execution of operations.

This neural network starts with the same front propagation as a feed-forward network but then goes on to remember all processed information to reuse it in the future. If the network's prediction is incorrect, then the system self-learns and continues working toward the correct prediction during backpropagation. This type of *ANN* is frequently used in text-to-speech conversions.

6.2.3.3 Convolutional Neural Networks (CNNs)

CNNs are one of the most popular models used today. This computational model uses a variation of multilayer perceptions and contains one or more convolutional layers that can be either entirely connected or pooled. These convolutional layers create feature maps that record a region of the image that's ultimately broken into rectangles and sent out for nonlinear processing.

The *CNN* model is particularly popular for image recognition. It has been used in many of the most advanced applications of artificial intelligence, including facial recognition, text digitization and natural language processing. Other use cases include paraphrase detection, signal processing and image classification.

6.2.3.4 Deconvolutional Neural Networks

Deconvolutional neural networks use a reversed *CNN* model process. They try to find lost features or signals that might have originally been considered unimportant to the *CNN* system's task. This network model can be used in image synthesis and analysis.

6.2.3.5 Modular Neural Networks

These contain multiple neural networks working separately from one another. The networks don't communicate or interfere with each other's activities during the computation process. Consequently, complex or big computational processes can be performed more efficiently.

6.2.4 Advantages of Artificial Neural Networks

- **Parallel Processing Abilities:** ANNs have parallel processing abilities, which means the network can perform more than one job at a time.
- **Information Storage:** *ANNs* store information on the entire network, not just in a database. This ensures that even if a small amount of data disappears from one location, the entire network continues to operate.
- **Non-Linearity:** The ability to learn and model nonlinear, complex relationships helps model the real-world relationships between input and output.
- **Fault Tolerance:** *ANNs* come with fault tolerance, which means the corruption or fault of one or more cells of the *ANN* won't stop the generation of output.
- **Gradual Corruption:** This means the network slowly degrades over time instead of degrading instantly when a problem occurs.
- **Unrestricted Input Variables:** No restrictions are placed on the input variables, such as how they should be distributed.
- **Observation-Based Decisions:** Machine learning means the *ANN* can learn from events and make decisions based on the observations.
- **Unorganized Data Processing:** Artificial Neural Networks are exceptionally good at organizing large amounts of data by processing, sorting and categorizing it.
- **Ability to Learn Hidden Relationships:** *ANNs* can learn the hidden relationships in data without commanding any fixed relationship. This means *ANNs* can better model highly volatile data and non-constant variance.
- **Ability to Generalize Data:** The ability to generalize and infer unseen relationships on unseen data means ANNs can predict the output of unseen data.

6.2.5 Disadvantages of Artificial Neural Networks

- **Lack of Rules:** The lack of rules for determining the proper network structure means the appropriate artificial neural network architecture can only be found through trial, error and experience.
- **Hardware Dependency:** The requirement of processors with parallel processing abilities makes neural networks dependent on hardware.
- **Numerical Translation:** The network works with numerical information, meaning all problems must be translated into numerical values before they can be presented to the *ANN*.
- **Inaccurate Results:** If not trained properly, *ANNs* can often produce incomplete or inaccurate results.
- **BlackBox Nature:** Because of their black box *AI* model, it can be challenging to grasp how neural networks make their predictions or categorize data.

6.3 BACKPROPAGATION NETWORKS

Backpropagation is the method of fine-tuning the weights of a neural network based on the error rate obtained in the previous epoch (i.e., iteration). Proper tuning of the weights allows you to reduce error rates and make the model reliable by increasing its generalization.

Backpropagation in neural network is a short form for "backward propagation of errors". It is a standard method of training artificial neural networks. This method helps to calculate the gradient of a loss function with respect to all the weights in the network.

6.3.1 The Working of Backpropagation Algorithm

The Backpropagation algorithm in neural network computes the gradient of the loss function for a single weight by the chain rule. It efficiently computes one layer at a time, unlike a native direct computation. It computes the gradient, but it does not define how the gradient is used. It generalizes the computation in the delta rule.

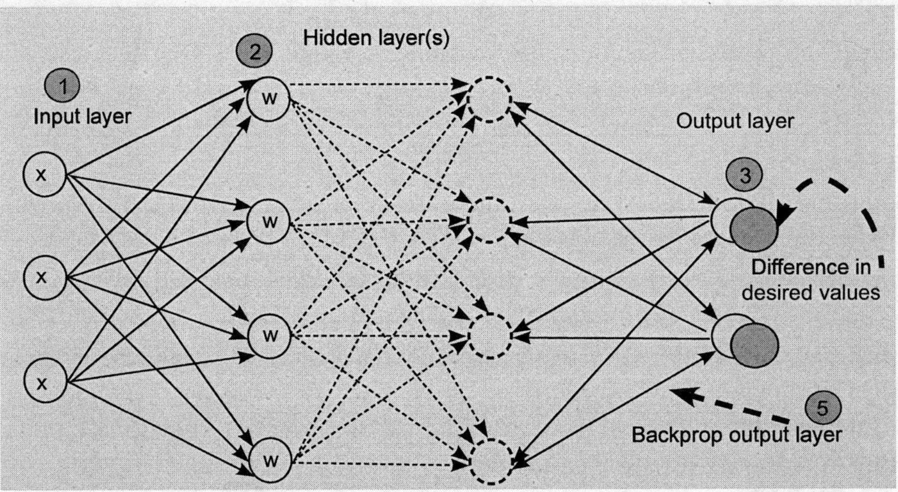

Fig. 6.3: The working of Backpropagation Algorithm

The figure 6.3 depicts the working of Backpropagation Algorithm and the process is as follows:

1. Inputs X, arrive through the preconnected path.
2. Input is modelled using real weights W. The weights are usually randomly selected.
3. Calculate the output for every neuron from the input layer, to the hidden layers, to the output layer.
4. Calculate the error in the outputs

   $\text{Error}_B = \text{Actual Output} - \text{Desired Output}$
5. Travel back from the output layer to the hidden layer to adjust the weights such that the error is decreased.

6.3.2 Advantages of Backpropagation

- Backpropagation is fast, simple and easy to program.
- It has no parameters to tune apart from the numbers of input.
- It is a flexible method as it does not require prior knowledge about the network.
- It does not need any special mention of the features of the function to be learned.

6.3.3 Disadvantages of Backpropagation

- The actual performance of backpropagation on a specific problem is dependent on the input data.
- Backpropagation algorithm in data mining can be quite sensitive to noisy data.
- You need to use the matrix-based approach for backpropagation instead of mini-batch.

6.3.4 Types of Backpropagation Networks

Two Types of Backpropagation Networks are:

- Static Back-propagation
- Recurrent Backpropagation

6.3.4.1 Static Back-Propagation

It is one kind of backpropagation network which produces a mapping of a static input for static output. It is useful to solve static classification issues like optical character recognition.

6.3.4.2 Recurrent Backpropagation

Recurrent Backpropagation in data mining is fed forward until a fixed value is achieved. After that, the error is computed and propagated backward.

6.4 CONVOLUTIONAL NEURAL NETWORKS (CNN)

6.4.1 What is a CNN?

A Convolutional Neural Network (CNN or ConvNet) is a deep learning algorithm specifically designed for any task where object recognition is crucial such as image classification, detection, and segmentation. Many real-life applications, such as self-driving cars, surveillance cameras, and more, use CNNs.

6.4.2 The importance of CNNs

These are several reasons why CNNs are important, as highlighted below:

- Unlike traditional machine learning models like *SVM* and decision trees that require manual feature extractions, *CNNs* can perform automatic feature extraction at scale, making them efficient.
- The convolutions layers make *CNNs* translation invariant, meaning they can recognize patterns from data and extract features regardless of their position, whether the image is rotated, scaled, or shifted.
- Multiple pre-trained *CNN* models such as *VGG*-16, ResNet50, Inceptionv3, and EfficientNet are proved to have reached state-of-the-art results and can be fine-tuned on news tasks using a relatively small amount of data.
- *CNNs* can also be used for non-image classification problems and are not limited to natural language processing, time series analysis, and speech recognition.

6.4.3 Architecture of a CNN

CNNs' architecture tries to mimic the structure of neurons in the human visual system composed of multiple layers, where each one is responsible for detecting a specific feature in the data. As illustrated in the image below, the typical CNN is made of a combination of four main layers:

- Convolutional layers
- Rectified Linear Unit (ReLU for short)
- Pooling layers
- Fully connected layers

Let's understand how each of these layers works using the following example of classification of the handwritten digit as depicted in below figure 6.4.

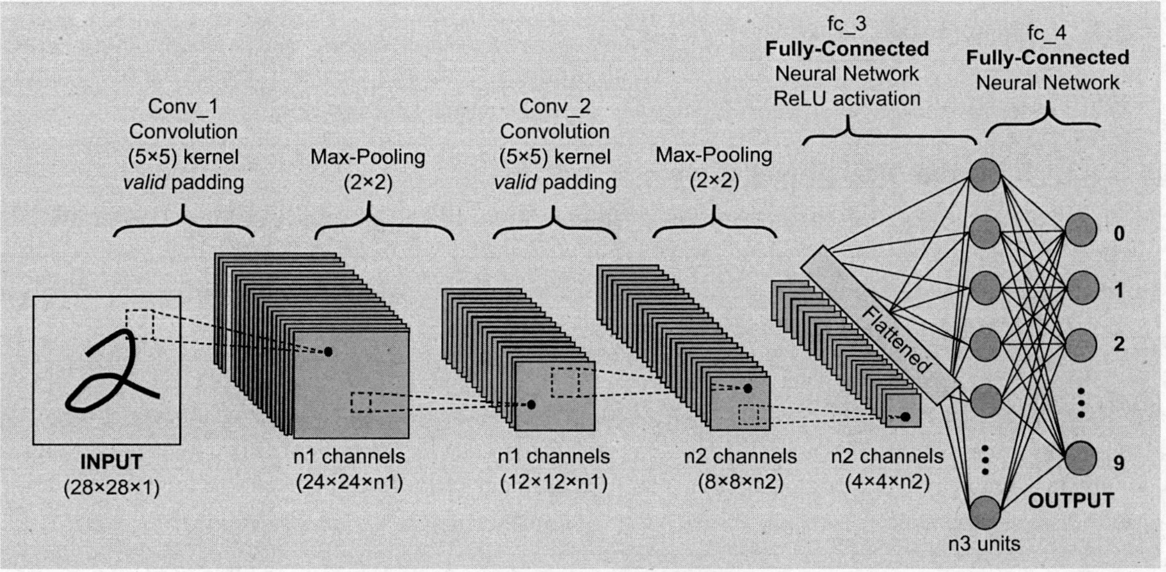

Fig 6.4: Classification of Handwritten Digit

Convolution Layers

This is the first building block of a *CNN*. As the name suggests, the main mathematical task performed is called convolution, which is the application of a sliding window function to a matrix of pixels representing an image. The sliding function applied to the matrix is called kernel or filter, and both can be used interchangeably.

In the convolution layer, several filters of equal size are applied, and each filter is used to recognize a specific pattern from the image, such as the curving of the digits, the edges, the whole shape of the digits, and more.

Let's consider this 32 × 32 grayscale image of a handwritten digit as shown in figure 6.5. The values in the matrix are given for illustration purposes.

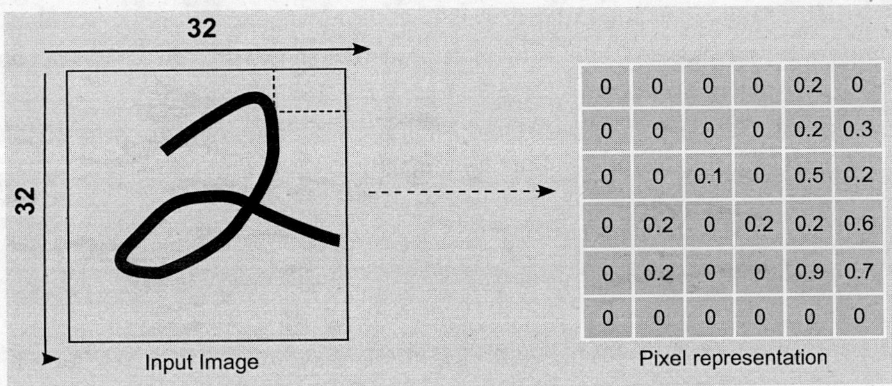

Fig. 6.5: 32 × 32 Grayscale Image of a Handwritten Digit

Also, let's consider the kernel used for the convolution. It is a matrix with a dimension of 3 × 3. The weights of each element of the kernel is represented in the grid. Zero weights are represented in the black grids and ones in the white grid.

Do we have to manually find these weights?

In real life, the weights of the kernels are determined during the training process of the neural network.

Using these two matrices, we can perform the convolution operation by taking applying the dot product, and work as follows:

1. Apply the kernel matrix from the top-left corner to the right.
2. Perform element-wise multiplication.
3. Sum the values of the products.
4. The resulting value corresponds to the first value (top-left corner) in the convoluted matrix.
5. Move the kernel down with respect to the size of the sliding window.
6. Repeat from step 1 to 5 until the image matrix is fully covered.

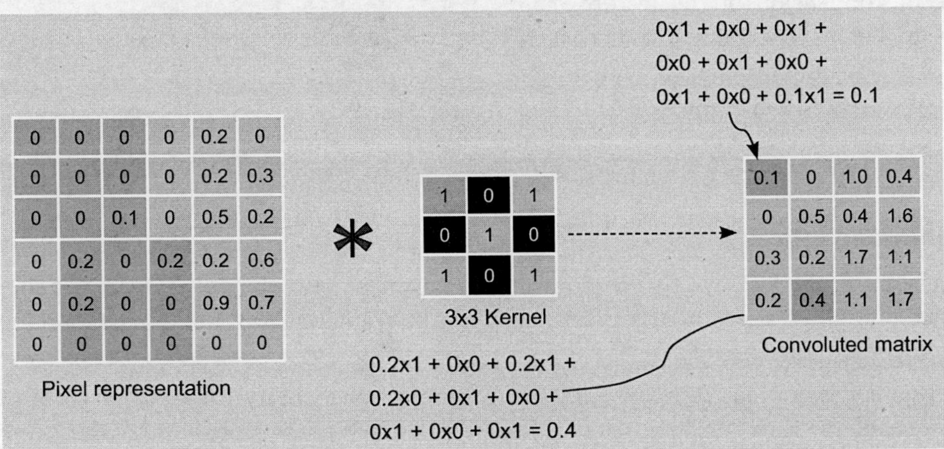

Fig 6.6: Pixel Representation to Convoluted Matrix Generation

The dimension of the convoluted matrix depends on the size of the sliding window. The higher the sliding window, the smaller the dimension. The figure 6.6 shows the conversion of data from pixel representation to convoluted matrix.

Another name associated with the kernel in the literature is feature detector because the weights can be fine-tuned to detect specific features in the input image.

For instance:

- Averaging neighboring pixels kernel can be used to blur the input image.
- Subtracting neighboring kernel is used to perform edge detection.

The more convolution layers the network has, the better the layer is at detecting more abstract features.

Activation Function

A ReLU activation function is applied after each convolution operation. This function helps the network learn non-linear relationships between the features in the image, hence making the network more robust for identifying different patterns. It also helps to mitigate the vanishing gradient problems.

Pooling Layer

The goal of the pooling layer is to pull the most significant features from the convoluted matrix. This is done by applying some aggregation operations, which reduces the dimension of the feature map (convoluted matrix), hence reducing the memory used while training the network. Pooling is also relevant for mitigating overfitting.

The most common aggregation functions that can be applied are:

- Max pooling which is the maximum value of the feature map.
- Sum pooling corresponds to the sum of all the values of the feature map.
- Average pooling is the average of all the values.

Below is an illustration of each of the previous example:

Also, the dimension of the feature map becomes smaller as the polling function is applied. The last pooling layer flattens its feature map so that it can be processed by the fully connected layer. The figure 6.7 depicts the data from Convoluted Matrix to Pooling Result.

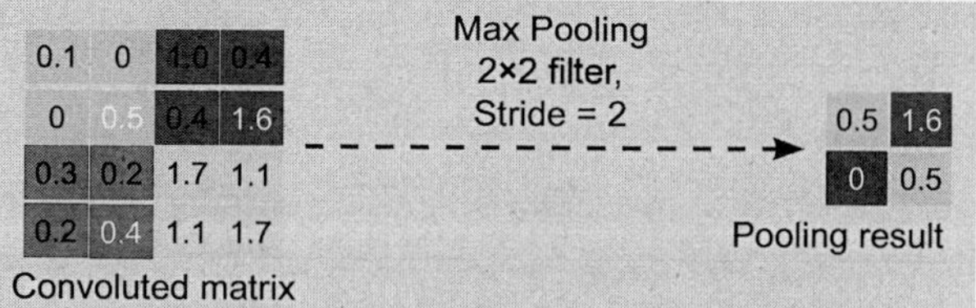

Fig 6.7: Convoluted Matrix to Pooling Result

Fully Connected Layers

These layers are in the last layer of the convolutional neural network, and their inputs correspond to the flattened one-dimensional matrix generated by the last pooling layer. ReLU activation functions are applied to them for non-linearity.

Finally, a softmax prediction layer is used to generate probability values for each of the possible output labels, and the final label predicted is the one with the highest probability score.

Dropout

Dropout is a regularization technic applied to improve the generalization capability of the neural networks with a large number of parameters. It consists of randomly dropping some neurons during the training process, which forces the remaining neurons to learn new features from the input data.

6.4.4 CNN Step-by-Step Implementation

Let's put everything we have learned previously into practice. This section will illustrate the end-to-end implementation of a convolutional neural network in TensorFlow applied to the CIFAR-10 dataset, which is a built-in dataset with the following properties:

- It contains 60.000 32 by 32 color images.
- The dataset has 10 different classes.
- Each class has 6000 images.
- There are overall 50.000 training images.
- And overall 10.000 testing images.

6.4.4.1 Working of CNN

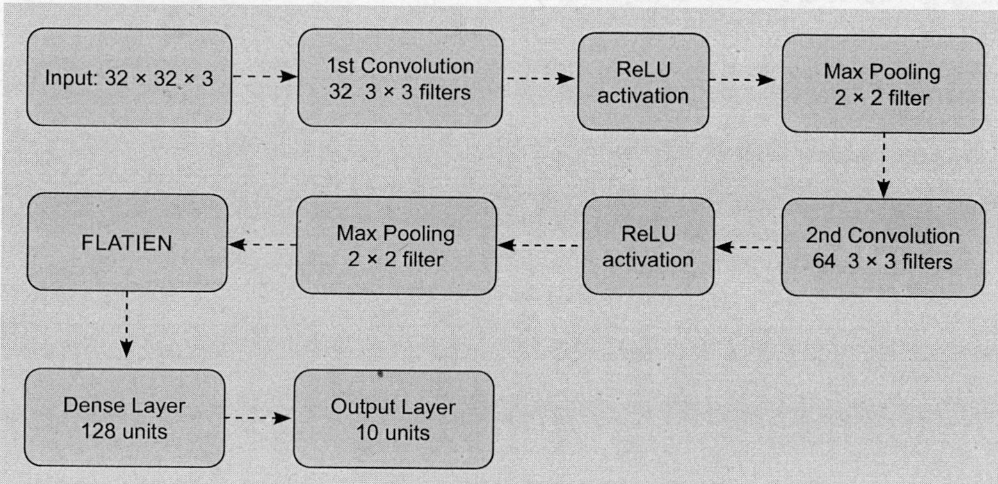

Fig. 6.8: Working process of CNN

The above figure 6.8 depicts the working process of CNN through the following steps:

- The input of the model is a 32 × 32 × 3 tensor, respectively, for the width, height, and channels.
- We will have two convolutional layers. The first layer applies 32 filters of size 3 × 3 each and a ReLU activation function. And the second one applies 64 filters of size 3 × 3.
- The first pooling layer will apply a 2 × 2 max pooling.
- The second pooling layer will apply a 2 × 2 max pooling as well.
- The fully connected layer will have 128 units and a ReLU activation function.
- Finally, the output will be 10 units corresponding to the 10 classes, and the activation function is a softmax to generate the probability distributions.

Load dataset

The built-in dataset is loaded from the keras.datasets() as follows:

```
(train_images, train_labels), (test_images, test_labels) = cf10_load_data()
```

- This code uses the Python programming language and is using the load_data() function from the cf10 module to load the CIFAR-10 dataset.
- The function returns two tuples, one containing the training images and labels, and the other containing the test images and labels.
- The code is using tuple unpacking to assign these values to the variables train_images, train_labels, test_images, and test_labels.
- This code is commonly used in machine learning and computer vision projects to load and preprocess image data for training and testing models.

Exploratory Data Analysis

This section focuses solely on showing some sample images since we already know the proportion of each class in both the training and testing data.

The helper function show_images() shows a total of 12 images by default and takes three main parameters:

- The training images.
- The class names.
- And the training labels.

```
import matplotlib.pyplot as plt
def show_images (train_images,
                 class_names,
                 train_labels,
                 nb_samples=12, nb_row=4):
plt.figure(figsize-(12, 12))
for i in range(nb_samples):
                 plt.subplot(nb_row, nb_row, 1+1)
                 plt.xticks([])
                 plt.yticks([])
                 plt.grid(False)
                 plt.imshow(train_images[i], cmap=plt.cm.binary)
                 plt.xlabel(class_names(train_labels[i][0]))
plt.show()
```

This code imports the matplotlib.pyplot library and defines a function called show_images.

- The function takes in four parameters: train_images, class_names, train_labels, nb_samples, and nb_row.
- The train_images parameter is a set of images used for training a machine learning model.
- The class_names parameter is a list of the names of the classes that the model is trying to classify the images into.

- The train_labels parameter is a set of labels corresponding to the train_images.
- The nb_samples parameter is the number of images to display, and nb_row is the number of rows to display the images in.
- The function then creates a figure with a size of 12 × 12 using plt.figure(figsize=(12, 12)).
- It then loops through nb_samples and creates a subplot for each image using plt.subplot(nb_row, nb_row, i + 1).
- The plt.xticks([]), plt.yticks([]), and plt.grid(False) functions remove the tick marks and grid lines from the plot.
- The plt.imshow(train_images[i], cmap=plt.cm.binary) function displays the image, and plt.xlabel(class_names[train_labels[i][0]]) adds a label to the image indicating its class.
- Finally, the function displays the plot using plt.show().

Now, we can call the function with the required parameters.

```
class_names = ['airplane', 'automobile', 'bird', 'cat', 'deer', 'dog', 'frog',
             'horse', 'ship', 'truck']
show_images (train_images, class_names, train_labels)
```

This code defines a list of class names for a computer vision classification problem.

- The classes are 'airplane', 'automobile', 'bird', 'cat', 'deer', 'dog', 'frog', 'horse', 'ship', and 'truck'.
- Then, the function show_images() is called with the arguments train_images, class_names, and train_labels.
- This function likely displays a set of images from the train_images dataset along with their corresponding labels from train_labels, using the class_names list to map the label indices to their corresponding class names.

A successful execution of the previous code generates the images below.

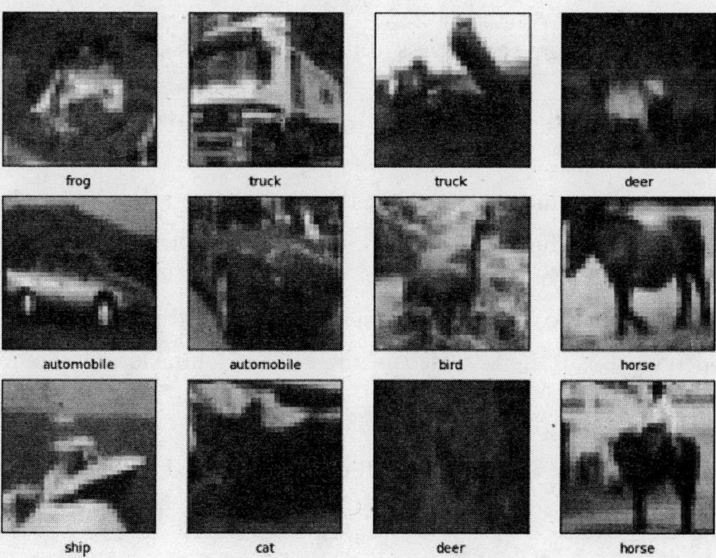

Fig. 6.8A: Data Pre-processing

Prior to training the model, we need to normalize the pixel values of the data in the same range (e.g. 0 to 1). This is a common preprocessing step when dealing with images to ensure scale invariance, and faster convergence during the training.

```
max_pixel_value = 255
train_images = train_images/max_pixel_value
test_images = test_images/max_pixel_value
```

- The first line sets the variable max_pixel_value to 255, which is the maximum value that a pixel can have in an image.
- The next two lines divide the train_images and test_images arrays by max_pixel_value.
- This is done to normalize the pixel values in the images to be between 0 and 1.
- Normalizing the pixel values can help improve the performance of machine learning models that are trained on these images.

Also, we notice that the labels are represented in a categorical format like cat, horse, bird, and so one. We need to convert them into a numerical format so that they can be easily processed by the neural network.

```
from tensorflow,keras.utils import to_categorical
train_labels = to_categorical (train_labels, len(class_names))
test_labels = to_categorical (test_labels, len(class_names))
```

- This code is using the to_categorical function from the tensorflow.keras.utils module to convert the labels of the training and testing data into one-hot encoded vectors.
- One-hot encoding is a technique used to convert categorical data into a format that can be used by machine learning algorithms.
- In this case, the labels are being converted into a binary vector where each element represents a unique class.
- The element corresponding to the class of the data point is set to 1, while all other elements are set to 0.
- The to_categorical function takes two arguments: the labels to be encoded and the number of classes.
- In this code, train_labels and test_labels are the labels of the training and testing data, respectively.
- len(class_names) is the number of unique classes in the data, which is used to determine the length of the one-hot encoded vectors.
- The resulting one-hot encoded labels are stored back into train_labels and test_labels.
- These encoded labels can then be used as input to a machine learning model.

Model Architecture Implementation

The next step is to implement the architecture of the network based on the previous description.

First, we define the model using the **Sequential**() class, and each layer is added to the model with the **add**() function.

```
from tensorflow.keras import Sequential
from tensorflow.keras.layers import conv20, NaxPooLing20, Flatten, Dense
# Variables
INPUT_SHAPE = (32, 32, 3)
FILTER1_SIZE = 32
FILTER2_SIZE = 64
FIKTER_SHAPE = (3, 3)
POOL_SHAPE = (2, 2)
FULLY_CONNECT_NUM = 128
NUM_CLASSES = Len (class_names)
# Model architecture implementation
model = Sequential()
model.add(Conv20(FILTER1_SIZE, FILTER_SHAPE, activation = 'relu', input_
shape = INPUTS_8))
model.add(MaxPooling20(POOL_SHAPE))
model.add(Conv20(FILTER_SIZE, FILTER_SHAPE, activation = 'rolu'))
model.add(MaxPooling20(POOL_SHAPE))
model.add(Platten())
model.add(Dense(FULLY_CONNECT_NUM, activation = 'relu'))
model.add(Dense(NUM_CLASSES, activation = 'softmax'))
```

- This code imports necessary modules from the TensorFlow Keras library, including Sequential, Conv2D, MaxPooling2D, Flatten, and Dense.
- It then defines several variables that will be used in the model architecture implementation.
- The model architecture implementation starts by creating a Sequential model.
- The first layer added to the model is a Conv2D layer with FILTER1_SIZE filters of size FILTER_SHAPE and an activation function of 'relu'.
- The input shape for this layer is specified as INPUT_SHAPE.
- The next layer added is a MaxPooling2D layer with a pool size of POOL_SHAPE.
- The same process is repeated for a second Conv2D layer with FILTER2_SIZE filters and a second MaxPooling2D layer.
- After the convolutional and pooling layers, a Flatten layer is added to convert the output of the previous layers into a 1D array.
- This is followed by two Dense layers, the first with FULLY_CONNECT_NUM neurons and an activation function of 'relu', and the second with NUM_CLASSES neurons and an activation function of 'softmax'.
- The final layer outputs a probability distribution over the possible classes.
- Overall, this code defines a convolutional neural network (CNN) model for image classification.

After applying the summary() function to the model, a comprehensive summary of the model's architecture with information about each layer, its type, output shape and the total number of trainable parameters are displayed.

model: 'sequential_3'

Layer (type)	output shape	param #
conv2d_2 (Conv2D)	(None, 30, 30, 32)	896
max_pooling2d_2 (MaxPooling2D)	(None, 15, 15, 32)	0
conv2d_3 (conv2D)	(None, 13, 13, 64)	18496
max_pooling2d_3 (MaxPooling2D)	(None, 6, 6, 64)	0
flatten_1 (Flatten)	(None, 2304)	0
dense_1 (Dense)	(None, 128)	295040
dense_2 (Dense)	(None, 10)	1290

Model Training

All the resources are finally available to configure and trigger the training of the model. This is done respectively with the **compile**() and **fit**() functions which takes the following parameters:

- The Optimizer is responsible for updating the model's weights and biases. In our case, we are using the Adam optimizer.
- The loss function is used to measure the misclassification errors, and we are using the Crosentropy().
- Finally, the metrics is used to measure the performance of the model, and accuracy, precision, and recall will be displayed in our use case.

```
from tensorflow.keras.metrics import Precision, Recall
BATCH_SIZE = 32
EPOCHS = 30
METRICS = meteics = ['accuracy',
                   Precision(name='precision'),
                   Recall(name='recall')]
model.compile(optimizer='adam',
                   loss='categorical_crossentropy',
                   metric = METRICS)
# Train the model
training_history = model.fit(train_images, train_labels,
                   epochs=EPOCHS, batch_size=BATCH_SIZE,
                   validation_data=(test-images, test_labels))
```

- This code imports the Precision and Recall metrics from the tensorflow.keras.metrics module.
- It then sets the batch size and number of epochs for training the model.
- The METRICS variable is a list of metrics to be used during training, including accuracy, precision, and recall.
- The Precision and Recall metrics are given names for identification purposes.
- The model.compile() function compiles the model with the Adam optimizer and categorical cross-entropy loss function.
- The metrics parameter is set to the METRICS list defined earlier.

- Finally, the model.fit() function trains the model using the specified batch size and number of epochs.
- The training data is passed in as train_images and train_labels, and the validation data is passed in as test_images and test_labels.
- The training history is stored in the training_history variable.

Model Evaluation

After the model training, we can compare its performance on both the training and testing datasets by plotting the above metrics using the show_performance_curve() helper function in two dimensions.

- The horizontal axis (x) is the number of epochs.
- The vertical one (y) is the underlying performance of the model.
- The curve represents the value of the metrics at a specific epoch.

For better visualization, a vertical red line is drawn through the intersection of the training and validation performance values along with the optimal value.

```
def show_performance_curve(training_result, metric, metric_label):
train_perf = training_result.history[str(metric)]
validation_perf = training_result.history['val_'+str(metric)]
intersection_idx = np.argwhere(np.isclose(train_perf,
validation_perf, atol=1e-2)).flatten()[0]
intersection_value = train_perf[intersection_idx]
plt.plot(train_perf, label=metric_label)
plt.plot(validation_perf, label = 'val_'+str(metric))
plt.axvline(x=intersection_idx, color='r', linestyle='--', label='Intersection')
plt.annotate(f'Optimal Value: {intersection_value:.4f}',
xy=(intersection_idx, intersection_value),
xycoords='data',
fontsize=10,
color='green')
plt.xlabel('Epoch')
plt.ylabel(metric_label)
plt.legend(loc='lower right')
```

- This code defines a function called show_performance_curve that takes in three arguments: training_result, metric, and metric_label.
- The function first extracts the training and validation performance values for the specified metric from the training_result object using the history attribute.
- It then finds the index of the first intersection point between the two performance curves using the argwhere and isclose functions from the NumPy library.

- The intersection point is defined as the point where the difference between the training and validation performance values is less than or equal to $1e - 2$.
- Next, the function plots the training and validation performance curves using the plot function from the Matplotlib library.
- It also adds a vertical line at the intersection point using the axvline function and annotates the optimal value at the intersection point using the annotate function.
- Finally, the function adds labels to the x and y axes and a legend to the plot.
- Overall, this function is useful for visualizing the performance of a machine learning model during training and identifying the optimal value of a specified metric.

Then, the function is applied for both the accuracy and the precision of the model.

```
show_performance_curve(training_history, 'accuracy', 'accuracy')
```

- This code calls the function show_performance_curve with three arguments: training_history, 'accuracy', and 'accuracy'.
- The first argument, training_history, is likely a variable that holds information about the performance of a machine learning model during training.
- The second and third arguments, both 'accuracy', specify that the function should plot a curve of the model's accuracy over time.

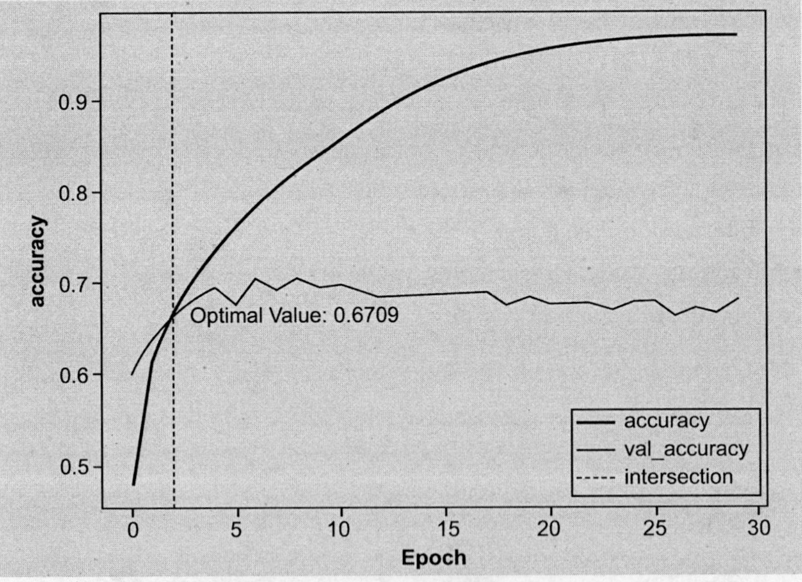

Fig. 6.9: Performance Curve with Accuracy

The above figure 6.9 shows the Performance Curve with Accuracy parameter.

```
show_performance_curve(training_history, 'precision', 'precision')
```

- This code calls the function show_performance_curve with three arguments: training_history, 'precision', and 'precision'.

- The training_history argument is likely a variable that holds information about the performance of a machine learning model during training.
- The second and third arguments, both 'precision', specify that the precision metric should be used to plot the performance curve.
- The precision metric is a measure of how many of the predicted positive cases are actually positive.
- Overall, this code is likely used to visualize the precision performance of a machine learning model during training.

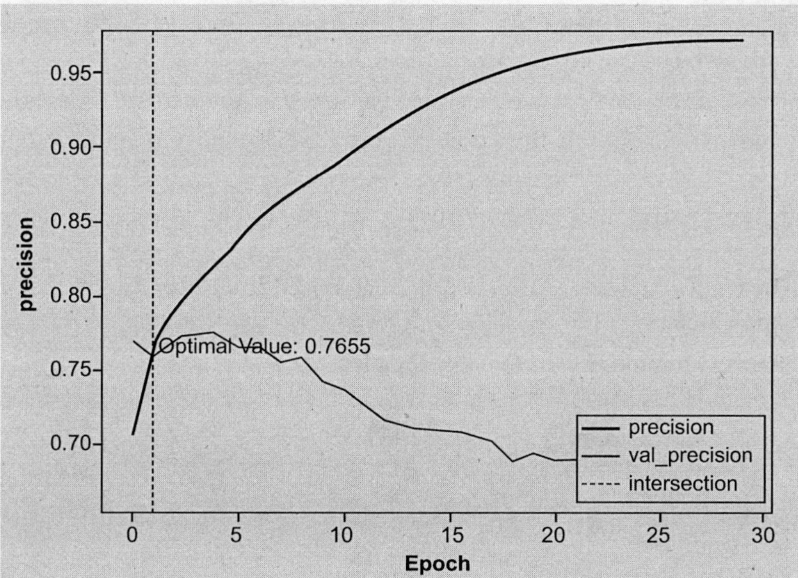

Fig. 6.10: Performance Curve with Accuracy

The above figure 6.10 shows the Performance Curve with Precision parameter.

After training the model without any fine-tuning and pre-processing, we end up with:

- An accuracy score of 67.09%, meaning that the model correctly classifies 67% of the samples out of every 100 samples.
- And, a precision of 76.55%, meaning that out of each 100 positive predictions, almost 77 of them are true positives, and the remaining 23 are false positives.
- These scores are achieved respectively at the third and second epochs for accuracy and precision.

These two metrics give a global understanding of the model behavior.

What if we want to know for each class which ones are the model good at predicting and those that the model struggles with?

This can be achieved from the confusion matrix, which shows for each class the number of correct and wrong predictions. The implementation is given below. We start by making predictions on the test data, then compute the confusion matrix and show the final result.

from sklearn.metrics import confusion_matrix, ConfusionMatrixDisplay

test_predictions = model.predict(test_images)

```
test_predicted_labels = np.argmax(test_predictions, axis=1)
test_true_labels = np.argmax(test_labels, axis=1)
cm – confusion matrix(test true labels, test_predicted_labels)
emd – ConfusionMatrixDisplay(confusion_matrix=cm)
emd.plot(include_values=True, cmap='viridis', ax=None, xticks_rotation='horizontal')
plt.show()
```

- This code snippet is used to generate a confusion matrix for a machine learning model's predictions on a test dataset.
- First, the necessary libraries are imported: sklearn.metrics for the confusion matrix and ConfusionMatrixDisplay for displaying the matrix.
- Next, the model's predictions are generated using model.predict(test_images).
- The np.argmax() function is then used to convert the predicted and true labels from one-hot encoded format to integer format.
- The confusion matrix is then generated using confusion_matrix(test_true_labels, test_predicted_labels).
- Finally, the ConfusionMatrixDisplay function is used to display the confusion matrix with the specified parameters.
- The plt.show() function is used to show the plot.

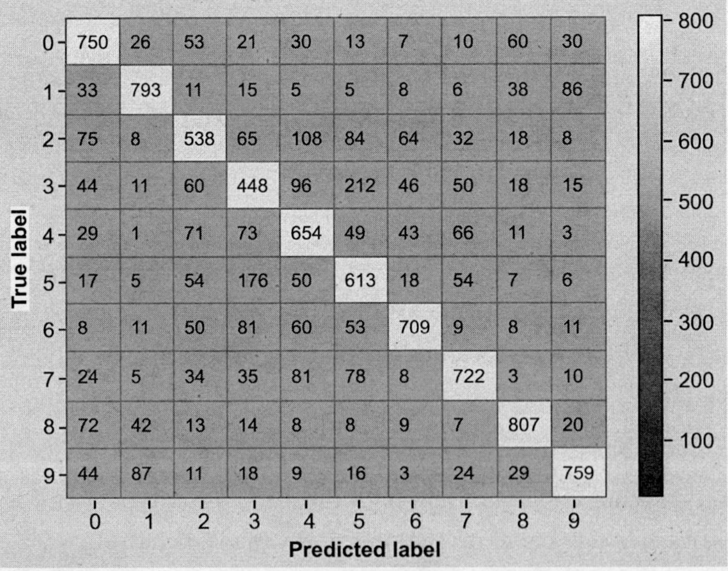

Fig. 6.11: Confusion Matrix

The above figure 6.11 shows the confusion matrix which shows more accurate prediction.

- Classes 0, 1, 6, 7, 8, 9, respectively, for airplane, automobile, frog, horse, ship, and truck have the highest values at the diagonal. This means that the model is better at predicting those classes.
- On the other hand, it seems to struggle with the remaining classes:

- The classes with the highest off-diagonal values are those the model confuses the good classes with. For instance, it confuses birds (class 2) with an airplane, and automobile with trucks (class 9).

6.5 RECURRENT NETWORKS

A Recurrent Neural Network (*RNN*) is the type of Artificial Neural Network (*ANN*) that is used in Apple's Siri and Google's voice search. *RNN* remembers past inputs due to an internal memory which is useful for predicting stock prices, generating text, transcriptions, and machine translation.

In the traditional neural network, the inputs and the outputs are independent of each other, whereas the output in *RNN* is dependent on prior elementals within the sequence. Recurrent networks also share parameters across each layer of the network. In Feedforward Networks, there are different weights across each node. Whereas *RNN* shares the same weights within each layer of the network and during Gradient Descent, the weights and basis are adjusted individually to reduce the loss.

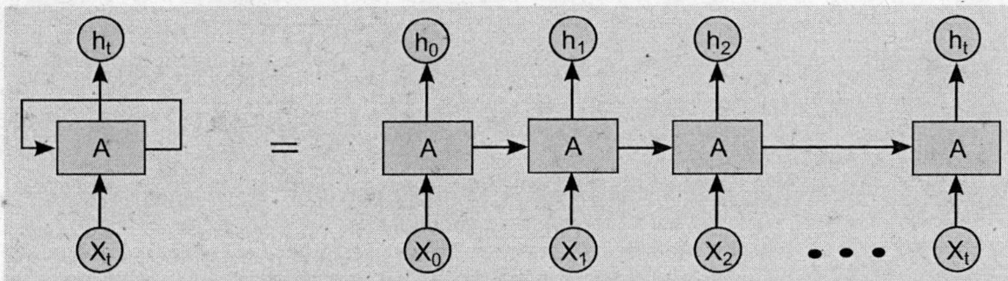

Fig. 6.12: Recurrent Neural Networks

The above figure 6.12 is a simple representation of recurrent neural networks. If we are forecasting stock prices using simple data [45, 56, 45, 49, 50, ...], each input from $\boldsymbol{X_0}$ to $\boldsymbol{X_t}$ will contain a past value. For example, $\boldsymbol{X_0}$ will have 45, $\boldsymbol{X_1}$ will have 56, and these values are used to predict the next number in a sequence.

6.5.1 Working of Recurrent Neural Networks

In *RNN*, the information cycles through the loop, so the output is determined by the current input and previously received inputs.

In the figure 6.13 the input layer **X** processes the initial input and passes it to the middle layer ***A***. The middle layer consists of multiple hidden layers, each with its activation functions, weights, and biases. These parameters are standardized across the hidden layer so that instead of creating multiple hidden layers, it will create one and loop it over.

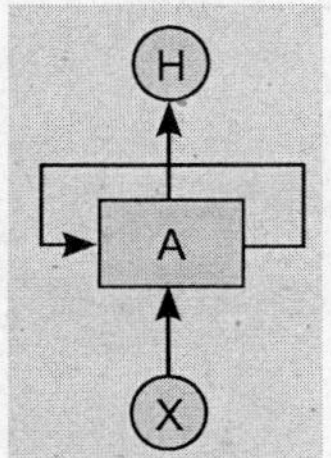

Fig. 6.13: Recurrent Neural Network

Instead of using traditional **Backpropagation,** recurrent neural networks use **Backpropagation Through Time** (*BPTT*) algorithms to determine the gradient. In backpropagation, the model adjusts the parameter by calculating errors from the output to the input layer. *BPTT* sums the error at each time step as *RNN* shares parameters across each layer.

6.5.2 Types of Recurrent Neural Networks

Feedforward networks have single input and output, while recurrent neural networks are flexible as the length of inputs and outputs can be changed. This flexibility allows *RNNs* to generate music, sentiment classification, and machine translation.

There are four types of *RNN* based on different lengths of inputs and outputs as depicted in figure 6.14.

- **One-to-one** is a simple neural network. It is commonly used for machine learning problems that have a single input and output.
- **One-to-many** has a single input and multiple outputs. This is used for generating image captions.
- **Many-to-one** takes a sequence of multiple inputs and predicts a single output. It is popular in sentiment classification, where the input is text and the output is a category.
- **Many-to-many** takes multiple inputs and outputs. The most common application is machine translation.

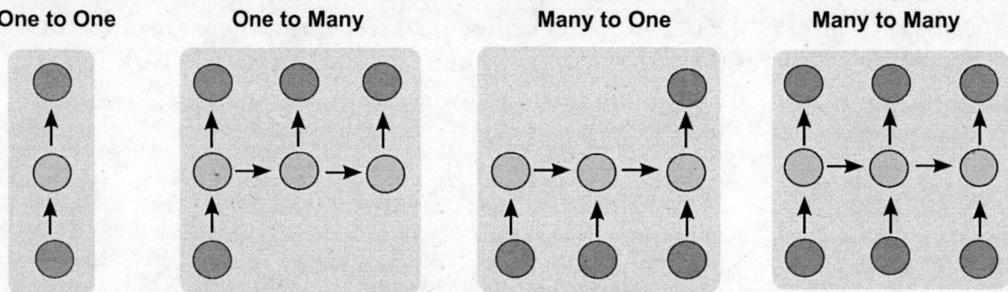

Fig. 6.14: Types of RNNs

6.5.3 Recurrent Neural Networks Architectures

6.5.3.1 Bidirectional Recurrent Neural Networks (BRNN)

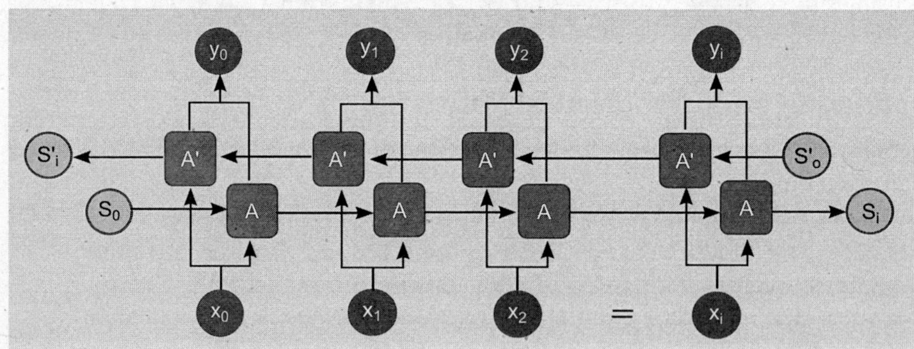

Fig. 6.15: Bidirectional Recurrent Neural Network

A typical *RNN* relies on past and present events. However, there can be situations where a prediction depends on past, present, and future events.

For example, predicting a word to be included in a sentence might require us to look into the future, i.e., a word in a sentence could depend on a future event. Such linguistic dependencies are customary in several text prediction tasks.

Thus, capturing and analysing both past and future events is helpful.

To enable straight (past) and reverse traversal of input (future), Bidirectional *RNNs* or *BRNNs* are used. As depicted in figure 6.15, a *BRNN* is a combination of two *RNNs* – one *RNN* moves forward, beginning from the start of the data sequence, and the other, moves backward, beginning from the end of the data sequence. The outputs of the two RNNs are usually concatenated at each time step, though there are other options, e.g. summation. The individual network blocks in a *BRNN* can either be a traditional *RNN*, *GRU*, or *LSTM* depending upon the use-case.

6.5.3.2 Gated Recurrent Units

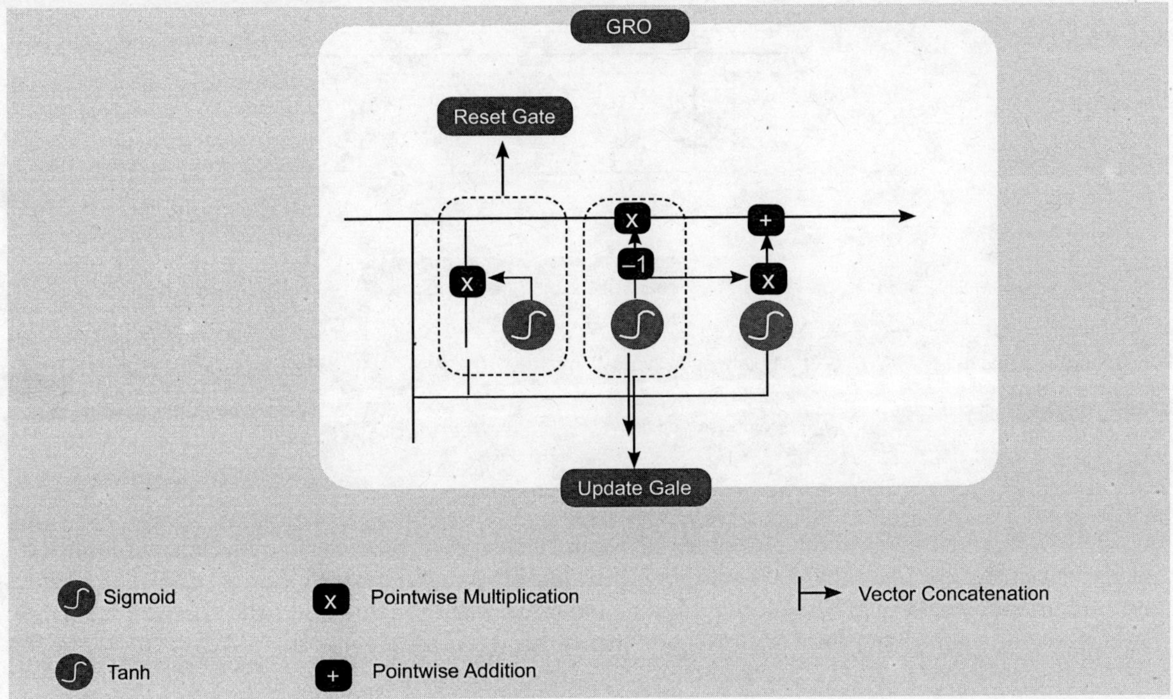

Fig. 6.16: Gated Recurrent Units

There can be scenarios where learning from the immediately preceding data in a sequence is insufficient. Consider a case where you are trying to predict a sentence from another sentence that was introduced a while back in a book or article. In this case, remembering the immediately preceding data and the earlier ones is crucial. An RNN, owing to the parameter sharing mechanism, uses the same weights at every time step. Thus, back propagation makes the gradient either explodes or vanishes, and the neural network doesn't learn much from the data, which is far from the current position.

GRU uses update and reset gate as shown in figure 6.16. Basically, these are two vectors which decide what information should be passed to the output. The special thing about them is that they can be trained to keep long-term information without washing it through time or remove information which is irrelevant to the prediction.

- The update gate is responsible for determining the amount of previous information that needs to pass along the next state.

- The reset gate is used from the model to decide how much of the past information is needed to neglect.

6.5.3.3 Long Short Term Memory (LSTM)

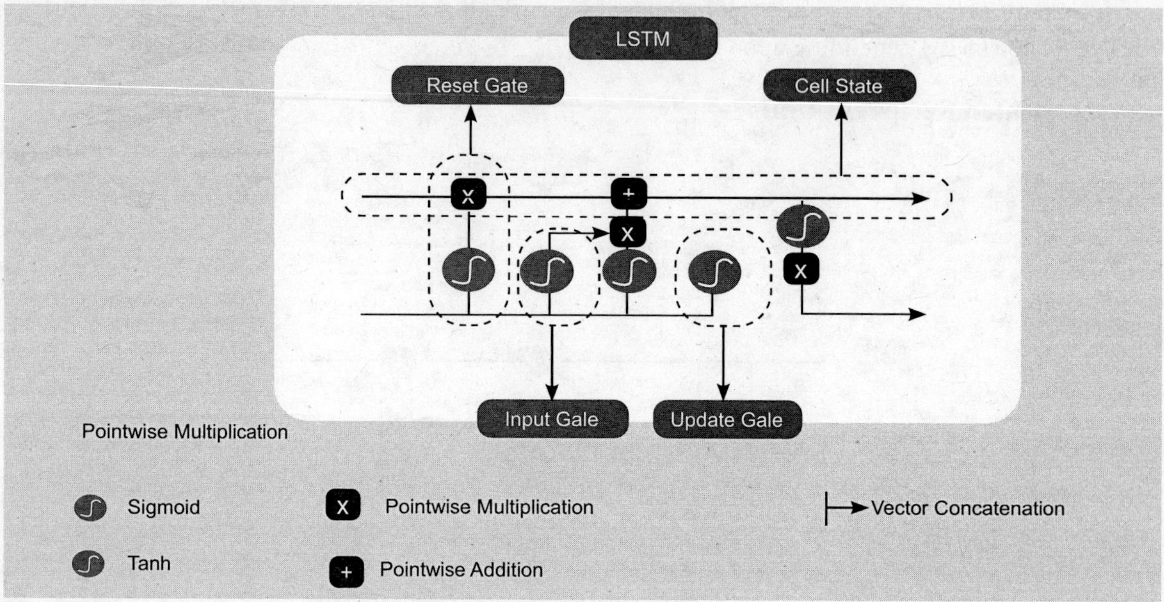

Fig. 6.17: Long Short-Term Memory

A *LSTM* is another variant of Recurrent Neural Network that is capable of learning long-term dependencies. Unlike in an *RNN*, where there's a simple layer in a network block, an *LSTM* block does some additional operations. Using input, output, and forget gates, it remembers the crucial information and forgets the unnecessary information that it learns throughout the network.

- Input gate finds which value from input should be used to modify the memory.
- Forget gate learns what details to be discarded from the block.
- Output gate discovers the input and the memory of the block is used to decide the output.

The key difference between *GRU* and *LSTM* is that *GRU's* architecture has two gates that are reset and update while *LSTM* has three gates that are input, output, forget as depicted in figure 6.17. *GRU* is less complex than *LSTM* because it has less number of gates. Hence, if the dataset is small then *GRU* is preferred otherwise LSTM for the larger dataset.

6.5.4 Advantages of Recurrent Neural Network

Recurrent Neural Networks (*RNNs*) have several advantages over other types of neural networks, including:

Ability To Handle Variable-Length Sequences

RNNs are designed to handle input sequences of variable length, which makes them well-suited for tasks such as speech recognition, natural language processing, and time series analysis.

Memory Of Past Inputs

RNNs have a memory of past inputs, which allows them to capture information about the context of the input sequence. This makes them useful for tasks such as language modeling, where the meaning of a word depends on the context in which it appears.

Parameter Sharing

RNNs share the same set of parameters across all time steps, which reduces the number of parameters that need to be learned and can lead to better generalization.

Non-Linear Mapping

RNNs use non-linear activation functions, which allows them to learn complex, non-linear mappings between inputs and outputs.

Sequential Processing

RNNs process input sequences sequentially, which makes them computationally efficient and easy to parallelize.

Flexibility

RNNs can be adapted to a wide range of tasks and input types, including text, speech, and image sequences.

Improved Accuracy

RNNs have been shown to achieve state-of-the-art performance on a variety of sequence modelling tasks, including language modelling, speech recognition, and machine translation.

These advantages make *RNNs* a powerful tool for sequence modelling and analysis, and have led to their widespread use in a variety of applications, including natural language processing, speech recognition, and time series analysis.

6.5.5 Disadvantages of Recurrent Neural Network

Although Recurrent Neural Networks (*RNNs*) have several advantages, they also have some disadvantages. Here are some of the main disadvantages of *RNNs*:

Vanishing and Exploding Gradients

RNNs can suffer from the problem of vanishing or exploding gradients, which can make it difficult to train the network effectively. This occurs when the gradients of the loss function with respect to the parameters become very small or very large as they propagate through time.

Computational Complexity

RNNs can be computationally expensive to train, especially when dealing with long sequences. This is because the network has to process each input in sequence, which can be slow.

Difficulty in Capturing Long-Term Dependencies

Although *RNNs* are designed to capture information about past inputs, they can struggle to capture long-term dependencies in the input sequence. This is because the gradients can become very small as they propagate through time, which can cause the network to forget important information.

Lack of Parallelism

RNNs are inherently sequential, which makes it difficult to parallelize the computation. This can limit the speed and scalability of the network.

Difficulty in Choosing the Right Architecture

There are many different variants of *RNNs*, each with its own advantages and disadvantages. Choosing the right architecture for a given task can be challenging, and may require extensive experimentation and tuning.

Difficulty in Interpreting the Output

The output of an *RNN* can be difficult to interpret, especially when dealing with complex inputs such as natural language or audio. This can make it difficult to understand how the network is making its predictions.

6.5.6 Applications of Recurrent Neural Networks

- Prediction Problems
- Language Modelling and Generating Text
- Machine Translation
- Speech Recognition
- Generating Image Descriptions
- Video Tagging
- Text Summarization
- Call Center Analysis
- Face detection, *OCR* Applications as Image Recognition
- Other applications like Music Composition

Quiz Questions

1. Which of the following consists of a single layer of neurons that process inputs, compute a weighted total, and then apply an activation function to get an output?
   (*a*) Process (*b*) Program
   (*c*) Perceptron (*d*) All of the above
2. Which of the following has several layers of neurons, including one or more hidden layers in between the input and output layers?
   (*a*) Single-Layer Perceptron (*b*) Multi-Layer Perceptron
   (*c*) Single-Layer Process (*d*) Multi-Layer Process
3. Which of the following is a Machine Learning model designed to imitate the function and structure of the human brain?

(a) Neural Network (b) Artificial Network
(c) Deep Network (d) None of the above

4. What is the full form of ANN?
(a) Advanced Neural Networks (b) Advanced Neural Neurons
(c) Artificial Neural Neurons (d) Artificial Neural Networks

5. Which of the following neural networks pass information in one direction, through various input nodes, until it makes it to the output node?
(a) Feed Forward Neural Networks (b) Recurrent Neural Networks
(c) Convolutional Neural Networks (d) Modular Neural Networks

6. Which of the following neural networks save the output of processing nodes and feed the result back into the model?
(a) Feed Forward Neural Networks (b) Recurrent Neural Networks
(c) Convolutional Neural Networks (d) Modular Neural Networks

7. Which of the following neural networks don't communicate or interfere with each other's activities during the computation process?
(a) Feed Forward Neural Networks (b) Recurrent Neural Networks
(c) Convolutional Neural Networks (d) Modular Neural Networks

8. Which of the following neural networks uses a variation of multilayer perceptions and contains one or more convolutional layers that can be either entirely connected or pooled?
(a) Feed Forward Neural Networks (b) Recurrent Neural Networks
(c) Convolutional Neural Networks (d) Modular Neural Networks

9. Which of the following method fine tunes the weights of a neural network based on the error rate obtained in the previous epoch (i.e., iteration).
(a) Backpropagation (b) Forward Propagation
(c) Reverse Propagation (d) None of the above

10. Which of the following backpropagation network produces a mapping of a static input for static output?
(a) Recurrent Backpropagation (b) Static Backpropagation
(c) Reverse Backpropagation (d) None of the above

11. Which of the following backpropagation in data mining is fed forward until a fixed value is achieved?
(a) Recurrent Backpropagation (b) Static Backpropagation
(c) Reverse Backpropagation (d) None of the above

12. In which layerseveral filters of equal size are applied, and each filter is used to recognize a specific pattern from the image, such as the curving of the digits, the edges, the whole shape of the digits, and more?
(a) Pooling Layer (b) Fully Connected Layer
(c) Convolutional Layer (d) None of the above

13. Which layer is used to pull the most significant features from the convoluted matrix?
(a) Pooling Layer (b) Fully Connected Layer
(c) Convolutional Layer (d) None of the above

14. Which of the following Recurrent Neural Networks relies on past and present events?
    (*a*) Gated Recurrent Units
    (*b*) Bidirectional Recurrent Neural Networks
    (*c*) Long Short-Term Memory
    (*d*) None of the above
15. Which of the following Recurrent Neural Networks is capable of learning long term dependencies?
    (*a*) Gated Recurrent Units
    (*b*) Bidirectional Recurrent Neural Networks
    (*c*) Long Short-Term Memory
    (*d*) None of the above

ANSWERS

1.(*c*)	2.(*b*)	3.(*a*)	4.(*d*)	5.(*a*)	6.(*b*)	7.(*d*)	8.(*c*)	9.(*a*)	10. (*b*)
11.(*a*)	12.(*c*)	13.(*a*)	14.(*b*)	15.(*c*)					

Instance-Based Learning

Objectives

1. Describe the process of instance-based learning.
2. Explain the usage of *K* Nearest Neighbors algorithm.
3. Elucidate the usage of radial basis function.

Outcomes

1. Acquire knowledge on instance-based learning.
2. Implement *K* Nearest Neighbors algorithm.
3. Acquire knowledge on the usage of radial basis function.

7.1 INTRODUCTION

Instance-Based Learning, also known as lazy learning, is a machine learning algorithm that stores the training instances and uses them to make predictions or decisions when new data is encountered. Instead of developing a model during the training phase, instance-based learning relies on the stored instances as the representation of the learned knowledge. It learns directly from the training examples and generalizes the knowledge to make future predictions.

7.1.1 Working of Instance-Based Learning

In Instance-Based Learning, the training instances are stored in memory and utilized to compute the output for new instances. When a new instance is encountered, the algorithm finds the closest stored instances (based on similarity measures such as distance or similarity functions) and uses their labels or values to make predictions or decisions for the new instance. The algorithm generally involves the following steps:

1. Store the training instances in memory.
2. When a new instance is encountered, calculate the similarity between the new instance and the stored instances.
3. Based on the closest stored instances, make predictions or decisions for the new instance.

7.1.2 Benefits of Instance-Based Learning

- **Flexibility:** Instance-based learning algorithms can handle complex and non-linear relationships between input variables and output values.
- **Adaptability:** Instance-based learning algorithms can adapt and update the learned knowledge as new instances are encountered, making it suitable for environments with evolving data.
- **Interpretability:** Instance-based learning provides transparency in decision-making as it relies on the stored instances for predictions, allowing users to understand the reasoning behind the decisions.
- **Efficiency:** Instance-based learning avoids the need for model training, resulting in faster processing times for new instances.
- **Robustness:** Instance-based learning is less affected by outliers or noise in the data, as it makes predictions based on the nearest neighbors rather than the entire data distribution.

7.2 *K*-NEAREST NEIGHBOURS LEARNING

K-Nearest Neighbours (*KNN*) is a type of supervised learning machine learning algorithm and is used for both regression and classification tasks.

KNN is used to make predictions on the test data set based on the characteristics of the current training data points. This is done by calculating the distance between the test data and training data, assuming that similar things exist within close proximity.

The algorithm will have stored learned data, making it more effective at predicting and categorising new data points. When a new data point is inputted, the *KNN* algorithm will learn its characteristics/ features. It will then place the new data point at closer proximity to the current training data points that share the same characteristics or features.

7.2.1 What is the '*k*' in *KNN*?

The '*K*' in *KNN* is a parameter that refers to the number of nearest neighbors. *K* is a positive integer and is typically small in value and is recommended to be an odd number.

In simple terms, the *K*-value creates an environment for the data points. This makes it easier to assign which data point belongs to which category. The example below shows 3 graphs in figure 7.1. The first, the 'Initial Data' is a graph where data points are plotted and clustered into classes, and a new example to classify is present. In the 'Calculate Distance' graph, the distance from the new example data

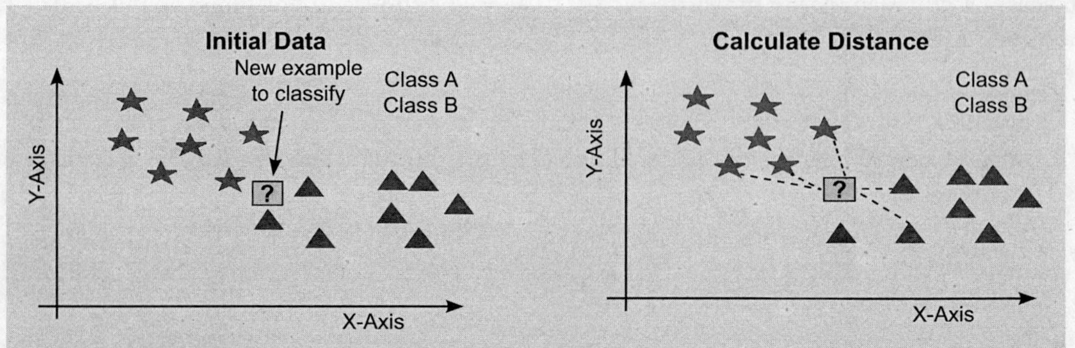

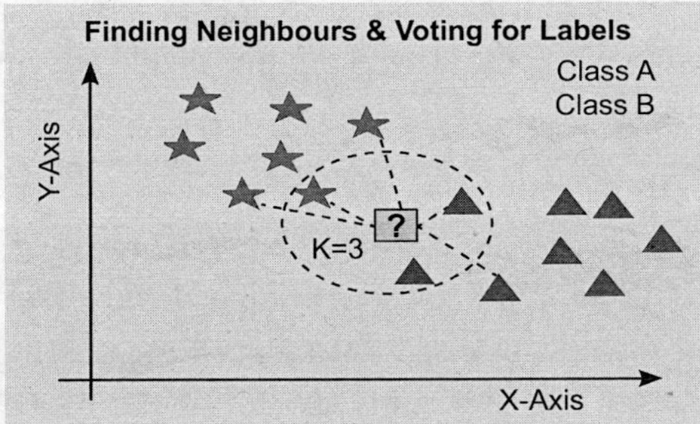

Fig. 7.1: *K* Nearest Neighbor

point to the closest trained data points is calculated. However, this still does not categorise the new example data point. Therefore, using *k*-value, essentially created a neighborhood where we can classify the new example data point.

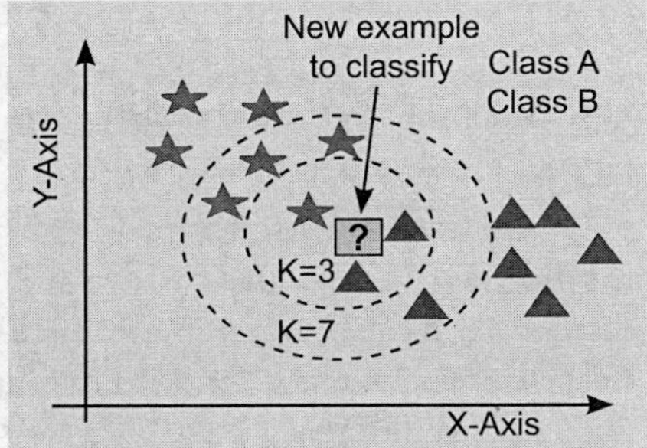

Fig. 7.2: Allocation of New Data Points in KNN

We would say that $k = 3$ and the new data point will belong to Class *B* as there are more trained Class *B* data points with similar characteristics to the new data point in comparison to Class *A*.

If we increase the *k*-value to 7, we will see that the new data point will belong to Class *A* as there are more trained Class *A* data points with similar characteristics to the new data point in comparison to Class *B* as depicted in figure 7.2.

The *k*-value is typically a small number because, as we increase the *k*-value, the error rate also increases. The below figure 7.3 shows this:

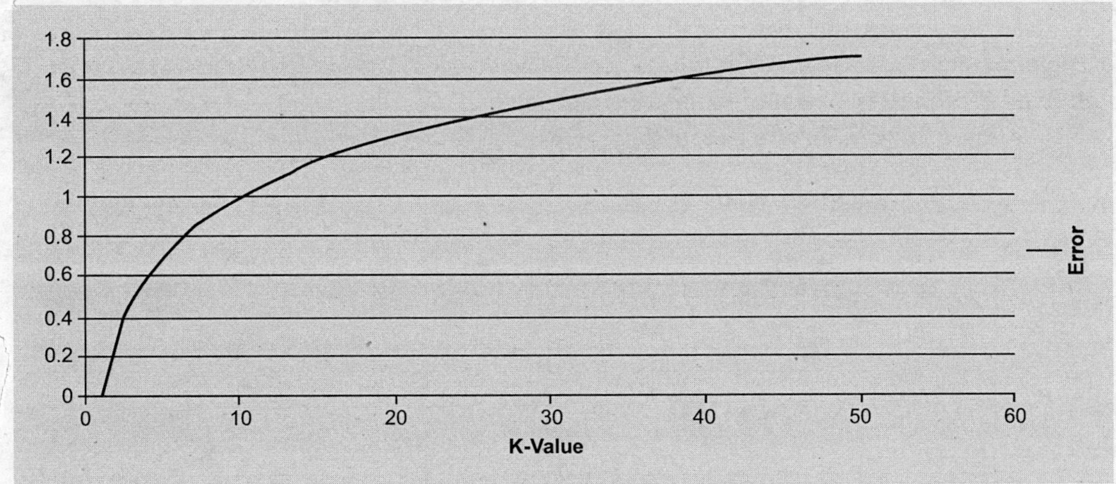

Fig. 7.3: Error Rate in KNN

However, If the *k*-value is small then it causes a low bias but a high variance, leading to overfitting of the model. It is also recommended that the *k*-value is an odd number. This is because if we are trying to classify a new data point and we only have an even number of categories/classes (e.g., Class A and Class B) it can produce inaccurate outputs. Therefore, it is highly recommended to choose a K-value with an odd number to avoid a tie.

7.2.2 Calculating the Distance

KNN calculates the distance between data points in order to classify new data points. The most common methods used to calculate this distance in *KNN* are Euclidian, Manhattan, and Minkowski.

Euclidean Distance is the distance between two points using the length of a line between the two points. The formula for Euclidean Distance is the square root of the sum of the squared differences between a new data point (x) and an existing trained data point (y).

Manhattan Distance is the distance between two points is the sum of the absolute difference of their Cartesian coordinates. The formula for Manhattan Distance is the sum of the lengths between a new data point (x) and an existing trained data point (y) using a line segment on the coordinate axes.

Minkowski Distance is the distance between two points in the normed vector space and is a generalization of the Euclidean distance and the Manhattan distance. In the formula for Minkowski Distance when $p = 2$, we get Euclidian distance, also known as L_2 Distance. When $p = 1$ we get Manhattan distance, also known as L_1 distance, city-block distance, and *LASSO*.

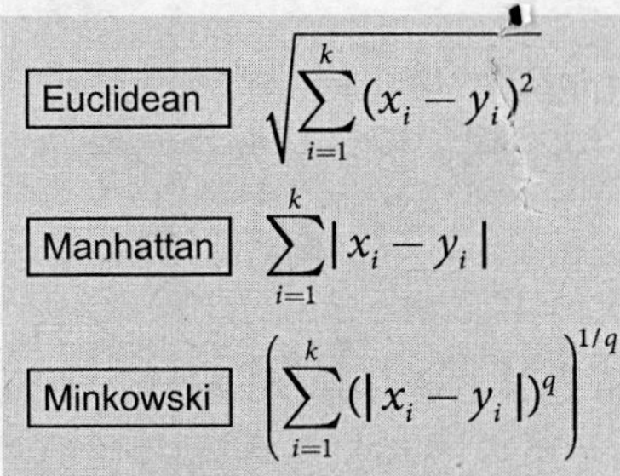

Fig 7.4: Distance Functions

The figure 7.4 is the formulas:

7.2.3 Working of KNN Algorithm

1. Load in your dataset.
2. Choose a k-value. An odd number is recommended to avoid a tie.
3. Calculate the distance between the new data point and the neighboring existing trained data points.
4. Find the K nearest neighbor to the new data point

Below figure 7.5 gives an overview of these steps:

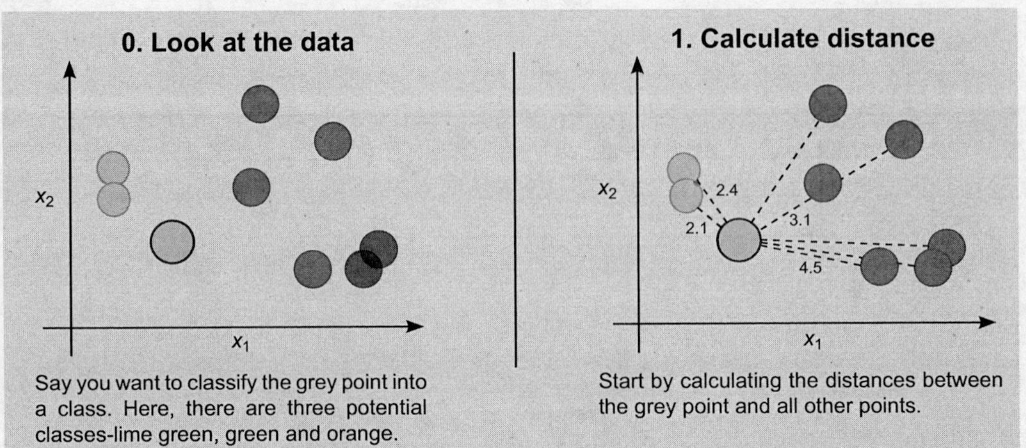

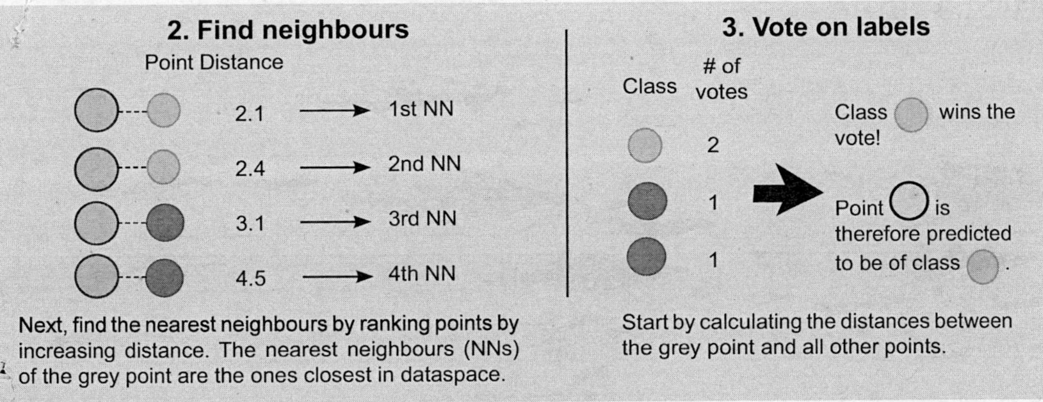

Fig. 7.5: Working of KNN

7.2.4 Advantages of KNN

- Very easy to implement.
- This algorithm can be used for both classification and regression.
- Since data is not previously assumed, it is very useful in cases of nonlinear data.
- The algorithm ensures relatively high accuracy.

7.2.5 Disadvantages of KNN

- It is a bit more expensive as it stores the entire training data.
- High memory storage requirements for this algorithm.
- Higher sets of values may lead to inaccurate predictions.
- Highly sensitive to the scale of the data.

7.2.6 Applications of KNN

- Speech Recognition
- Handwriting Detection
- Image Recognition
- Video Recognition
- Credit Ratings
- Video Recognition

7.2.7 KNN Algorithm Classification Implementation

Import libraries

```
import numpy as np
import matplotlib.pyplot as plt
import pandas as pd
```

Load the Iris Dataset

```
url = "https://archive.ics.uci.edu/ml/machine-learning-databases/iris/iris.data"
# Assign the column namesnames = ['sepal-length', 'sepal-width', 'petal-length',
'petal-width', 'Class']
# Read the dataset in
dataset = pd.read_csv(url, names=names)
dataset
```

	sepal-length	sepal-width	petal-length	petal-width	class
0	5.1	3.5	1.4	0.2	Iris-setosa
1	4.9	3.0	1.4	0.2	Iris-setosa
2	4.7	3.2	1.3	0.2	Iris-setosa
3	4.6	3.1	1.5	0.2	Iris-setosa
4	5.0	3.6	1.4	0.2	Iris-setosa
...	...	...	...	...	...
145	6.7	3.0	5.2	2.3	Iris-virginica
146	6.3	2.5	5.0	1.9	Iris-virginica
147	6.5	3.0	5.2	2.0	Iris-virginica
148	6.2	3.4	5.4	2.3	Iris-virginica
149	5.9	3.0	5.1	1.8	Iris-virginica
150 row × 5 column					

Preprocessing the data

We do this to split our dataset into its attributes and labels. The *X* variable will contain the first four columns of the dataset, which we refer to as the attributes and the *y* variable will contain the last column, which we refer to as the labels.

```
X = dataset.iloc[:, :-1].values
y = dataset.iloc[:, 4].values
```

Train Test Split

In this step, we are going to divide the dataset into training and test splits. This gives us an idea of how well the algorithm learned the training data and how well it performs on the testing data.

```
from sklearn.model_selection import train_test_split
X_train, X_test, y_train, y_test = train_test_split(X, y, test_size=0.20)
```

Feature Scaling

Feature scaling is an important element in preprocessing the data before making predictions. This method is used to normalise the range of features of the data.

```
from sklearn.preprocessing import StandardScaler
scaler = StandardScaler()
scaler.fit(X_train)
X_train = scaler.transform(X_train)
X_test = scaler.transform(X_test)
```

Making Predictions with KNN

First we need to import the KNeighborsClassifier class from the sklearn.neighbors library. We then choose our k-value, in this example, I have chosen 7. Remember that it is highly recommended to choose an odd value to avoid ties.

```
from sklearn.neighbors import KNeighborsClassifier
classifier = KNeighborsClassifier(n_neighbors=7)
classifier.fit(X_train, y_train)
```

We then move onto making predictions on our test dataset.

```
y_pred = classifier.predict(X_test)
```

Accuracy of the algorithm

With sklearn.metrics, we can classification_report to evaluate the accuracy of the algorithm, looking at precision, recall and f_1 – score.

```
from sklearn.metrics import classification_report
print(classification_report(y_test, y_pred))
```

	precision	recall	fl-score	support
Iris-setosa	1.00	1.00	1.00	12
Iris-versicolor	1.00	0.83	0.91	12
Iris-virginica	0.75	1.00	0.86	6
accuracy			0.93	30
macro avg	0.92	0.94	0.92	30
weighted avg	0.95	0.93	0.94	30

From this, we can see that the *KNN* algorithm classified 30 data points with an average total of 95% on precision, 93% on recall, and 94% on f_1 – score.

Finding the right k-value

In this example, *I* chose a *k*-value of 7. However, if we wanted to check what the best k-value is, we can produce a graph that shows the different *k*-values and the error rate it produces.

I will be looking at *k*-values between 1 and 30. A loop will be executed from 1 to 30, where during each iteration the mean error is calculated and added to the error list.

```
error = []
# Calculating the error rate for K-values between 1 and 30
for i in range(1, 30):
    knn = KNeighborsClassifier(n_neighbors=i)
    knn.fit(X_train, y_train)
    pred_i = knn.predict(X_test)
    error.append(np.mean(pred_i != y_test))
```

Plotting the k-value against error rate graph:

```
plt.figure(figsize=(12, 5))
plt.plot(range(1, 30), error, color='red', marker='o',
        markerfacecolor='yellow', markersize=10)
plt.title('Error Rate K Value')
plt.xlabel('K Value')
plt.ylabel('Mean Error')
```

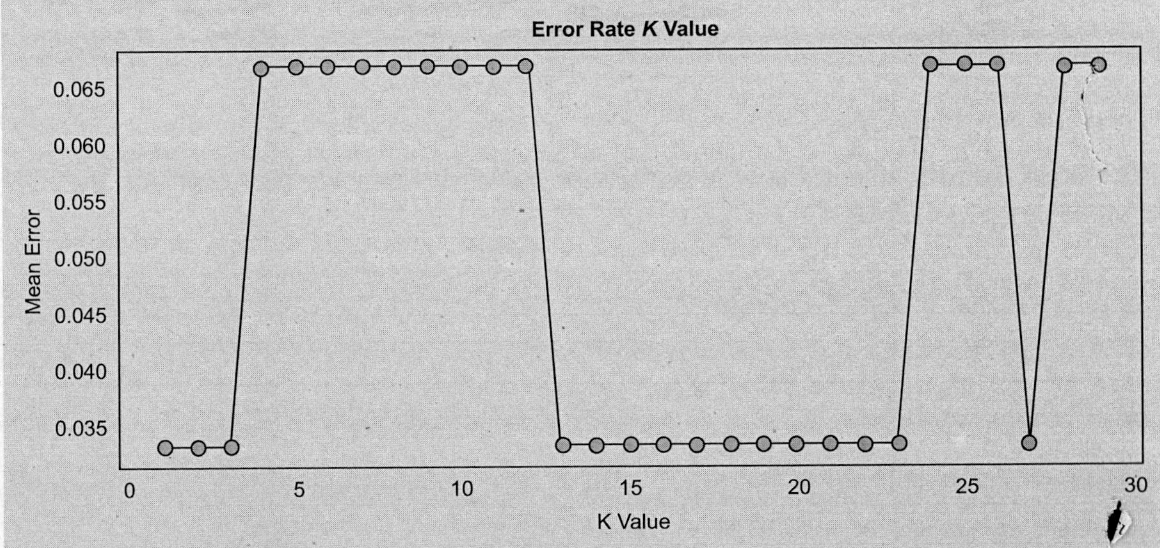

Fig. 7.6: Error Rate K Value

From this above figure 7.6, we can see that the *k*-values that give us a Mean Error of 0 are predominantly between k-value 13 – 23.

7.3 LOCALLY WEIGHTED REGRESSION (LWR) LEARNING

Locally Weighted Regression (*LWR*) is a memory-based method that performs a regression around a point of interest using only training data that are local to that point.

7.3.1 Parametric Learning Algorithm

An algorithm that has a fixed number of parameters that fit the data. Linear regression is an example of parametric learning.

In the figure 7.7, data is normally distributed with a specific and limited number of independent variables (parameters).

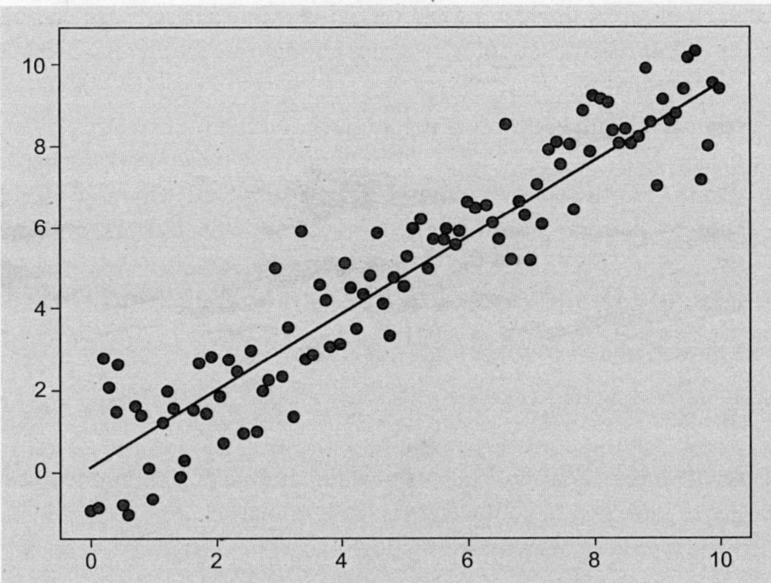

Fig. 7.7: Regression with Linear Distributed Data

7.3.2 Non-Parametric Learning Algorithm

An algorithm in which the number of parameters grows with the size of the training set.

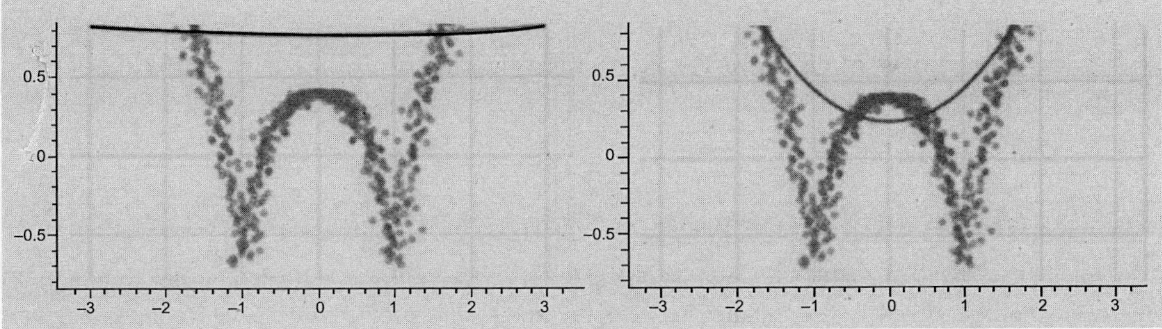

Fig. 7.8: Regression with Non-Linear Distributed Data

In the above figure 7.8, it's clear that there is not a linear distribution and if the prediction would be calculated as before (we have done in linear regression), then we will have a weak prediction by large prediction error as obvious by the red line which shows linear regression.

In this case, we can also apply the regression model and it is called locally weighted regression. We can apply LOESS or LOWESS (Locally Weighted Scatterplot Smoothing) when the relationship between independent and dependent variables is non-linear such as in the above figure.

7.3.3 Locally Weighted Regression

Locally Weighted Regression Learning methods are non-parametric and the current prediction is done by local functions. The basic idea behind *LWR* is that instead of building a global model for the whole function space, for each point of interest a local model is created based on neighbouring data of the query point. For this purpose, each data point becomes a weighting factor which expresses the influence of the data point for the prediction.

In general, data points that are in the close neighbourhood to the current query point are receiving a higher weight than data points that are far away. *LWR* is also called lazy learning because the processing of the training data is shifted until a query point needs to be answered. This approach makes *LWR* a very accurate function approximation method where it is easy to add new training points.

7.3.4 Advantages and Disadvantages of Locally Weighted Regression

Advantages:

- It is a simple algorithm that works on the same idea of minimizing the least-squared error function.
- It can give excellent results when we have non-linear data points, and features are less, i.e., 2 or 3, and we want to incorporate all the features in our analysis.
- Since it's a non-parametric algorithm, there is no training phase.

Disadvantages:

- Doesn't work very well for high-dimensional data.
- Uses local fitting of data points at high computational costs.
- It's very prone to the effect of outliers.

7.3.5 Applications of Locally Weighted Regression

- Time Series Analysis
- Robotics and Control Systems
- Anomaly Detection

7.4 RADIAL BASIS FUNCTION

The Radial Basis Function (RBF) is a mathematical function that takes a real-valued input and outputs a real-valued output based on the distance between the input value projected in space from an imaginary fixed point placed elsewhere. This function is popularly used in many machine learning and deep learning algorithms such as Support Vector Machines, Artificial Neural Networks, etc.

7.4.1 Radial Basis Function Network

Radial Basis Function Network (RBFN) was formulated by Broomhead and Lowe in 1988. Since Radial basis functions (RBFs) have only one hidden layer, the convergence of optimization objective is much faster, and despite having one hidden layer RBFs are proven to be universal approximators.

RBF networks have many applications like function approximation, interpolation, classification and time series prediction. All these applications serve various industrial interests like stock price prediction, anomaly detection in data, fraud detection in financial transaction etc.

RBFNs are a common type of use in artificial neural networks for function approximation problems. Radial-based function networks are distinguished from other neural networks due to their global approximation and fast learning speed. Radial Based Function Neural Networks (RBFNN) are also a type of feed-forward network trained using a supervised training algorithm. The main advantage of the RBF network is that it has only one hidden layer and uses the radial basis function as the activation function. These functions are very powerful in approximation.

7.4.2 Working of RBFNs

- RBFNs perform classification by measuring the input's similarity from the training set.
- RBFNs have an input vector that feeds to the input layer. They have a layer of RBF neurons.
- The function finds the weighted sum of the inputs, and the output layer has one node per category or class of data.
- The neurons in the hidden layer contain the Gaussian transfer functions, which have outputs that are inversely proportional to the distance from the neuron's center.
- The network's output is a linear combination of the input's radial-basis functions and the neuron's parameters.

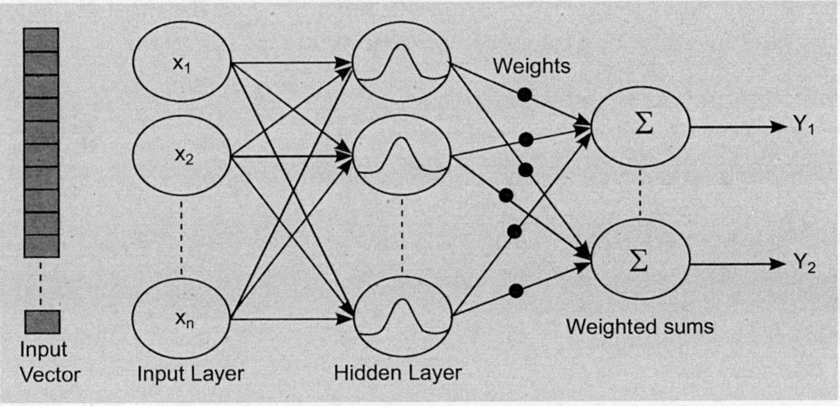

Fig. 7.9: Radial Based Function Network

The above figure 7.9 depicts the Radial Based Function Network which includes the following layers:

Input Vector

The input vector is the *n*-dimensional vector you are trying to classify. The entire input vector is shown for each of the RBF neurons.

RBF Neurons

Each RBF neuron stores a 'prototype' vector, just one of the vectors from the training set. Each RBF neuron compares the input vector to its prototype and outputs a value between 0 and 1 which is a measure of similarity. If the input is equal to the prototype, the output of the RBF neuron will be 1. As the distance between the input and the prototype increases, the response decreases exponentially towards 0. The shape of the response of the RBF neuron is a bell curve, as shown in the network geometry diagram. The value of a neuron's response is also called the "activation" value. The prototype vector is also often called the "centre" of a neuron since it is the value at the centre of the bell curve.

The input layer transforms the data into hidden neurons that contain radial basis activation functions. This function generally calculates the distance between the network inputs and the centres of the hidden layer. The output assembly of the hidden layers is provided with some weight as the output of the RBFNN.

The output of the network consists of a set of nodes, one per category that we are trying to classify. Each output node computes a sort of score for the associated category. Typically, a classification decision is made by assigning the input to the category with the highest score.

The score is computed by taking a weighted sum of the activation values from every RBF neuron. By weighted sum, we mean that an output node associates a weight value with each of the RBF neurons, and multiplies the neuron's activation by this weight before adding it to the total response. Because each output node is computing the score for a different category, every output node has its own set of weights. The output node will typically give a positive weight to the RBF neurons that belong to its category, and a negative weight to the others.

Each RBF neuron computes a measure of the similarity between the input and its prototype vector (taken from the training set). Input vectors which are more similar to the prototype return a result closer to 1. There are different possible choices of similarity functions, but the most popular is based on the Gaussian. Below is the equation for a Gaussian with a one-dimensional input.

$$f(x) = \frac{1}{\sigma\sqrt{2\pi}} e - \frac{(x-\mu)^2}{2\sigma^2}$$

Where x is the input, μ is the mean, and σ is the standard deviation.

7.4.3 Advantages of RBFN

- Easy Design.
- Good Generalization.
- Faster Training.
- Only one hidden layer.
- A straightforward interpretation of the meaning or function of each node in the hidden layer.

7.4.4 Disadvantages of RBFN

- They require a good choice of radial basis function and its parameters, which can be challenging.
- They can also suffer from the curse of dimensionality, as the number of required hidden neurons grows exponentially with the dimensionality of the input space.

7.4.5 Applications of RBFN

- Finite element or spectral methods for the solution of partial differential equations.
- Neural networks with radial basis functions, and machine learning.
- Approximations on spheres.
- Statistical approximations, where positive definite kernels are very important.
- Geophysical research and many engineering applications.

Quiz Questions

1. Which of the following is a machine learning algorithm that stores the training instances and uses them to make predictions or decisions when new data is encountered?
   (*a*) KNN (*b*) K-Means
   (*c*) Instance Based Learning (*d*) Random Forest

2. Which of the following is used to make predictions on the test data set based on the characteristics of the current training data points?
   (*a*) KNN (*b*) K-Means
   (*c*) Instance Based Learning (*d*) Random Forest

3. The distance between two points using the length of a line between the two points is known as
   (*a*) Manhattan Distance (*b*) Euclidean Distance
   (*c*) Minkowski Distance (*d*) None of the above

4. Which of the following is the distance between two points is the sum of the absolute difference of their Cartesian coordinates?
   (*a*) Manhattan Distance (*b*) Euclidean Distance
   (*c*) Minkowski Distance (*d*) None of the above

5. Which of the following is the distance between two points in the normed vector space and is a generalization of the Euclidean distance and the Manhattan distance?
   (*a*) Manhattan Distance (*b*) Euclidean Distance
   (*c*) Minkowski Distance (*d*) None of the above

6. Which of the following is a memory-based method that performs a regression around a point of interest using only training data that are local to that point.
   (*a*) Linear Regression (*b*) Logistic Regression
   (*c*) Locally Weighted Regression (*d*) None of the above

7. Which of the following algorithm has a fixed number of parameters that fit the data?
   (*a*) Non-Parametric Learning (*b*) Parametric Learning
   (*c*) Linear Regression (*d*) None of the above

8. In which of the following algorithm the number of parameters grows with the size of the training set?
   (*a*) Non-Parametric Learning (*b*) Parametric Learning
   (*c*) Linear Regression (*d*) None of the above

9. Which of the following is a mathematical function that takes a real-valued input and outputs a real-valued output based on the distance between the input value projected in space from an imaginary fixed point placed elsewhere?
   (*a*) Parametric Function (*b*) Non-Parametric Function
   (*c*) Linear Function (*d*) Radial Basis Function

10. What is the full form of RBFN?

(*a*) Radio Broad Functional Network
(*b*) Radial Basis Function Network
(*c*) Radio Breadth Functional Neuron
(*d*) None of the above

ANSWERS

1.(*c*)	2.(*a*)	3.(*b*)	4.(*a*)	5.(*c*)	6.(*c*)	7.(*b*)	8.(*a*)	9.(*d*)	10. (*b*)

8 Combining Classifiers

Objectives

1. **Understanding Classifier Ensembles:** Gain a comprehensive understanding of ensemble methods in machine learning, including the rationale behind combining multiple classifiers.
2. **Exploration of Ensemble Techniques:** Explore various ensemble techniques such as bagging, boosting, stacking, and hybrid methods, understanding their strengths, weaknesses, and applications.
3. **Implementation Skills:** Develop practical implementation skills in building ensemble models using popular machine learning libraries such as Scikit-learn, TensorFlow, or PyTorch.

Outcomes

1. **Improved Predictive Performance:** Combining multiple classifiers often leads to better predictive performance compared to using individual classifiers. By leveraging the strengths of different algorithms and mitigating their weaknesses, ensemble methods can produce more accurate and robust predictions.
2. **Reduced Overfitting:** Ensemble methods can help reduce overfitting by averaging out the predictions of multiple models trained on different subsets of data or using different algorithms. This leads to more generalizable models that perform well on unseen data.
3. **Increased Stability:** Ensemble methods are often more stable than individual models, particularly when dealing with noisy or uncertain data. By aggregating predictions from multiple models, ensemble methods can smooth out fluctuations and errors inherent in any single model.

8.1 COMBINING CLASSIFIERS

The simplest way of combining classifier output is to allow each classifier to make its own prediction and then choose the plurality prediction as the "final" output. This simple voting scheme is easy to implement and easy to understand, but it does not always produce the best possible results.

Now then, once I have a number of estimates for the one case, what is the final decision? **How can I combine the decisions of the *N* sub-systems?** As a quick answer I can take the average of the decisions and use this. But, are there different ways of making the most out of my sub-systems? Of course, there are! Think outside the box!

Multiclassifiers

When there are several classifiers with a common objective it is called a multiclassifier. In Machine Learning multiclassifiers are sets of different classifiers which make estimates and are fused together, obtaining a result that is a combination of them. Lots of terms are used to refer to multiclassifiers: multi-models, multiple classifier systems, combining classifiers, decision committe, etc.

They can be divided into two big groups:

- **Ensemble methods:** Refers to sets of systems that combine to create a new system using the same learning technique. Bagging and Boosting are the most extended ones.
- **Hybrid methods:** Takes a set of different learners and combines them using new learning techniques. Stacking (or Stacked Generalization) is one of the main hybrid multi classifiers.

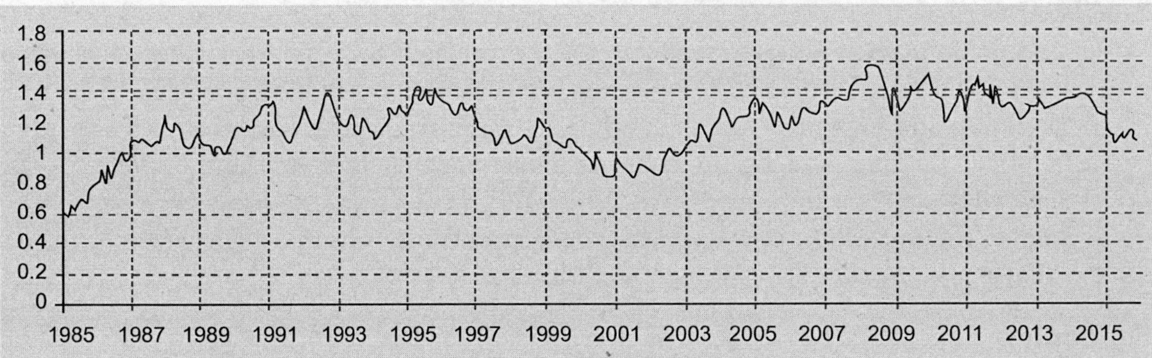

Fig. 8.1: EURUSD: Classification Problem

Bagging, also known as bootstrap aggregation, is the ensemble learning method that is commonly used to reduce variance within a noisy dataset. In bagging, a random sample of data in a training set is selected with replacement—meaning that the individual data points can be chosen more than once.

Boosting is a method used in machine learning to reduce errors in predictive data analysis. Data scientists train machine learning software, called machine learning models, on labelled data to make guesses about labelled data.

Boosting improves machine models' predictive accuracy and performance by converting multiple weak learners into a single strong learning model. Machine learning models can be weak learners or strong learners:

Weak learners

Weak learners have low prediction accuracy, similar to random guessing. They are prone to overfitting—that is, they can't classify data that varies too much from their original dataset. For example, if you train the model to identify cats as animals with pointed ears, it might fail to recognize a cat whose ears are curled.

Strong learners

Strong learners have higher prediction accuracy. Boosting converts a system of weak learners into a single strong learning system. For example, to identify the cat image, it combines a weak learner that guesses for pointy ears and another learner that guesses for cat-shaped eyes. After analyzing the animal image for pointy ears, the system analyzes it once again for cat-shaped eyes. This improves the system's overall accuracy.

How does boosting work in Machine Learning

To understand how boosting works, let's describe how machine learning models make decisions. Although there are many variations in implementation, data scientists often use boosting with decision-tree algorithms:

Decision trees

Decision trees are data structures in machine learning that work by dividing the dataset into smaller and smaller subsets based on their features. The idea is that decision trees split up the data repeatedly until there is only one class left. For example, the tree may ask a series of yes or no questions and divide the data into categories at every step.

Boosting ensemble method

Boosting creates an ensemble model by combining several weak decision trees sequentially. It assigns weights to the output of individual trees. Then it gives incorrect classifications from the first decision tree a higher weight and input to the next tree. After numerous cycles, the boosting method combines these weak rules into a single powerful prediction rule.

Boosting compared to bagging

Boosting and bagging are the two common ensemble methods that improve prediction accuracy. The main difference between these learning methods is the method of training. In bagging, data scientists improve the accuracy of weak learners by training several of them at once on multiple datasets. In contrast, boosting trains weak learners one after another.

8.2 HOW IS TRAINING IN BOOSTING DONE?

The training method varies depending on the type of boosting process called the boosting algorithm. However, an algorithm takes the following general steps to train the boosting model:

Step 1: The boosting algorithm assigns equal weight to each data sample. It feeds the data to the first machine model, called the base algorithm. The base algorithm makes predictions for each data sample.

Step 2: The boosting algorithm assesses model predictions and increases the weight of samples with a more significant error. It also assigns a weight based on model performance. A model that outputs excellent predictions will have a high amount of influence over the final decision.

Step 3: The algorithm passes the weighted data to the next decision tree.

Step 4: The algorithm repeats steps 2 and 3 until instances of training errors are below a certain threshold.

8.3 ADABOOST ALGORITHM

AdaBoost algorithm, short for Adaptive Boosting, is a Boosting technique used as an Ensemble Method in Machine Learning. It is called Adaptive Boosting as the weights are re-assigned to each instance, with higher weights assigned to incorrectly classified instances.

There are many machine learning algorithms to choose from for your problem statements. One of these algorithms for predictive modelling is called AdaBoost.

AdaBoost algorithm, short for Adaptive Boosting, is **a Boosting technique used as an Ensemble Method in Machine Learning**. It is called Adaptive Boosting as the weights are re-assigned to each instance, with higher weights assigned to incorrectly classified instances.

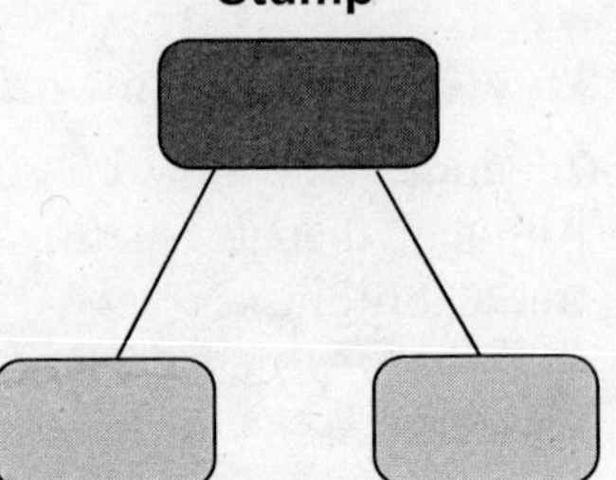

Fig. 8.2: AdaBoost Algorithm Stumping

What this algorithm does is that it builds a model and gives equal weights to all the data points. It then assigns higher weights to points that are wrongly classified. Now all the points with higher weights are given more importance in the next model. It will keep training models until and unless a lower error is received.

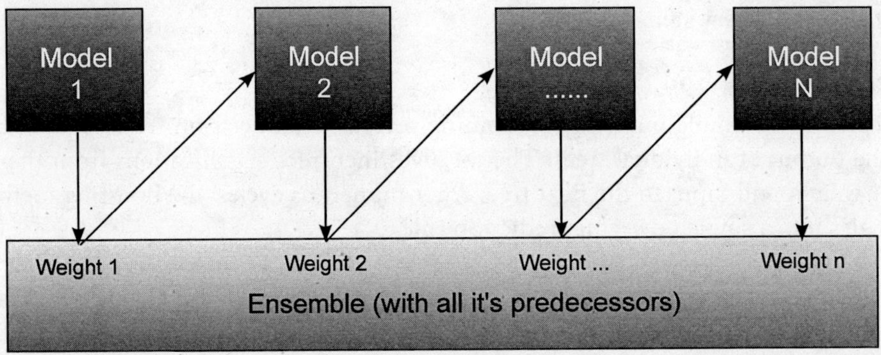

Fig. 8.3: AdaBoost Algorithm Evaluations Process

Let's take an example to understand this, suppose you built a decision tree algorithm on the Titanic dataset, and from there, you get an accuracy of 80%. After this, you apply a different algorithm and check the accuracy, and it comes out to be 75% for KNN and 70% for Linear Regression.

We see the accuracy differs when we build a different model on the same dataset. But what if we use combinations of all these algorithms to make the final prediction? We'll get more accurate results by taking the average of the results from these models. We can increase the prediction power in this way

Here we will be more focused on mathematics intuition.

There is another ensemble learning algorithm called the gradient boosting algorithm. In this algorithm, we try to reduce the error instead of wights, as in AdaBoost. But in this article, we will only be focussing on the mathematical intuition of AdaBoost.

8.4 GRADIENT BOOSTING

Gradient Boosting It is a popular boosting algorithm in machine learning used for classification and regression tasks. Boosting is one kind of ensemble Learning method which trains the model sequentially and each new model tries to correct the previous model. It combines several weak learners into strong learners.

Gradient Boosting is a powerful boosting algorithm that combines several weak learners into strong learners, in which each new model is trained to minimize the loss function such as mean squared error or cross-entropy of the previous model using gradient descent. In each iteration, the algorithm computes the gradient of the loss function with respect to the predictions of the current ensemble and then trains a new weak model to minimize this gradient. The predictions of the new model are then added to the ensemble, and the process is repeated until a stopping criterion is met.

In contrast to *AdaBoost*, the weights of the training instances are not tweaked, instead, each predictor is trained using the residual errors of the predecessor as labels. There is a technique called the **Gradient Boosted Trees** whose base learner is CART (Classification and Regression Trees). The below diagram explains how gradient-boosted trees are trained for regression problems.

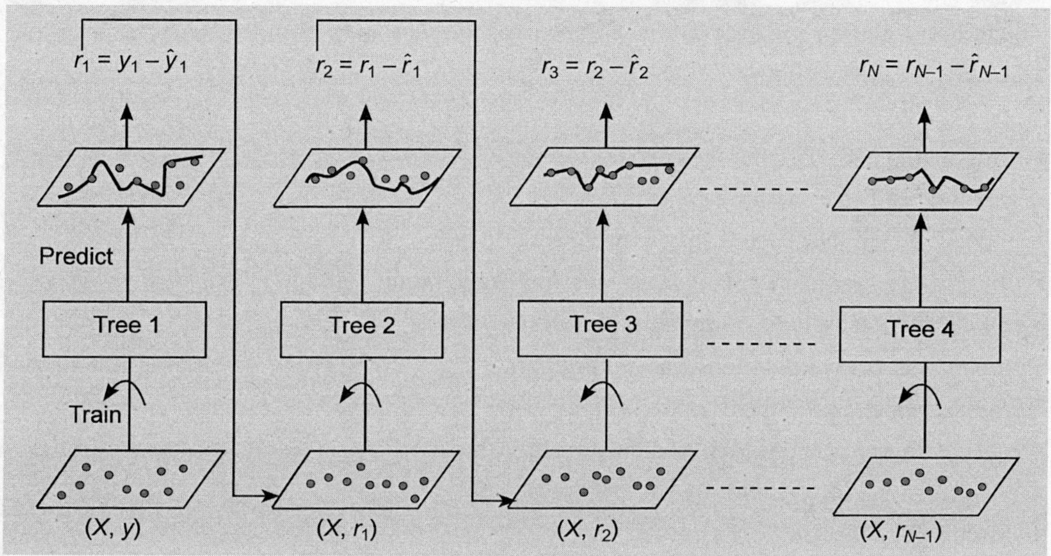

Fig. 8.3A: Gradient Boosted Trees for Regression

The ensemble consists of *M* trees. Tree1 is trained using the feature matrix *X* and the labels y. The predictions labeled y_1(hat) are used to determine the training set residual errors r_1. Tree2 is then trained using the feature matrix X and the residual errors r_1 of Tree1 as labels. The predicted results r1(hat) are then used to determine the residual r_2. The process is repeated until all the M trees forming the ensemble are trained. There is an important parameter used in this technique known as **Shrinkage. Shrinkage** refers to the fact that the prediction of each tree in the ensemble is shrunk after it is multiplied by the learning rate (eta) which ranges between 0 to 1. There is a trade-off between eta and the number of estimators, decreasing learning rate needs to be compensated with increasing estimators in order to reach certain model performance. Since all trees are trained now, predictions can be made. Each tree predicts a label and the final prediction is given by the formula,

$$y(\text{pred}) = y_1 + (\text{eta} * r_1) + (\text{eta} * r_2) + ... + (\text{eta} * rN)$$

8.5 GRADIENT BOOSTING ALGORITHM

Step 1: Let's assume *X*, and *Y* are the input and target having *N* samples. Our goal is to learn the function $f(x)$ that maps the input features *X* to the target variables *y*. It is boosted trees i.e the sum of trees.

The loss function is the difference between the actual and the predicted variables.

Step 2: We want to minimize the loss function $L(f)$ with respect to f.

If our gradient boosting algorithm is in M stages then To improve the algorithm can add some new estimator as having.

Step 3: Steepest Descent

For M stage gradient boosting, The steepest Descent findswhere is constant and known as step length and is the gradient of loss function $L(f)$.

Step 4: Solution

The gradient Similarly for M trees:

The current solution will be:

Example: 1 Classifiaction

Steps:

- Import the necessary libraries
- Setting SEED for reproducibility
- Load the digit dataset and split it into train and test.
- Instantiate Gradient Boosting classifier and fit the model.
- Predict the test set and compute the accuracy score.

Python Code as a solution to the above problem:

```
# Import models and utility functions
fromsklearn.ensembleimportGradientBoostingClassifier
fromsklearn.model_selectionimporttrain_test_split
fromsklearn.metricsimportaccuracy_score
fromsklearn.datasetsimportload_digits
# Setting SEED for reproducibility
SEED = 23
# Importing the dataset
X, y = load_digits(return_X_y=True)
# Splitting dataset
train_X, test_X, train_y, test_y=train_test_split(X, y,
                    test_size=0.25,
                    random_state=SEED)
  # Instantiate Gradient Boosting Regressor
  gbc=GradientBoostingClassifier(n_estimators=300,
          learning_rate=0.05,
          random_state=100,
          max_features=5)
  # Fit to training set
```

gbc.fit(train_X, train_y)
# Predict on test set
pred_y=gbc.predict(test_X)
# accuracy
acc=accuracy_score(test_y, pred_y)
print("Gradient Boosting Classifier accuracy is : {:.2f}".format(acc))

Output:

Gradient Boosting Classifier accuracy is: 0.98

Example: 2 Regression

Steps:

- Import the necessary libraries
- Setting SEED for reproducibility
- Load the diabetes dataset and split it into train and test.
- Instantiate Gradient Boosting Regressor and fit the model.
- Predict on the test set and compute RMSE.
- Sample code of Python for the example as follows:
- # Import the necessary libraries
- **from**sklearn.ensemble**import**GradientBoostingRegressor
- **from**sklearn.model_selection**import**train_test_split
- **from**sklearn.metrics**import**mean_squared_error
- **from**sklearn.datasets**import**load_diabetes
- # Setting SEED for reproducibility
- SEED =23
- # Importing the dataset
- X, y = load_diabetes(return_X_y=True)
- # Splitting dataset
- train_X, test_X, train_y, test_y=train_test_split(X, y,
- test_size=0.25,
- random_state=SEED)
- # Instantiate Gradient Boosting Regressor
- gbr=GradientBoostingRegressor(loss='absolute_error',
- learning_rate=0.1,
- n_estimators=300,
- max_depth=1,
- random_state=SEED,

- max_features=5)
- # Fit to training set
- gbr.fit(train_X, train_y)
- # Predict on test set
- pred_y=gbr.predict(test_X)
- # test set RMSE
- test_rmse=mean_squared_error(test_y, pred_y) **(1/2)
- # Print rmse
- print('Root mean Square error: {:.2f}'.format(test_rmse))

Output:

Root mean Square error: 56.39

8.6 HOW THE GRADIENT BOOSTING ALGORITHM WORKS?

Gradient boosting algorithm is one of the most powerful algorithms in the field of machine learning. As we know that the errors in machine learning algorithms are broadly classified into two categories i.e. Bias Error and Variance Error. As gradient boosting is one of the boosting algorithms it is used to minimize bias error of the model.

Unlike, Adaboosting algorithm, the base estimator in the gradient boosting algorithm cannot be mentioned by us. The base estimator for the Gradient Boost algorithm is fixed and i.e. *Decision Stump.* Like, AdaBoost, we can tune the *n*_estimator of the gradient boosting algorithm. However, if we do not mention the value of *n*_estimator, the default value of *n*_estimator for this algorithm is 100.

Gradient boosting algorithm can be used for predicting not only continuous target variable (as a Regressor) but also categorical target variable (as a Classifier). When it is used as a regressor, the cost function is Mean Square Error (MSE) and when it is used as a classifier then the cost function is Log loss.

Manual Example for understanding the algorithm:

Let us now understand the working of the Gradient Boosting Algorithm with the help of one example. In the following example, Age is the Target variable whereas LikesExercising, GotoGym, DrivesCar are independent variables. As in this example, the target variable is continuous, GradientBoostingRegressor is used here.

Likes Exercising	Goto Gym	Drives Car	Age
False	True	True	14
False	True	False	15
False	True	False	16
True	True	True	26
False	True	True	36
True	False	False	50

Likes Exercising	Goto Gym	Drives Car	Age
True	True	True	69
True	False	False	72
True	False	True	73

1st-Estimator

For estimator-1, the root level (level 0) will consist of all the records. The predicted age at this level is equal to the mean of the entire Age column i.e. 41.33(addition of all values in Age column divided by a number of records i.e. 9). Let us find out what is the MSE for this level. MSE is calculated as the mean of the square of errors. Here error is equal to actual age-predicted age. The predicted age for the particular node is always equal to the mean of age records of that node. So, the MSE of the root node of the 1st estimator is calculated as given below.

MSE = (Σ(Agei –mu)2)/9=577.11

The cost function hers is MSE and the objective of the algorithm here is to minimize the MSE.

Now, one of the independent variables will be used by the Gradient boosting to create the Decision Stump. Let us suppose that the LikesExercising is used here for prediction. So, the records with False LikesExercising will go in one child node, and records with True LikesExercising will go in another child node as shown below.

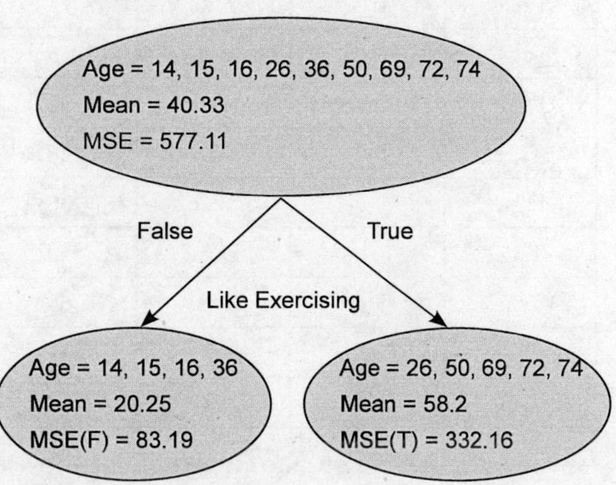

Let us find the means and MSEs of both the nodes of level 1. For the left node, the mean is equal to 20.25 and MSE is equal to 83.19. Whereas, for the right node, the mean is equal to 58.2 and MSE is equal to 332.16. Total MSE for level 1 will be equal to the addition of all nodes of level 1 i.e. 83.19 + 332.16 = 415.35. We can see here, the cost function i.e. MSE of level 1 is better than level 0.

2nd-Estimator

Let us now find out the estimator-2. Unlike AdaBoost, in the Gradient boosting algorithm, residues (agei – mu)of the first estimator are taken as root nodes as shown below. Let us suppose for this estimator another dependent variable is used for prediction. So, the records with False GotoGym will go in one child node, and records with True GotoGym will go in another child node as shown below.

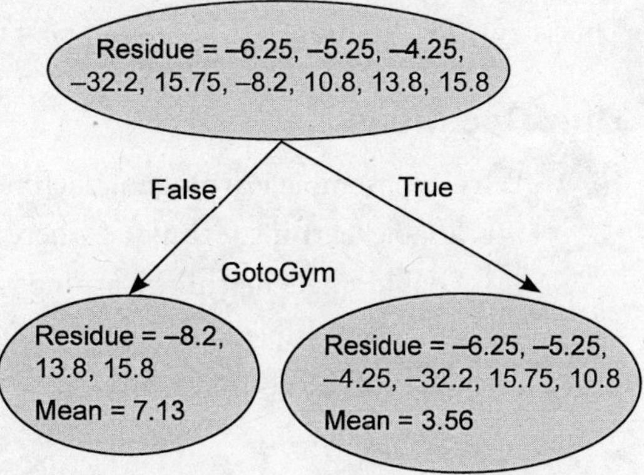

The prediction of age here is slightly tricky. First, the age will be predicted from estimator 1 as per the value of LikeExercising, and then the mean from the estimator is found out with the help of the value of

GotoGym and then that means is added to age-predicted from the first estimator and that is the final prediction of Gradient boosting with two estimators.

Let us consider if we want to predict the age for the following records:

Likes Exercising	Goto Gym	Drives Car
False	True	True

Here, LikesExercising is equal to False. So, the predicted age from the first estimator will be 20.25 (i.e. mean of the left node of the first estimator). Now we need to check what is the value of GotoGym for the second predictor and its value is True. So, the mean of True GotoGym in the 2nd estimator is –3.56. This will be added to the prediction of the first estimator i.e. 20.25. So final prediction of this model will be 20.25 + (–3.56) = 16.69.

Let us predict of ages of all records we have in the example.

Likes Exercising	Goto Gym	Drives Car	Age	Prediction from 1st Estimator	Mean from 2nd Estimator	Final Prediction	Final Residues
False	True	True	14	20.25	–3.56	16.69	–2.69
False	True	False	15	20.25	–3.56	16.69	–1.69
False	True	False	16	20.25	–3.56	16.69	–0.69
True	True	True	26	58.2	–3.56	54.64	28.64
False	True	True	36	20.25	–3.56	16.09	19.31
True	False	False	50	58.2	7.13	65.33	–15.33
True	True	True	69	58.2	–3.56	54.64	14.36
True	False	False	72	58.2	7.13	65.33	6.67
True	False	True	73	58.2	7.13	65.33	7.67

Let us now find out the Final MSE for above all 9 records.

$MSE = ((-2.69)^2 + (-1.69)^2 + (-0.69)^2 + (-28.64)^2 + (19.31)^2 + (-15.33)^2 + (14.36)^2$

$+ (6.67)^2 + (7.67)^2)/9 = 194.2478$

So, we can see that the final MSE is much better than the MSE of the root node of the 1st Estimator. This is only for 2 estimators. There can be *n* number of estimators in gradient boosting algorithm.

Quiz Questions

1. What is ensemble learning in machine learning?
   (*a*) Enable learning technique where multiple machine learning models are combined.
   (*b*) Enable single machine learning is performed.
   (*c*) Enable Multiple Machines are learning from same mechanism.
   (*d*) None of the above.

2. What are the two main categories of ensemble methods?
   (*a*) The two categories of Boosting and Capture.
   (*b*) The two main categories are Bagging and Boosting.
   (*c*) The two categories of Swell and Bagging.
3. What is Bagging?
   (*a*) Kill and Shoot
   (*b*) Ensure and Pickup
   (*c*) Bootstrap Aggregating and involves in training data
   (*d*) None of the above
4. What is Boosting?
   (*a*) Model to reduce errors and optimize the model.
   (*b*) Boosting is an ensemble technique model trained sequentially.
   (*c*) Which uses multiple models to optimize the model.
   (*d*) None of the above
5. Name a popular Bagging ensemble method.
   (*a*) Random Forest is popular bagging ensemble method.
   (*b*) The ensemble method is *K*-Mean algorithm.
   (*c*) It is suitable to Decision Tree implementation.
   (*d*) None of the above
6. Name a widely used Boosting algorithm.
   (*a*) Adaptive Boosting is a widely used boosting algorithm.
   (*b*) It is used primarily to reduce the variance in unsupervised learning.
   (*c*) Primarily provides unpredictive accuracy during training.
   (*d*) None of the above
7. What is Stacking in ensemble learning?
   (*a*) Stacking involves in training a meta-model for predictions for multiple models.
   (*b*) Collecting of Heap with some models.
   (*c*) Making sticking in his craw.
   (*d*) None of the above
8. What is the difference between Bagging and Boosting?
   (*a*) Sticking in his craw to perform guest object.
   (*b*) While Bagging trains multiple models independently combines their predictions.
   (*c*) Boosting is the process trains models randomly on different models.
   (*d*) None of the above
9. Can ensemble methods be used with any type of base learner?
   (*a*) Yes, It is ensemble methods which will be type of base learner.

(*b*) No, it performs on non-neural network methods to adopt support vector mechanism.
(*c*) Possibly suitable answers to take any decision.
(*d*) None of the above

10. What is the concept of Diversity in ensemble learning?
(*a*) Not shows difference between base learners and high diversity.
(*b*) Allows Higher Diversity in models.
(*c*) Diversity is essential differ from each one identifies different types of errors.
(*d*) Not suitable any above answers.

ANSWERS

1.(*a*)	2.(*b*)	3.(*c*)	4.(*b*)	5.(*a*)	6.(*a*)	7.(*a*)	8.(*b*)	9.(*a*)	10. (*c*)

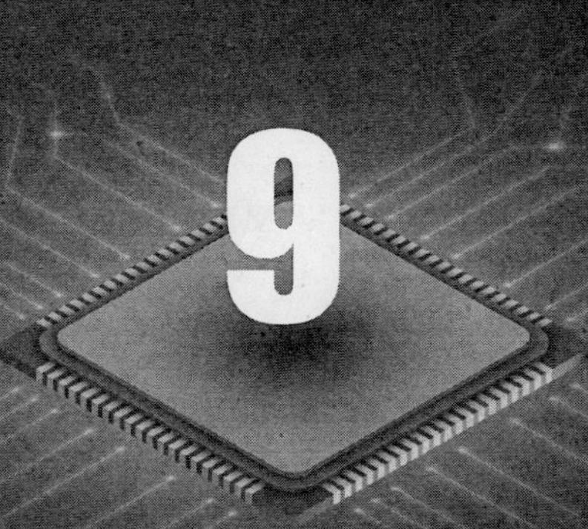

9 Support Vector Machine-I

Objectives

1. **Maximizing Margin:** SVM aims to find the hyperplane that maximizes the margin between different classes in the feature space. This margin represents the distance between the hyperplane and the nearest data points from each class, providing better generalization and robustness to new data.
2. **Effective Separation:** SVM seeks to separate classes by finding the hyperplane that best divides the data points into distinct classes. This separation is achieved by maximizing the distance between the hyperplane and the nearest data points of each class, known as support vectors.
3. **Handling Non-linearity:** SVM can handle non-linear separation by using a technique called the kernel trick. By mapping the input features into a higher-dimensional space, SVM can find a linear separation boundary in this new space, effectively separating non-linearly separable data.

Outcomes

1. **Understanding of Ensemble Learning Techniques:** Students will gain a comprehensive understanding of various ensemble learning techniques such as bagging, boosting, stacking, and fusion methods.
2. **Familiarity with Base Classifiers:** Students will become familiar with different base classifiers that can be combined, including decision trees, support vector machines, neural networks, *k*-nearest neighbours, etc.
3. **Knowledge of Diversity and Ensemble Methods:** Students will learn about the importance of diversity among base classifiers and how to achieve it using techniques such as bootstrap sampling, feature selection, or using different learning algorithms.

9.1 THEORY OF SVM

SVM are based on statistical learning theory. They can be used for learning to predict future data [25]. SVM are trained by solving a constrained quadratic optimization problem. SVM, implements mapping of inputs onto a high dimensional space using a set of nonlinear basis functions.

Support Vector Machine Explained :Support Vector Machine (SVM) is probably one of the most popular ML algorithms used by data scientists. SVM is powerful, easy to explain, and generalizes well in many cases. In this article, I'll explain the rationales behind SVM and show the implementation in

Python. For simplicity, I'll focus on binary classification problems in this article. However, SVM supports multi-classification.

9.2 GENERAL IDEAS BEHIND SVM

SVM seeks the best decision boundary which separates two classes with the highest generalization ability (why focus on generalization? I'll explain it later in the kernel section). The first question one asks is how does SVM define optimality.

Unlike logistic regression, which defines optimality by overall probability, SVM wants the **smallest distance between data points and the decision boundary to be as large as possible.** In other words, if you imagine the decision boundary as the central line of a street, SVM prefers an 8-line highway rather than a country road. The width of the street is called the **margin**.

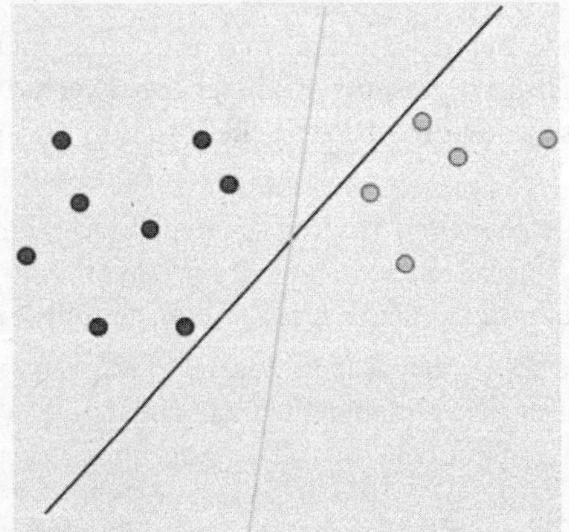

Fig. 9.1: Which decision boundary should we pick? from *MIT*

optimal margin

optimal hyperplane

Fig. 9.2: Support-Vector Network

Support Vector Machines(SVM): Machine learning involves predicting and classifying data and to do so we employ various machine learning algorithms according to the dataset.

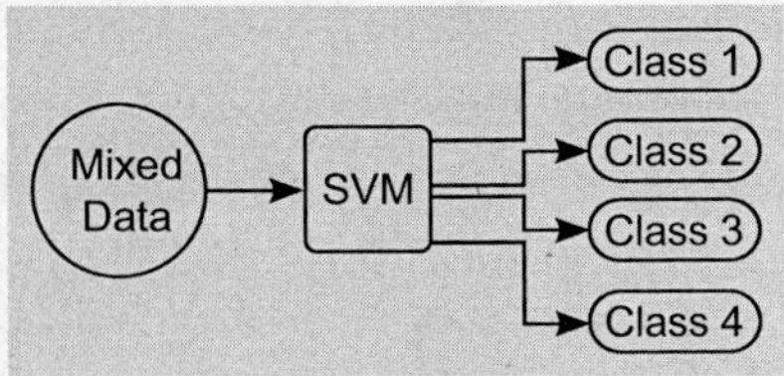

Fig. 9.3: SVM classifier

SVM or Support Vector Machine is a linear model for classification and regression problems. It can solve linear and non-linear problems and work well for many practical problems. The idea of SVM is simple: The algorithm creates a line or a hyperplane which separates the data into classes.

In this blog post I plan on offering a high-level overview of SVMs. I will talk about the theory behind SVMs, it's application for non-linearly separable datasets and a quick example of implementation of SVMs in Python as well. In the upcoming articles I will explore the maths behind the algorithm and dig under the hood.

At first approximation what SVMs do is to find a separating line(or hyperplane) between data of two classes. SVM is an algorithm that takes the data as an input and outputs a line that separates those classes if possible.

Lets begin with a problem. Suppose you have a dataset as shown below and you need to classify the red rectangles from the blue ellipses(let's say positives from the negatives). So your task is to find an ideal line that separates this dataset in two classes (say red and blue).

But, it becomes less scary once I started to think of support vector machine as a "*road machine*", which separates the left,right-side cars, buildings, pedestrians and makes the widest lane as possible. And those cars, buildings, really close to the street is the support vectors.Feeling better. Let's get started of understanding how this "*road machine*" works.

This blog covers three parts:

1. What is the support vector machine.
2. How does it work in linear separable scenarios.
3. How does it work in linear non-separable scenarios.

What is Support Vector Machine

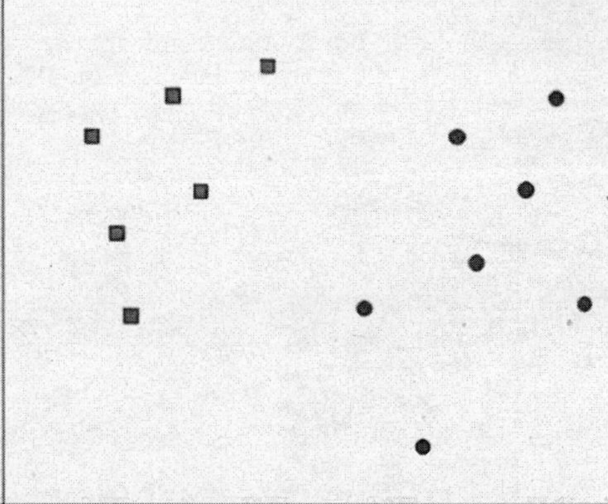

Fig. 9.4: Find an ideal line/ hyperplane that separates this dataset into red and blue categories. Support Vector Machine

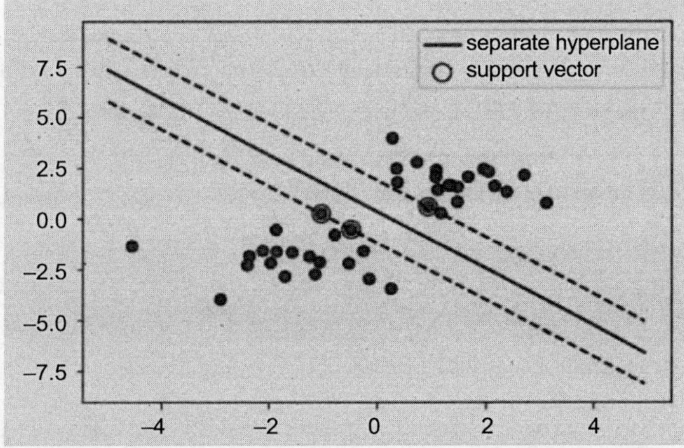

Fig. 9.5: Support vector performing above and below range of centre line values with different colours

Back to the ML world, those cars, building, pedestrians all become dots now. Red dots stand for objects on the left side of the street; green dots stand for those on the right. The street becomes dashed and solid lines.

9.3 SVM IN LINEAR SEPARABLE CASES

Obviously, infinite lines exist to separate the red and green dots in the example above. SVM needs to find the optimal line with the constraint of correctly classifying either class:

1. **Follow the constraint:** only look into the **separate hyperplanes** (e.g. separate lines), hyperplanes that classify classes correctly.
2. **Conduct optimization:** pick up the one that maximizes the **margin**.

I will illustrate the concept of separate hyperplane and margin, but the explanation of solving the optimization with the constraint will not be covered in this post.

So what is a **Hyperplane**?

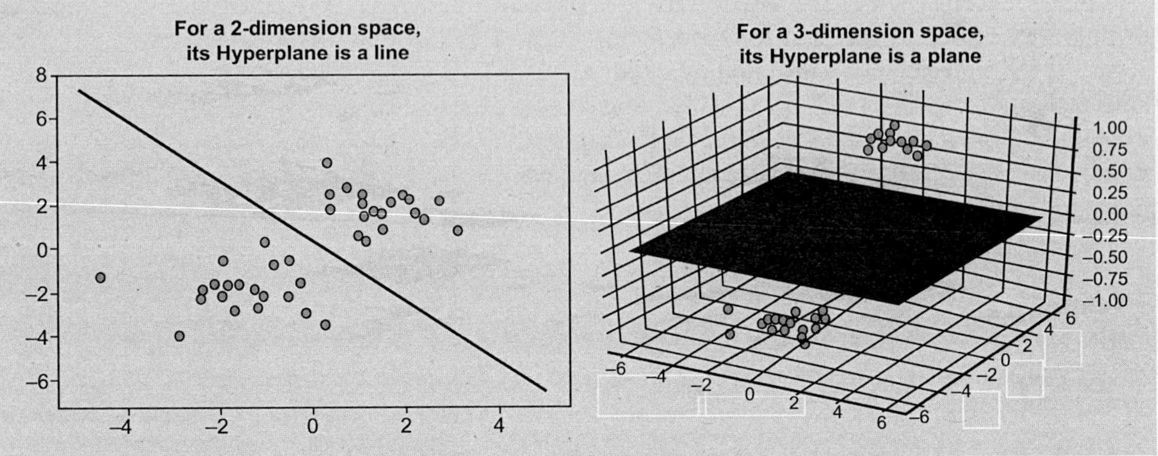

Fig. 9.5: Showing 2d and 3d values of values represented in a graph

y-perplane is an (*n* minus 1) - dimensional subspace for an *n*-dimensional space. For a 2-dimension space, its hyperplane will be 1-dimension, which is just a line. For a 3-dimension space, its hyperplane will be 2-dimension, which is a plane that slice the cube. Okay, you got the idea.

$$\beta_0 + \beta_1 * x_1 + \beta_2 * x_2 + ... + \beta_n * x_n = 0$$

Any Hyperplane can be written mathematically as above.

$$\beta_0 + \beta_1 * x_1 + \beta_2 * x_2 = 0$$

For a 2-dimensional space, the Hyperplane, which is the line.

$$\beta_0 + \beta_1 * x_1 + \beta_2 * x_2 > 0$$

The dots above this line, are those x_1, x_2 satisfy the formula above.

$$\beta_0 + \beta_1 * x_1 + \beta_2 * x_2 < 0$$

The dots below this line, similar logic.

What is a Separating Hyperplane?

Assuming the label *y* is either 1 (for green) or –1 (for red), all those three lines below are separating hyperplanes. Because they all share the same property — above the line, is green; below the line, is red.

This property can be written in math again as followed:

$\beta_0 + \beta_1 * x_1 + \beta_2 * x_2 > 0$ if $y = 1$ theGreen

$\beta_0 + \beta_1 * x_1 + \beta_2 * x_2 > 0$ if $y = -1$ theRed

If we further generalize these two into one, it becomes:

$$y * (\beta_0 + \beta_1 * x_1 + \beta_2 * x_2) > 0$$

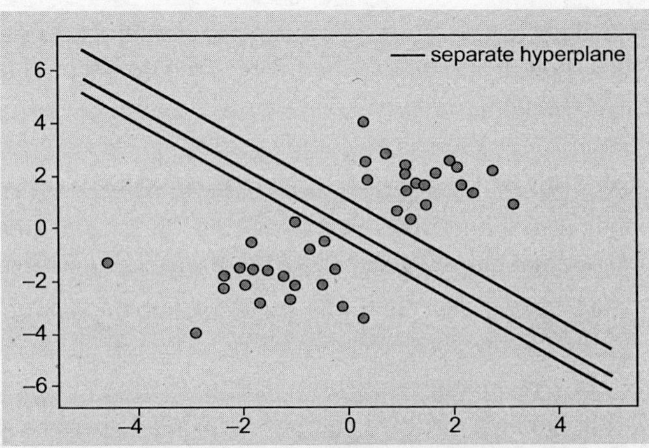

Fig. 9.6: Showing separate hyperplane showing with different colours to show the datapoint

Separate hyperplane constraint is written mathematically above. In the perfect scenario — linear separable scenario, this constraint can be met by SVM. But in the non-separable scenario, we will need to loosen it.

So margin?

- Let's say we have a hyperplane — line *X*.
- Calculate the perpendicular distance from all those 40 dots to line *X*, it will be 40 different distances.
- Out of the 40, the smallest distance, that's our margin!

The distance between either side of the dashed line to the solid line is the margin. We can think of this optimal line as the mid-line of the widest stretching we can possibly have between red and green dots.

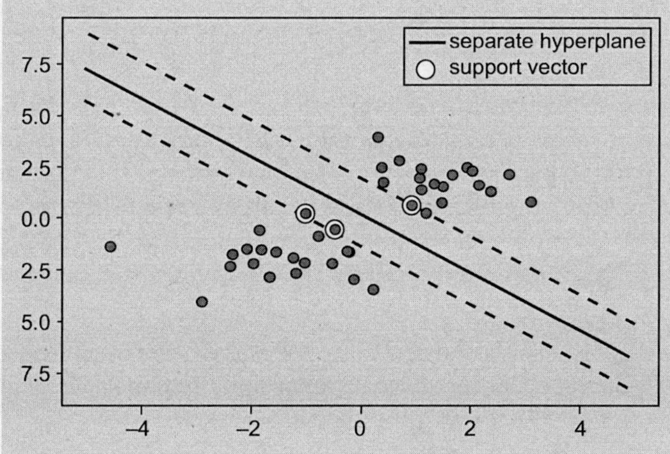

Fig. 9.7: Support vector showing different colours with different hyperplane

To sum up, SVM in the linear separable cases:

- Constrain/ensure that each observation is on the correct side of the Hyperplane.
- Pick up the optimal line so that the distance from those closest dots to the Hyperplane, so-called margin, is maximized.

Soft Margin

Two types of misclassifications are tolerated by SVM under soft margin:

1. The dot is on the wrong side of the decision boundary but on the correct side/on the margin (shown in left).
2. The dot is on the wrong side of the decision boundary and on the wrong side of the margin (shown in right).

Applying Soft Margin, SVM tolerates a few dots to get misclassified and tries to balance the trade-off between finding a line that maximizes the margin and minimizes the misclassification.

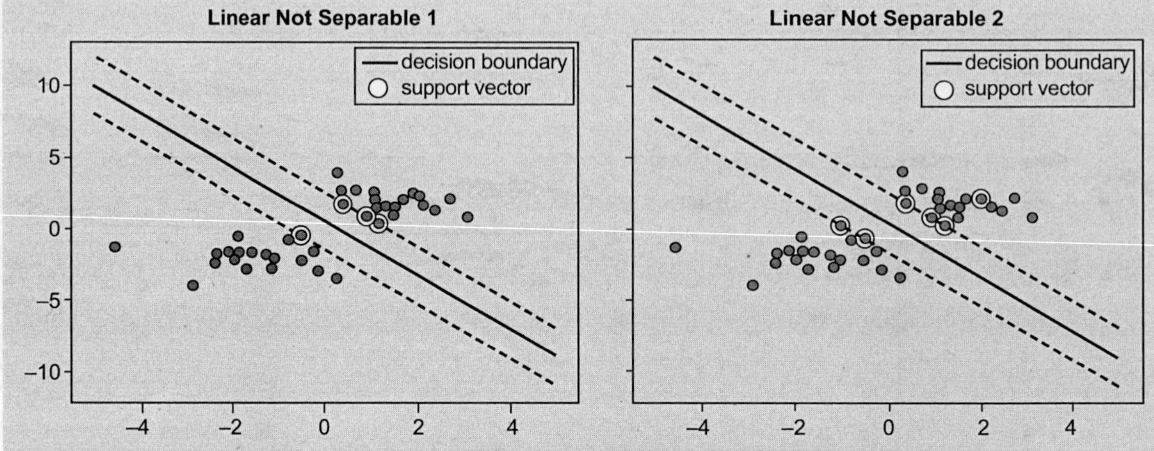

Fig. 9.8: Two lines not linear separable I 2 graphs

Degree of tolerance: How much tolerance(soft) we want to give when finding the decision boundary is an important hyper-parameter for the SVM (both linear and nonlinear solutions). In Sklearn, it is represented as the penalty term — 'C'. The bigger the C, the more penalty SVM gets when it makes misclassification. Therefore, the narrower the margin is and fewer support vectors the decision boundary will depend on.

VC dimension

Vapnik–Chervonenkis theory (also known as VC theory) was developed during 1960–1990 by Vladimir Vapnik and Alexey Chervonenkis. The theory is a form of computational learning theory, which attempts to explain the learning process from a statistical point of view.

VC dimension, short for Vapnik-Chervonenkis dimension, is a measure of the complexity of a machine learning model. It is named after the mathematicians Vladimir Vapnik and Alexey Chervonenkis, who developed the concept in the 1970s as part of their work on statistical learning theory.

VC dimension is defined as the largest number of points that can be shattered by a binary classifier without misclassification. In other words, it is a measure of the model's capacity to fit arbitrary labeled datasets. The more complex the model, the higher its VC dimension.

Quiz Questions

1. What is ensemble learning in machine learning?
   (*a*) Enable learning technique in machine learning for classifiers and regressions are trained in machine learning.
   (*b*) Not at all useful method for machine learning.
   (*c*) Not useful to perform regressions and other classifier problems.
   (*d*) None of the above answers.
2. What are the two main types of ensemble learning techniques?
   (*a*) One of the main ensemble techniques bootstrap and boosting algorithm.
   (*b*) Not suitable for bootstrap and boosting algorithms to work.

(*c*) Not essential algorithm for bagging and boosting algorithms.
(*d*) None of the above answers.

3. In bagging, how are individual models trained?
(*a*) Not essential for training with data replacement.
(*b*) It performs bagging on individual data models trained independently on random subsets of training data.
(*c*) Not at all suitable implementing essential data replacement.
(*d*) None of above answers.

4. What is an example of a bagging algorithm?
(*a*) Not suitable for bagging algorithm for multiple decision trees which are trained on subsets of data.
(*b*) Not acceptable to implement on bagging algorithm data sets.
(*c*) Suitable for Random Forest for multiple decision trees to train averaging or voting combined procedure.
(*d*) None of the above answers

5. How does boosting differ from bagging?
(*a*) It is a boosting model are trained sequentially.
(*b*) Not useful boosting model incorrect the errors made by previous errors.
(*c*) Boosting is a method of merging different types of predictions.
(*d*) None of the above answers

6. What is an example of a boosting algorithm?
(*a*) Adaptive Boosting is an example of a boosting algorithm where the weak learns are trained sequentially and pays more attention one weak learners.
(*b*) Random Forest is not in boosting algorithm.
(*c*) Not collecting combine multiple weak learners in a sequential method.
(*d*) None of the above answers.

7. What is the concept behind stacking in ensemble learning?
(*a*) Stacking is one of the most popular ensemble machine learning techniques used to predict multiple nodes to build a new model and improve model performance.
(*b*) Stacking involves training multiple diverse models and then using a meta-learner to combine their predictions.
(*c*) Ensemble learning is a machine learning technique that enhances accuracy and resilience in forecasting by merging predictions from multiple models.
(*d*) None of the above answers.

8. How does stacking differ from bagging and boosting?
(*a*) Stacking combines models of different types or with different hyperparameters, whereas bagging and boosting typically use the same type of model accessibility investigate.
(*b*) If you want to reduce the overfitting or variance of your model, you use bagging and if you are looking to reduce underfitting or bias, you use boosting.
(*c*) Not Bagging decreases variance, not bias, and solves over-fitting issues in a model.
(*d*) None of the above answers.

9. What is a common technique for combining predictions in ensemble learning?
   (*a*) A common technique for combining predictions in ensemble learning is averaging or voting, where predictions from multiple regression problem solutions.
   (*b*) Not discover common techniques for combining predictions for ensemble learning.
   (*c*) Wewilldiscover common techniques for combining predictions for ensemble learning.
   (*d*) None of the answers above.
10. Why might ensemble methods outperform individual models?
   (*a*) The ensemble of all models with relatively high and low accuracy yields an average result that may or may not outperform all base models.
   (*b*) Ensemble methods can outperform individual models because they reduce the variance.
   (*c*) Ensemble methods offer several advantages over single models, such as improved accuracy and performance.
   (*d*) None of the above answers.

ANSWERS

1.(*a*)	2.(*a*)	3.(*b*)	4.(*c*)	5.(*a*)	6.(*a*)	7.(*b*)	8.(*a*)	9.(*a*)	10. (*b*)

10 Support Vector Machine

Objectives

1. **Multi-Class Classification:** Extend SVM to handle multi-class classification tasks using techniques like one-vs-one and one-vs-rest.
2. **Practical Applications and Implementations:** Explore real-world applications of SVM in various domains such as image recognition, text categorization, bioinformatics, finance, Gain practical experience by implementing SVM algorithms using machine learning libraries such as Scikit-learn, TensorFlow, or PyTorch.
3. **Advanced Topics:** Delve into advanced topics such as support vector regression (SVR), epsilon-SVM, nu-SVM, and other variants of SVM. Learn about the theoretical underpinnings of SVM, including Mercer's theorem and the relationship between SVM and other machine learning algorithms.

Outcomes

1. **Kernel Tricks and Nonlinear Classification:** Understanding how kernel tricks transform non-linearly separable data into a higher-dimensional space for effective classification by SVM.
2. **Regularization and Overfitting:** Understanding the role of regularization in SVM to prevent overfitting, including techniques like cross-validation and grid search.
3. **Applications and Case Studies:** Exploring real-world applications of SVM in various domains such as image classification, text classification, bioinformatics, and finance through case studies and projects.

10.1 MATHEMATICALLY,

the VC dimension of a binary classifier is defined as follows:

VC dimension, short for Vapnik-Chervonenkis dimension, is a measure of the complexity of a machine learning model. It is named after the mathematicians Vladimir

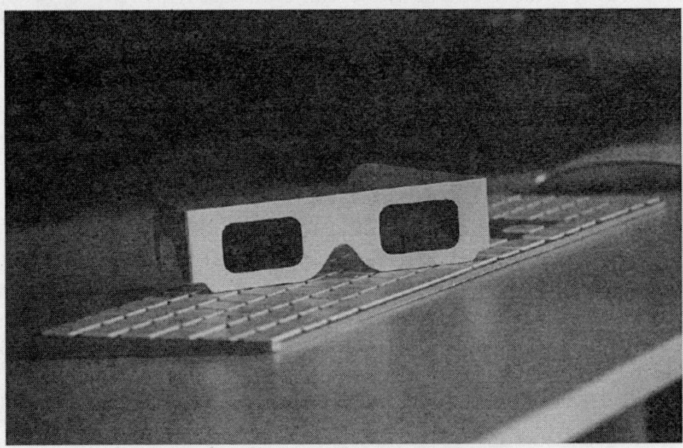

Fig. 10.1: Chervenak Dimension

Vapnik and Alexey Chervonenkis, who developed the concept in the 1970s as part of their work on statistical learning theory.

VC dimension is defined as the largest number of points that can be shattered by a binary classifier without misclassification. In other words, it is a measure of the model's capacity to fit arbitrary labeled datasets. The more complex the model, the higher its *VC* dimension.

Given a set of *n* points $S = \{x_1, x_2, \ldots, x_n\}$ in a *d*-dimensional space and a binary classifier *h*, the *VC* dimension of *h* is the largest integer *d* such that there exists a set of *d* points that can be shattered by *h*, i.e., for any labeling of the d points, there exists a hypothesis *h* in *H* that correctly classifies them.

Formally, the *VC* dimension of *h* is:

$VC(h) = \max\{d|$ there exists a set of d points that can be shattered by $h\}$

VC dimension has important implications for machine learning models. It is related to the model's generalization ability, *i.e.*, its ability to perform well on unseen data. A model with a low *VC* dimension is less complex and is more likely to generalize well, while a model with a high *VC* dimension is more complex and is more likely to overfit the training data.

VC dimension is used in various areas of machine learning, such as support vector machines (*SVMs*), neural networks, decision trees, and boosting algorithms. In *SVMs*, the *VC* dimension is used to bound the generalization error of the model. In neural networks, the *VC* dimension is related to the number of parameters in the model and is used to determine the optimal number of hidden layers and neurons. In decision trees, the *VC* dimension is used to measure the complexity of the tree and to prevent overfitting.

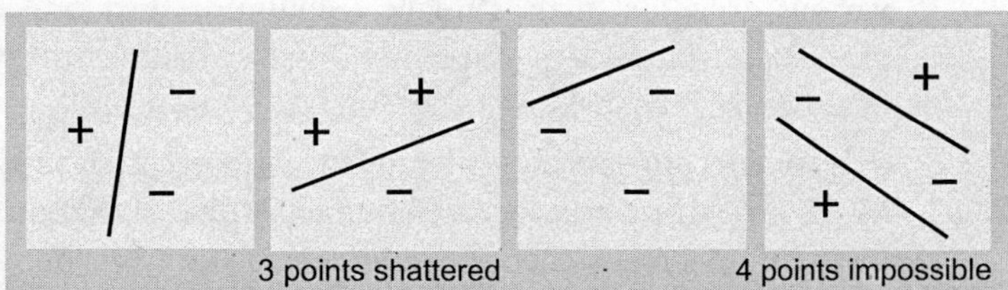

Fig. 10.2: Training VC dimension data

10.2 LIMITATIONS TO VC DIMENSION

However, there are some limitations to *VC* dimension. First, it only applies to binary classifiers and cannot be used for multi-class classification or regression problems. Second, it assumes that the data is linearly separable, which is not always the case in real-world datasets. Third, it does not take into account the distribution of the data and the noise level in the dataset.

The most powerful model according to *VC* dimension is the *SVM* with a Gaussian kernel, which has an infinite *VC* dimension. This means that the model has the capacity to fit any labeled dataset perfectly. However, this does not necessarily mean that it is the best model for all problems, as it can be computationally expensive and may not generalize well to unseen data.

10.3 FINITE VC DIMENSION

On the other hand, decision trees have a finite *VC* dimension, which makes them less complex and more likely to generalize well. However, they may not be suitable for datasets with high dimensionality or complex decision boundaries.

In summary, *VC* dimension is a powerful tool for measuring the complexity of machine learning models and for understanding their generalization ability. It has important implications for model selection, regularization, and optimization. However, it has some limitations and should be used in conjunction with other evaluation metrics and techniques.

Linearly Separable Data in Neural Networks

The concept of separability applies to binary classification problems. In them, we have two classes: one positive and the other negative. We say they're separable if there's a classifier whose decision boundary separates the positive objects from the negative ones.

If such a decision boundary is a linear function of the features, we say that the classes are linearly separable.

Since we deal with labeled data, the objects in a dataset will be linearly separable if the classes in the feature space are too.

10.4 LINEARLY SEPARABLE 2D DATA

We say a two-dimensional dataset is linearly separable if we can separate the positive from the negative objects with a straight line.

It doesn't matter if more than one such line exists. For linear separability, it's sufficient to find only one:

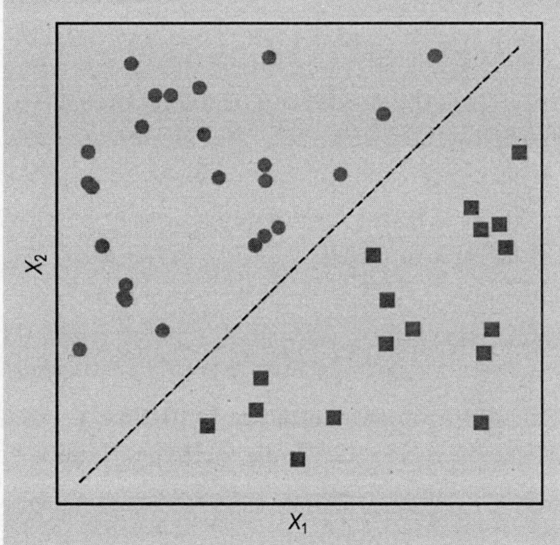

Fig. 10.3: Linearly spreader data in 2D plotting graph

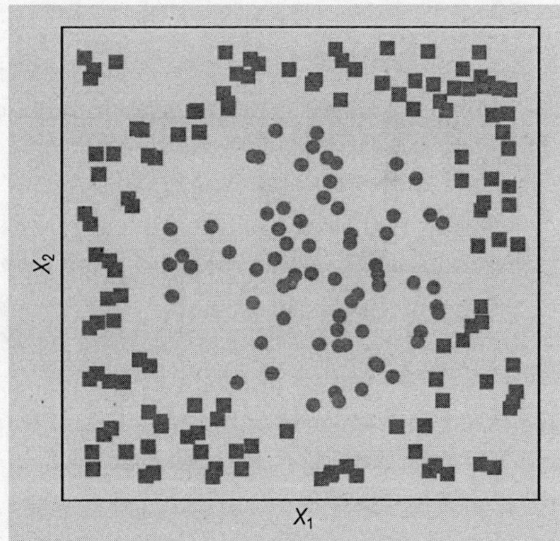

Fig. 10.3: Linearly Inspirable data in 2D plan graph

Linearly Separable – Dimensional Data

The equivalent of a 2D line is a hyperplane in - dimensional spaces. Assuming that the features are real, the equation of a hyperplane is: (1).

Where is the dot product (that also goes by the name of inner product) and is the vector orthogonal to the hyperplane. stands for an object from the feature space.

Mapping To Linearly Separable Spaces

In such cases, there's a way to make data linearly separable. **The idea is to map the objects from the original feature space in which the classes aren't linearly separable to a new one in which they are.**

Example

Let's consider as an example the 2D circular data from above. No straight line can separate the two classes faultlessly. However, while that's true in the original 2D space with features and, mapping to another could make the objects separable. Let's see if that's true for the mapping:

Since all the data points with are positive for equal to the positive circle radius while the rest are negative, the transformed data will be linearly separable. So, we can fit a linear SVM to the transformed set and obtain a linear model of, and conforming to Equation (1).

Issues

This approach has several issues. First, we have to design the mapping manually. **Sometimes, the correct transformation isn't straightforward to come by**. That's usually the case when we deal with complex data. Additionally, there may be multiple ways to make the data linearly separable, and it's not always clear which one is the most natural, the most interpretable, or the most efficient choice. For instance, all these mappings make the circular data from above linearly separable:

$$\begin{bmatrix} x_1 \\ x_2 \end{bmatrix} \rightarrow \begin{bmatrix} x_1 \\ \dfrac{x_2}{\sqrt{x_1^2 + x_2^2}} \end{bmatrix} \quad \begin{bmatrix} x_1 \\ x_2 \end{bmatrix} \rightarrow \left[\sqrt{x_1^2 + x_2^2}\right] \quad \begin{bmatrix} x_1 \\ x_2 \end{bmatrix} \rightarrow \left[\sqrt{x_1^2 + x_2^2}\right] \quad \begin{bmatrix} x_1 \\ x_2 \end{bmatrix} \rightarrow [(x_1^2 + x_2)^{\frac{1}{100}}]$$

Another problem is that **transforming the data before fitting the model can be overly inefficient.** If the dataset is large and the transformation is complex, mapping the whole set to the new feature space could take more time and memory than we can afford.

Finally, **if the data become linearly separable only in an infinite-dimensional space, we can't transform the data as the corresponding mapping would never complete.**

To solve these issues, we apply the kernel trick.

Linear Models

If the data are linearly separable, we can find the decision boundary's equation by fitting a linear model to the data. For example, a linear Support Vector Machine classifier finds the hyperplane with the widest margins.

Linear models come with three advantages. First, they're simple and operate with original features. So, it's easier to interpret them than the more complex non-linear models. Second, we can derive analytical solutions to the optimization problems that arise while fitting the models. In contrast, we can rely only on numerical methods to train a general non-linear model. And finally, it's easier to apply numerical methods to linear optimization problems than non-linear ones.

However, if the data aren't linearly separable, we can't enjoy the advantages of linear models.

Kernels

Let's go back to Equation (1) for a moment. Its key ingredient is the inner-product term $<w, x>$. It turns out that the analytical solutions to fitting linear models include the inner products <w, z> of the instances in the dataset.

When we apply a transformation mapping Ø, we change the inner-product terms in the original space to the inner products in another one: <Ø(x), Ø(z)>. But, we can evaluate them even without transforming the data. To do so, we use kernels.

A kernel is a function that maps a pair of original objects and into the inner product of their images Ø(x), Ø(z) and without actually calculating Ø(x) and Ø(x). So, **kernels allow us to skip the transformation step and find a linear decision boundary in another space by operating on the original features**.

For example: k\left ([x_1, x_2], [z_1, z_2]\right) = $x_1^2\, z_1^2 + 2\, x_1\, z_1\, x_2\, z_2 + x_2^2\, z_2^2$ is the inner product of [x_1^2, \sqrt{2x_1 x_2}, x_2^2] and [z_1^2, \sqrt {2z_1 z_2}, z_2^2]. So, if the separating decision boundary in the original space is a curve involving the terms x_1^2, x_2^2, or \sqrt {x_1 x_2}, or, it will be a plane in the transformed space. Therefore, training a linear model kernelized with will find it.

10.5 SUPPORT VECTOR MACHINE (SVM) ALGORITHM

Support Vector Machine (SVM) is a powerful machine learning algorithm used for linear or nonlinear classification, regression, and even outlier detection tasks. SVMs can be used for a variety of tasks, such as text classification, image classification, spam detection, handwriting identification, gene expression analysis, face detection, and anomaly detection. SVMs are adaptable and efficient in a variety of applications because they can manage high-dimensional data and nonlinear relationships.

SVM algorithms are very effective as we try to find the maximum separating hyperplane between the different classes available in the target feature.

Support Vector Machine

Support Vector Machine (SVM) is a supervised machine learning algorithm used for both classification and regression. Though we say regression problems as well it's best suited for classification. The main objective of the SVM algorithm is to find the optimal hyperplane in an N-dimensional space that can separate the data points in different classes in the feature space. The hyperplane tries that the margin between the closest points of different classes should be as maximum as possible. The dimension of the hyperplane depends upon the number of features. If the number of input features is two, then the hyperplane is just a line. If the number of input features is three, then the hyperplane becomes a 2-D plane. It becomes difficult to imagine when the number of features exceeds three.

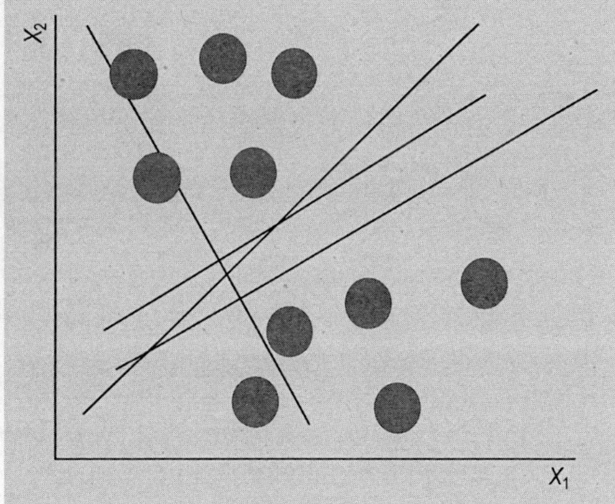

Fig. 10.4: Linearly separable Data Points

From the figure above it's very clear that there are multiple lines (our hyperplane here is a line because we are considering only two input features x_1, x_2) that segregate our data points or do a classification between red and blue circles. So how do we choose the best line or in general the best hyperplane that segregates our data points?

How does SVM work?

One reasonable choice as the best hyperplane is the one that represents the largest separation or margin between the two classes.

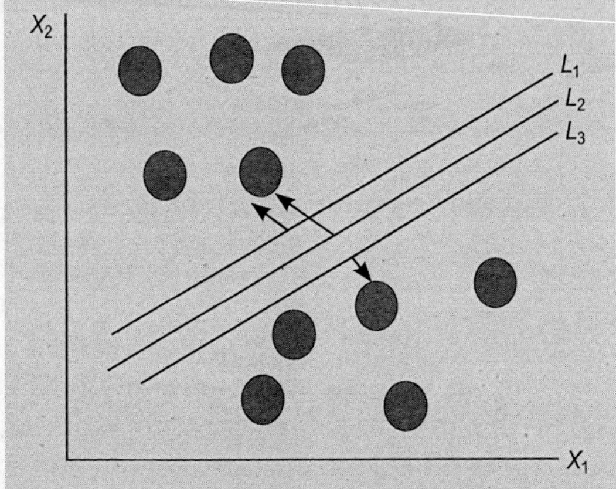

Fig. 10.5: Multiple hyperplanes separate the data from two classes

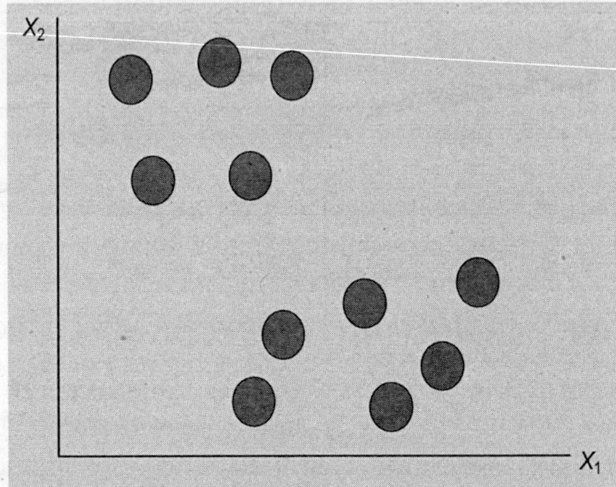

Fig. 10.6: Selecting hyperplane for data with outlier

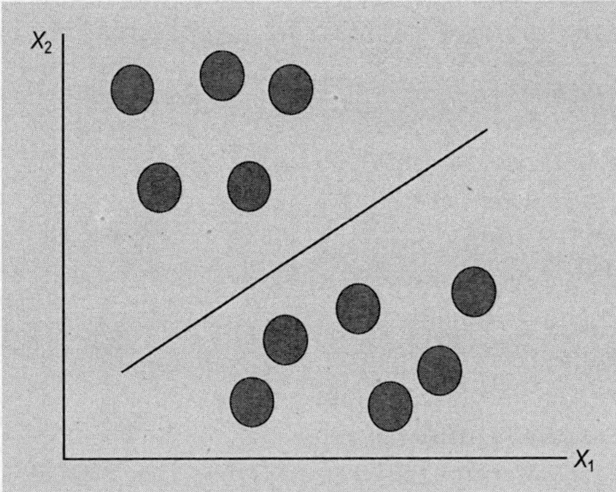

Fig. 10.7: Hyperplane which is the most optimized one

So in this type of data point what SVM does is, finds the maximum margin as done with previous data sets along with that it adds a penalty each time a point crosses the margin. So the margins in these types of cases are called **soft margins**. When there is a soft margin to the data set, the SVM tries to minimize ($1/margin$ + ^($\Sigma penalty$)). Hinge loss is a commonly used penalty. If no violations no hinge loss.If violations hinge loss proportional to the distance of violation.

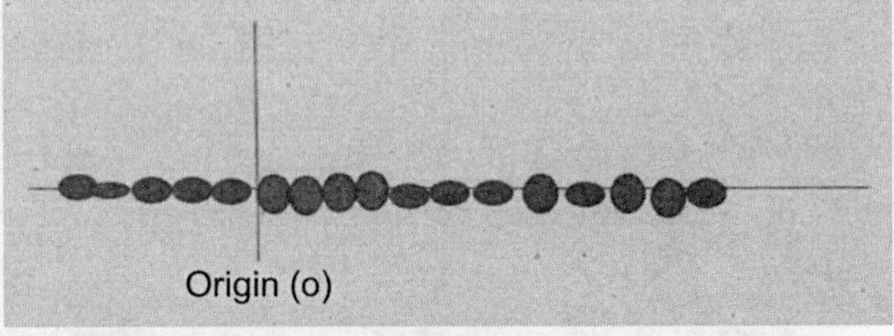

Fig. 10.8: Original 1D dataset for classification

Till now, we were talking about linearly separable data(the group of blue balls and red balls are separable by a straight line/linear line). What to do if data are not linearly separable?

Say, our data is shown in the figure above. SVM solves this by creating a new variable using a **kernel**. We call a point x_i on the line and we create a

New variable y as a function of distance from origin o. So if we plot this we get something like as shown below:

Support Vector Machine Terminology

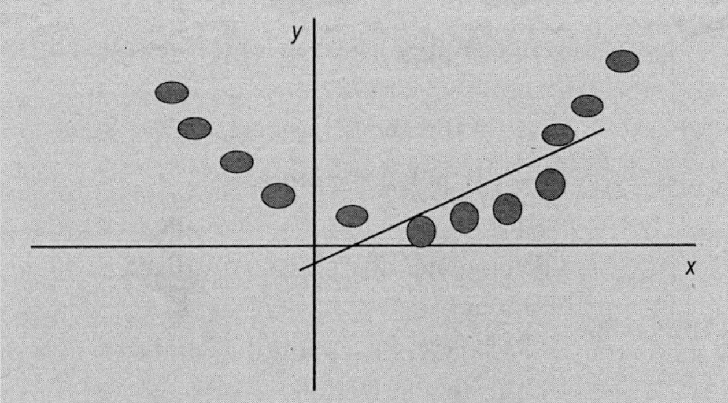

Fig. 10.9: Mapping 1D data to 2D to become able to separate the two classes

1. **Hyperplane:** Hyperplane is the decision boundary that is used to separate the data points of different classes in a feature space. In the case of linear classifications, it will be a linear equation.

   i.e. $wx + b = 0$.
2. **Support Vectors:** Support vectors are the closest data points to the hyperplane, which makes a critical role in deciding the hyperplane and margin.
3. **Margin:** Margin is the distance between the support vector and hyperplane. The main objective of the support vector machine algorithm is to maximize the margin. The wider margin indicates better classification performance.
4. **Kernel:** Kernel is the mathematical function, which is used in SVM to map the original input data points into high-dimensional feature spaces, so, that the hyperplane can be easily found out even if the data points are not linearly separable in the original input space. Some of the common kernel functions are linear, polynomial, radial basis function (RBF), and sigmoid.
5. **Hard Margin:** The maximum-margin hyperplane or the hard margin hyperplane is a hyperplane that properly separates the data points of different categories without any misclassifications.
6. **Soft Margin:** When the data is not perfectly separable or contains outliers, SVM permits a soft margin technique. Each data point has a slack variable introduced by the soft-margin SVM formulation, which softens the strict margin requirement and permits certain misclassifications or violations. It discovers a compromise between increasing the margin and reducing violations.
7. **C:** Margin maximisation and misclassification fines are balanced by the regularisation parameter C in SVM. The penalty for going over the margin or misclassifying data items is decided by it. A stricter penalty is imposed with a greater value of C, which results in a smaller margin and perhaps fewer misclassifications.
8. **Hinge Loss:** A typical loss function in SVMs is hinge loss. It punishes incorrect classifications or margin violations. The objective function in SVM is frequently formed by combining it with the regularisation term.

9. **Dual Problem:** A dual Problem of the optimisation problem that requires locating the Lagrange multipliers related to the support vectors can be used to solve SVM. The dual formulation enables the use of kernel tricks and more effective computing.

Quiz Questions

1. What are the disadvantages of SVM?
   (*a*) Disadvantages of SVM include the need for careful selection of hyperparameters, computational complexity.
   (*b*) Algorithm is not suitable for large data sets.
   (*c*) Long training time for large datasets. Difficult to understand and interpret the final model, variable weights and individual impact.
   (*d*) None of the above answers.
2. How does SVM handle outliers?
   (*a*) Compared to KNN, SVM is able to handle outliers pretty well.
   (*b*) SVM is generally robust to outliers, as it focuses on the support vectors closest to the decision boundary.
   (*c*) Not a SVM robust to outliers and easy to apply non-linear kernels to, but like linear regression with L_1 regularization.
   (*d*) None of the answers.
3. In SVM, what happens if the classes are not linearly separable?
   (*a*) If the classes are not linearly separable, SVM uses the kernel trick to map the input data into a higher-dimensional.
   (*b*) Nota linear classification cannot perfectly distinguish the two classes.
   (*c*) But what if the problem is not linearly separable? A single perceptron fails to solve the problem which is linearly inseparable.
   (*d*) None of answers is correct.
4. What is the difference between SVM and logistic regression?
   (*a*) Don't get confused between SVM and logistic regression.
   (*b*) SVM works well with unstructured and semi-structured data like text and images while logistic regression works with already identified independent variables.
   (*c*) While both SVM and logistic regression are used for classification.
   (*d*) None of the answers is correct.
5. How does SVM handle multi-class classification?
   (*a*) SVM handles multi-class classification using either the one-vs-one or one-vs-all approach. In the one-vs-one approach.
   (*b*) SVM doesn't support multiclass classification.
   (*c*) SVM handles multi-class classification using either the one-vs-one or one-vs-all approach. In the one-vs-one approach.
   (*d*) None of answers is correct.

6. What is the computational complexity of training an SVM?
   (*a*) The computational complexity of training an SVM is approximately O(n^2) to O(n^3).
   (*b*) Linear SVM has a complexity of O(n d).
   (*c*) Not SVMs typically perform better with high-dimensional and unstructured datasets.
   (*d*) None of the answers is correct.
7. What is the difference between SVM and *k*-NN (*k*-Nearest Neighbours)?
   (*a*) While both SVM and *k*-NN are used for classification, SVM finds a hyperplane that separates classes.
   (*b*) SVM and KNN exemplify several important trade-offs in machine learning (*ML*).
   (*c*) KNN is a voting-based algorithm that classifies an object based on the class of its nearest neighbours in the decision space.
   (*d*) None of above answers is correct.
8. What is the role of the bias term in SVM?
   (*a*) The bias term *b* is, indeed, a special parameter in SVM.
   (*b*) The bias term in SVM represents the offset of the decision boundary from the origin.
   (*c*) A SVM "learns" a hyperplane or plane or line which provides a maximum margin to the class boundary's.
   (*d*) None is correct.
9. How does SVM handle imbalanced datasets?
   (*a*) SVM can handle imbalanced datasets by adjusting the class weights or using techniques such as under-sampling.
   (*b*) The Support Vector Machine algorithm is effective for balanced classification.
   (*c*) Can't handle Random Under-Sampler (RU).
   (*d*) None is correct.
10. What evaluation metrics are commonly used to assess SVM performance?
   (*a*) Use appropriate evaluation metrics based on your problem.
   (*b*) SVM algorithm is not suitable for large data sets.
   (*c*) Common evaluation metrics for SVM include accuracy, precision, recall.
   (*d*) None of the answer is correct.

ANSWERS

1.(*a*)	2.(*b*)	3.(*a*)	4.(*b*)	5.(*c*)	6.(*a*)	7.(*a*)	8.(*b*)	9.(*a*)	10. (*c*)

11 Unsupervised Learning

Objectives

1. **Understanding Unsupervised Learning Concepts:** Students should grasp the fundamental concepts of unsupervised learning, including clustering, dimensionality reduction, density estimation, and anomaly detection.
2. **Algorithms and Techniques:** Familiarity with a range of unsupervised learning algorithms such as K-means clustering, hierarchical clustering, DBSCAN, PCA (Principal Component Analysis), t-SNE (t-Distributed Stochastic Neighbour Embedding), autoencoders, Gaussian Mixture Models (GMMs), and others.
3. **Mathematical Foundations:** Comprehension of the mathematical principles underlying unsupervised learning algorithms, including optimization methods, probability distributions, distance metrics, and manifold learning.

Outcomes

1. **Understanding the fundamental concepts of Unsupervised Learning:** Students should grasp the core principles of Unsupervised Learning, including clustering, dimensionality reduction, and density estimation.
2. **Exploring clustering algorithms:** Students should learn various clustering algorithms such as *K*-means, hierarchical clustering, DBSCAN, and Gaussian mixture models. They should understand the strengths, weaknesses, and applications of each algorithm.
3. **Mastering dimensionality reduction techniques:** Students should become proficient in dimensionality reduction techniques like Principal Component Analysis (PCA), t-distributed Stochastic Neighbour Embedding (t-SNE), and Autoencoders. They should understand how these techniques can be used for data visualization and feature extraction.

11.1 UNSUPERVISED MACHINE LEARNING

In the previous topic, we learned supervised machine learning in which models are trained using labeled data under the supervision of training data. But there may be many cases in which we do not have labeled data and need to find the hidden patterns from the given dataset. So, to solve such types of cases in machine learning, we need unsupervised learning techniques.

What is Unsupervised Learning?

As the name suggests, unsupervised learning is a machine learning technique in which models are not supervised using training dataset. Instead, models itself find the hidden patterns and insights from the given data. It can be compared to learning which takes place in the human brain while learning new things. It can be defined as:

> *Unsupervised learning is a type of machine learning in which models are trained using unlabeled dataset and are allowed to act on that data without any supervision.*

Unsupervised learning cannot be directly applied to a regression or classification problem because unlike supervised learning, we have the input data but no corresponding output data. The goal of unsupervised learning is to **find the underlying structure of dataset, group that data according to similarities, and represent that dataset in a compressed format.**

Example: Suppose the unsupervised learning algorithm is given an input dataset containing images of different types of cats and dogs. The algorithm is never trained upon the given dataset, which means it does not have any idea about the features of the dataset. The task of the unsupervised learning algorithm is to identify the image features on their own. Unsupervised learning algorithm will perform this task by clustering the image dataset into the groups according to similarities between images.

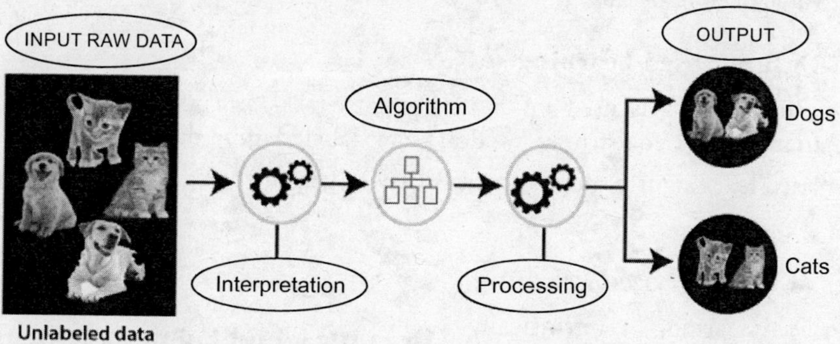

Fig. 11.1: Example of Unsupervised Learning

Types of Unsupervised Learning Algorithm

The unsupervised learning algorithm can be further categorized into two types of problems:

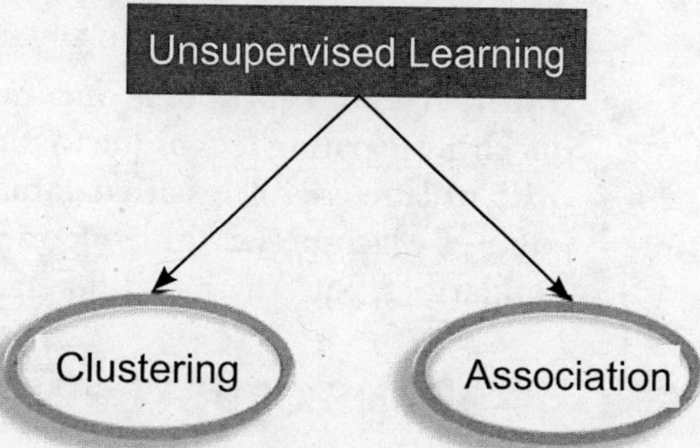

Fig. 11.2: Unsupervised Learning Types

- **Clustering:** Clustering is a method of grouping the objects into clusters such that objects with most similarities remains into a group and has less or no similarities with the objects of another group. Cluster analysis finds the commonalities between the data objects and categorizes them as per the presence and absence of those commonalities.
- **Association:** An association rule is an unsupervised learning method which is used for finding the relationships between variables in

the large database. It determines the set of items that occurs together in the dataset. Association rule makes marketing strategy more effective. Such as people who buy *X* item (suppose a bread) are also tend to purchase *Y* (Butter/Jam) item. A typical example of Association rule is Market Basket Analysis.

11.2 UNSUPERVISED LEARNING ALGORITHMS

Below is the list of some popular unsupervised learning algorithms:

- *K*-means clustering
- KNN (*k*-nearest neighbours)
- Hierarchal clustering
- Anomaly detection
- Neural Networks
- Principle Component Analysis
- Independent Component Analysis
- Apriori algorithm
- Singular value decomposition

Advantages of Unsupervised Learning

- Unsupervised learning is used for more complex tasks as compared to supervised learning because, in unsupervised learning, we don't have labeled input data.
- Unsupervised learning is preferable as it is easy to get unlabeled data in comparison to labeled data.

Disadvantages of Unsupervised Learning

- Unsupervised learning is intrinsically more difficult than supervised learning as it does not have corresponding output.
- The result of the unsupervised learning algorithm might be less accurate as input data is not labelled, and algorithms do not know the exact output in advance.
- **Unsupervised Learning is one kind of machine learning technique that deals with unlabeled, unclassified data.** This kind of Machine Learning algorithm help us to group unsorted information consistent with similarities, patterns, and differences with no prior training of knowledge.

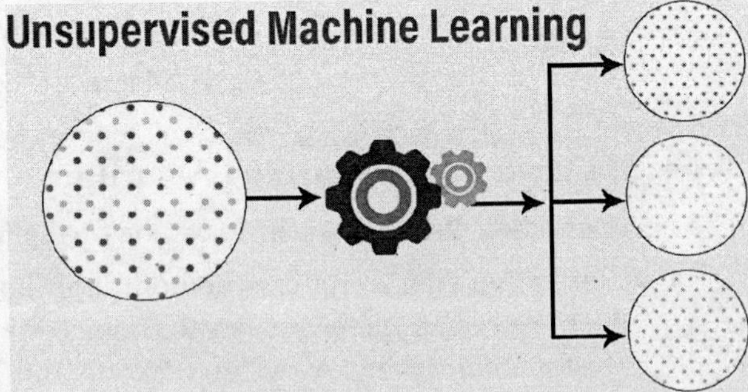

Fig. 11.3: Unsupervised Machine Learning Process

11.3 K-MEANS CLUSTERING

Clustering is an important concept when it comes to unsupervised learning. It mainly deals with finding a structure or pattern in a collection of uncategorized data. Unsupervised Learning Clustering algorithms will process your data and find natural clusters(groups) if they exist in the data. You can also modify how many clusters your algorithms should identify. It allows you to adjust the granularity of these groups.

Fig. 11.4: Clustering

Types of Clustering

- *Hierarchical clustering*
- *Partitioning clustering*

Hierarchical clustering is further subdivided into

- ***Agglomerative clustering***: It is a bottom-up approach where we begin with each element as a separate cluster and merge them into successively more massive clusters.
- ***Divisive clustering***: It is a top-down approach where we begin with the whole set and proceed to divide it into successively smaller clusters.

Partitioning clustering is further subdivided into

- ***K*-Means clustering**: In this method, the objects are divided into several clusters mentioned by the number "*K*". We can mention any value for "*K*" & Machine Learning will find that many clusters in our data.
- **Fuzzy *C*-Means clustering:** It is very similar to *k*-means in the sense that it clusters objects that have similar characteristics together. In *k*-means clustering, a single object cannot belong to two different clusters. But in *c*-means, objects can belong to more than one cluster.

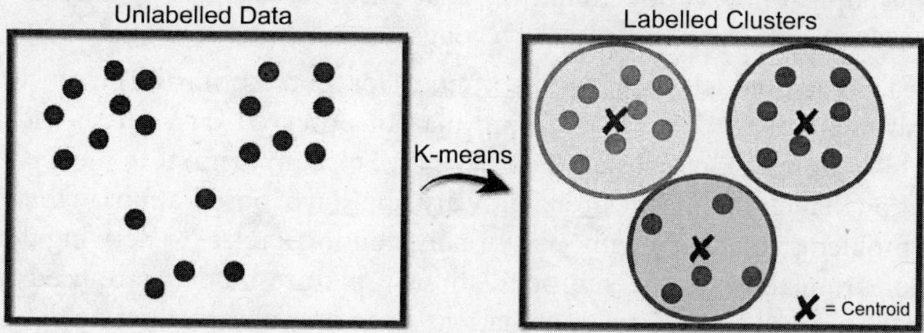

Fig. 11.5: Example of K-Mean Clustering Algorithm

K-Means Clustering is an Unsupervised Learning algorithm, which groups the unlabeled dataset into different clusters. **Here *K* defines the number of pre-defined clusters that needs to be created in the process, as if *K* = 2, there will be two clusters, and for *K* = 3, there will be three clusters, and so on.**

The *k*-means clustering algorithm mainly performs two tasks:

- Determines the best value for *K* center points or centroids by an iterative process.
- Assigns each data point to its closest *k*-center. Those data points which are near to the particular *k*-center, create a cluster.

The process *K*-Means Clustering follows is mentioned below:

- 1st, select the value of "*K*" that means fixing the number of clusters.
- 2nd, choosing some random *k* points or centroid to form the cluster. In this step we can choose any data points & it's not compulsory to choose data points which belongs to the dataset.
- 3rd, now we need to allocate all the data points to their nearest cluster. For that we can use either Euclidean-based distance or correlation-based distance method.
- 4th, till the time new data keep on coming we keep on repeating the 3rd step & allocate them to their nearest cluster.
- Finally, Compute the centroids for the clusters by taking the average of the all data points that belong to each cluster & our model will be created.

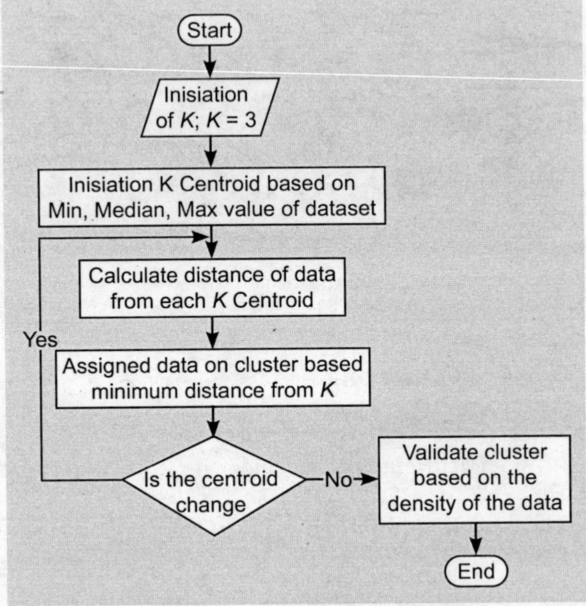

Fig. 11.6: Chart of K-Mean Algorithm implementation

11.4 MIXTURE MODEL

In statistics, a mixture model is a probabilistic model for representing the presence of subpopulations within an overall population, without requiring that an observed data set should identify the sub-population to which an individual observation belongs.

In statistics, a mixture model is a probabilistic model for representing the presence of subpopulations within an overall population, without requiring that an observed data set should identify the sub-population to which an individual observation belongs. Formally a mixture model corresponds to the mixture distribution that represents the probability distribution of observations in the overall population. However, while problems associated with "mixture distributions" relate to deriving the properties of the overall population from those of the sub-populations, "mixture models" are used to make statistical inferences about the properties of the sub-populations given only observations on the pooled population, without sub-population identity information.

Mixture models should not be confused with models for compositional data, *i.e.*, data whose components are constrained to sum to a constant value (1, 100%, etc.). However, compositional models can be thought of as mixture models, where members of the population are sampled at random. Conversely, mixture models can be thought of as compositional models, where the total size reading population has been normalized to 1.

General mixture model

A typical finite-dimensional mixture model is a hierarchical model consisting of the following components:

- N random variables that are observed, each distributed according to a mixture of K components, with the components belonging to the same parametric family of distributions (e.g., all normal, all Zipfian, etc.) but with different parameters.
- N random latent variables specifying the identity of the mixture component of each observation, each distributed according to a K-dimensional categorical distribution.
- A set of K mixture weights, which are probabilities that sum to 1.
- A set of K parameters, each specifying the parameter of the corresponding mixture component. In many cases, each "parameter" is actually a set of parameters. For example, if the mixture components are Gaussian distributions, there will be a mean and variance for each component. If the mixture components are categorical distributions (e.g., when each observation is a token from a finite alphabet of size V), there will be a vector of V probabilities summing to 1.

In addition, in a Bayesian setting, the mixture weights and parameters will themselves be random variables, and prior distributions will be placed over the variables. In such a case, the weights are typically viewed as a K-dimensional random vector drawn from a Dirichlet distribution (the conjugate prior of the categorical distribution), and the parameters will be distributed according to their respective conjugate priors.

Mathematically, a basic parametric mixture model can be described as follows:

K	= number of mixture components
N	= number of observations
$\theta_{i=1...K}$	= parameter of distribution of observation associated with component i
$\phi_{i=1...K}$	= mixture weight, *i.e.*, prior probability of a particular component i
ϕ	= K-dimensional vector composed of all the individual $\phi_{1...K}$; must sum to 1
$z_{i=1...N}$	= component of observation i
$x_{i=1...N}$	= observation i
$F(x\|\phi)$	= probability distribution of an observation, parametrized on θ
$z_{i=1...N}$	~ Categorical (ϕ)
$x_{i=1...N} \| z_{i=1...N}$	~ $F(\theta z_i)$

In a Bayesian setting, all parameters are associated with random variables, as follows:

K, N	= as above
$\theta_{i=1...K}, \phi_{i=1...K}, \phi$	= as above
α	= shared hyperparameter for component parameters

β = shared hyperparameter for mixture weights

$H(\theta|\alpha)$ = prior probability distribution of component parameters, parametrized on α

$\theta_{i=1...K} \sim H(\theta|\alpha)$

$\phi \sim$ Symmetric-Dirichlet$_K(\beta)$

$z_{i=1...N} | \phi \sim$ Categorical (ϕ)

$z_{i=1...N}|z_{i=1...N}, \theta_{i=1...N} \sim F(\theta z_i)$

This characterization uses F and H to describe arbitrary distributions over observations and parameters, respectively. Typically H will be the conjugate prior of F. The two most common choices of F are Gaussian aka "normal" (for real-valued observations) and categorical (for discrete observations). Other common possibilities for the distribution of the mixture components are:

- Binomial distribution, for the number of "positive occurrences" (e.g., successes, yes votes, etc.) given a fixed number of total occurrences.
- Multinomial distribution, similar to the binomial distribution, but for counts of multi-way occurrences (e.g., yes/no/maybe in a survey).
- Negative binomial distribution, for binomial-type observations but where the quantity of interest is the number of failures before a given number of successes occurs.
- Poisson distribution, for the number of occurrences of an event in a given period of time, for an event that is characterized by a fixed rate of occurrence.
- Exponential distribution, for the time before the next event occurs, for an event that is characterized by a fixed rate of occurrence.
- Log-normal distribution, for positive real numbers that are assumed to grow exponentially, such as incomes or prices.
- Multivariate normal distribution (aka multivariate Gaussian distribution), for vectors of correlated outcomes that are individually Gaussian-distributed.
- Multivariate Student's t-distribution, for vectors of heavy-tailed correlated outcomes[1]
- A vector of Bernoulli-distributed values, corresponding, e.g., to a black-and-white image, with each value representing a pixel; see the handwriting-recognition example below

Whenever I encounter any recommendation engine on a website, I can't wait to break it down and understand how it works. It's one of the many great things about being a data scientist! Artificial Intelligence has revolutionized how we approach data analysis and has led to the development of powerful algorithms such as *k*-means clustering. *K*-means clustering, a part of the unsupervised learning family in *AI*, is used to group similar data points together in a process known as clustering. Clustering helps us understand our data in a unique way – by grouping things together into – you guessed it – clusters.

In this article, we will cover *k*-means clustering one of the most commonly used clustering methods) and its components comprehensively. We'll look at clustering, why it matters, and its applications before diving deep into *k*-means clustering (including how to perform it in Python on a real-world dataset).

Learning Objectives

1. Get introduced to *K*-Means Clustering.
2. Understand the properties of clusters and the various evaluation metrics for clustering.

3. Get acquainted with some of the many real-world applications of *K*-Means Clustering.
4. Implement *K*-Means Clustering in Python on a real-world dataset.

And if you want to work directly on the Python code, jump straight here. We have a live coding window where you can build your own *k*-means clustering algorithm without leaving this article!

To learn more about clustering and other machine learning algorithms (both supervised and unsupervised) check out the following courses–

- Machine Learning Certification Course for Beginners
- Applied Machine Learning Course
- Certified AI & ML Blackbelt+Program

11.5 EM ALGORITHM IN MACHINE LEARNING

The EM algorithm is considered a latent variable model to find the local maximum likelihood parameters of a statistical model, proposed by Arthur Dempster, Nan Laird, and Donald Rubin in 1977. The EM (Expectation-Maximization) algorithm is one of the most commonly used terms in machine learning to obtain maximum likelihood estimates of variables that are sometimes observable and sometimes not. However, it is also applicable to unobserved data or sometimes called latent. It has various real-world applications in statistics, including obtaining the **mode of the posterior marginal distribution of parameters in machine learning and data mining applications.**

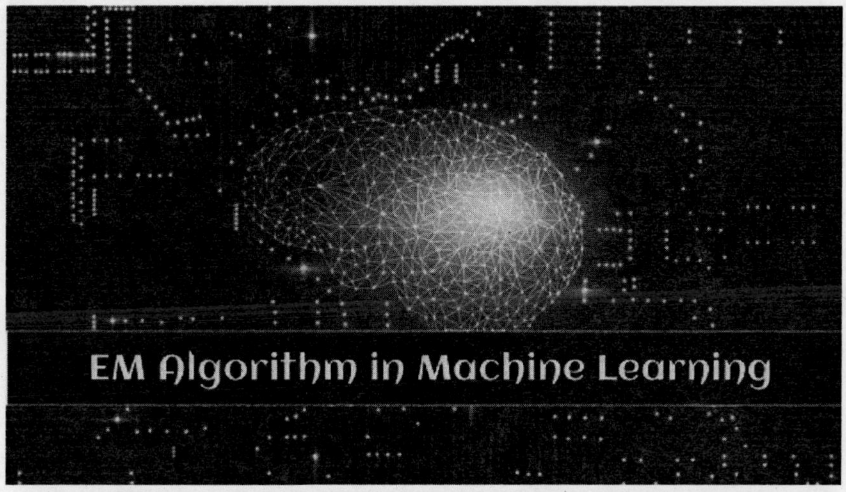

Fig. 11.7: EM (Expectation-Maximization) algorithm for Machine Learning

In most real-life applications of machine learning, it is found that several relevant learning features are available, but very few of them are observable, and the rest are unobservable. If the variables are observable, then it can predict the value using instances. On the other hand, the variables which are latent or directly not observable, for such variables Expectation-Maximization (EM) algorithm plays a vital role to predict the value with the condition that the general form of probability distribution governing those latent variables is known to us. In this topic, we will discuss a basic introduction to the EM algorithm, a flow chart of the EM algorithm, its applications, advantages, and disadvantages of *EM* algorithm, etc.

EM Algorithm

The *EM* algorithm is the combination of various unsupervised *ML* algorithms, such as the ***k*-means clustering algorithm**. Being an iterative approach, it consists of two modes. In the first mode, we estimate the missing or latent variables. Hence it is referred to as the **Expectation/estimation step (E-step)**. Further, the other mode is used to optimize the parameters of the models so that it can explain the data more clearly. The second mode is known as the **maximization-step or *M*-step.**

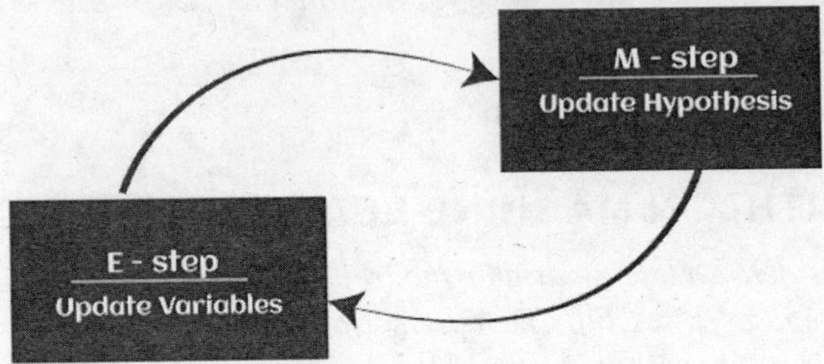

Fig. 11.8: EM steps and their relationship

- **Expectation step (*E*-step):** It involves the estimation (guess) of all missing values in the dataset so that after completing this step, there should not be any missing value.
- **Maximization step (*M*-step):** This step involves the use of estimated data in the *E*-step and updating the parameters.
- **Repeat** *E*-step and *M*-step until the convergence of the values occurs.

Steps in EM Algorithm

The *EM* algorithm is completed mainly in 4 steps, which include ***Initialization Step, Expectation Step, Maximization Step, and convergence Step***. These steps are explained as follows:

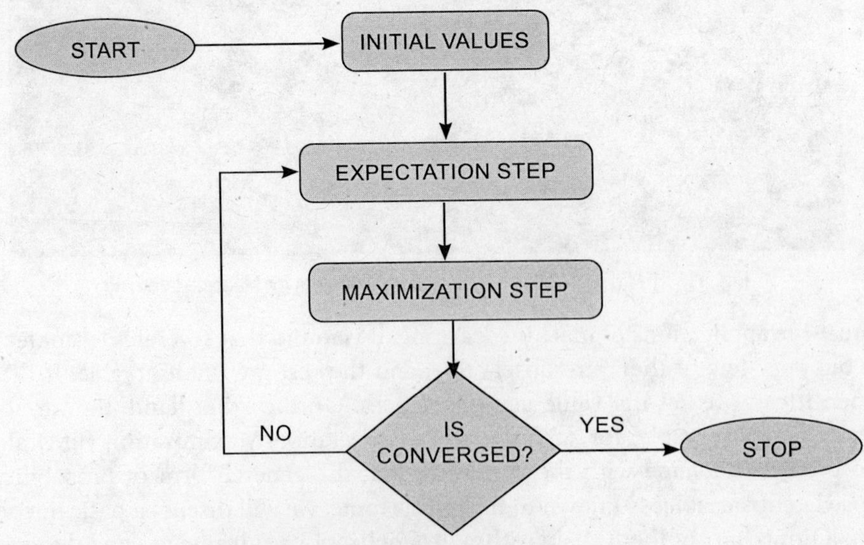

Fig. 11.9: Flow-chart showing Exception evaluation

- **1st Step:** The very first step is to initialize the parameter values. Further, the system is provided with incomplete observed data with the assumption that data is obtained from a specific model.
- **2nd Step:** This step is known as Expectation or *E*-Step, which is used to estimate or guess the values of the missing or incomplete data using the observed data. Further, *E*-step primarily updates the variables.
- **3rd Step:** This step is known as Maximization or *M*-step, where we use complete data obtained from the 2nd step to update the parameter values. Further, *M*-step primarily updates the hypothesis.
- **4th step:** The last step is to check if the values of latent variables are converging or not. If it gets "yes", then stop the process; else, repeat the process from step 2 until the convergence occurs.

Quiz Questions

1. What is Unsupervised Learning?
   (*a*) Unsupervised Learning is a type of machine learning where the model is trained on unlabelled data.
   (*b*) Dimensionality reduction algorithm is not unsupervised learning.
   (*c*) Unsupervised algorithm only processes "features" and does not process tags. Dimensionality reduction algorithm is not unsupervised learning.
   (*d*) None is correct
2. Name two common tasks in Unsupervised Learning.
   (*a*) Among the options, speech recognition is not an application of unsupervised machine learning as it usually involves supervised learning techniques.
   (*b*) Unsupervised machine learning is the process of inferring underlying hidden patterns from historical data. Within such an approach, a machine learning model tries to find any similarities, differences, patterns, and structure in data by itself. No prior human intervention is needed.
   (*c*) Dimensionality Reduction, the task of reducing the number of input features in a dataset.
   (*d*) None of the above answers.
3. What is Clustering?
   (*a*) Non-clustered indexes have a structure separate from the data rows.
   (*b*) Clustering is the task of dividing the unlabelled data or data points into different clusters such that similar data points fall in the same cluster than those which differ from the others.
   (*c*) The *K*-nearest neighbour method.
   (*d*) The *K*-nearest neighbour method.
4. Explain the K-means algorithm briefly?
   (*a*) *K*-Means clustering is an unsupervised learning algorithm.
   (*b*) The *k*-means clustering algorithm mainly performs two tasks.

(*c*) K-Means clustering is an unsupervised learning algorithm.

(*d*) k-means has trouble clustering data where clusters are of varying sizes and density.

5. What is Dimensionality Reduction?

(*a*) Dimensionality reduction, or dimension reduction, is the transformation of data from a high-dimensional space into a low-dimensional space so that the low-dimensional representation retains some meaningful properties of the original data.

(*b*) Principal Component Analysis (PCA) is a dimensionality reduction technique widely used in data analysis and machine learning.

(*c*) Not dimensionality Reduction is a technique used in Unsupervised Learning to reduce the number of features in the data while retaining its essential information.

(*d*) Dimensionality reduction, or dimension reduction, is the transformation of data from a high-dimensional space into a low-dimensional space so that the low-dimensional representation retains some meaningful properties of the original data, ideally close to its intrinsic dimension.

6. Name a popular Dimensionality Reduction technique.

(*a*) Nonlinear dimensionality reduction, also known as manifold learning.

(*b*) There are two common dimensionality reduction techniques: feature selection and feature extraction.

(*c*) Principal Component Analysis (PCA) is a popular Dimensionality Reduction technique used to reduce the dimensionality of the dataset while preserving most of its variance.

(*d*) Dimensionality reduction is a process and technique to reduce the number of dimensions or features.

7. What is Anomaly Detection?

(*a*) Anomaly Detection is a task in Unsupervised Learning where the model identifies instances in the data that deviate significantly from the norm or expected behaviour.

(*b*) Anomaly detection identifies suspicious activity that falls outside of your established normal patterns of behaviour.

(*c*) However, these types of micro clusters can often be identified more readily by a cluster analysis algorithm.

(*d*) In business data, three main time-series data anomalies exist.

8. How is Anomaly Detection useful in real-world applications?

(*a*) Anomaly Detection is useful in various real-world applications such as fraud detection in finance.

(*b*) It can be useful for detecting fraud, intrusion, defects, or outliers in various domains.

(*c*) Applications of anomaly detection include fraud detection in financial transactionsdifficulty in choosing a suitable neural network structure for a specific task.

9. What are the evaluation metrics used for assessing clustering algorithms?

(*a*) The two most popular evaluation metrics for clustering algorithms are the Silhouette coefficient and Dunn's Index.

(*b*) Davies–Bouldin Index.

(*c*) Common external evaluation metrics include the Rand index, the Adjusted Rand index.

(*d*) Adjusted Rand Index are commonly used metrics to evaluate clustering model performance.

10. Can Unsupervised Learning algorithms handle labelled data?

(*a*) Unsupervised Learning algorithms can handle labelled data, but they typically ignore the labels during the training process as they are designed to work with unlabelled data.

(*b*) *K*-nearest neighbour method is not a clustering method.

(*c*) The evaluation metrics which do not require any ground truth labels to calculate the efficiency of the clustering algorithm could be used for the computation of the performance evaluation.

(*d*) Accuracy, confusion matrix, log-loss, and AUC-ROC are some of the most popular metrics.

ANSWERS

1.(*a*)	2.(*c*)	3.(*b*)	4.(*a*)	5.(*a*)	6.(*c*)	7.(*a*)	8.(*a*)	9.(*b*)	10. (*a*)

Index

Chapter wise Datasets

2.2.1b

2.2.2b

2.3.1b

2.3.2b

2.4.1b

2.4.2b

3.2.1b

3.2.2b

3.3.1b

3.3.2b

4.2.1b

4.2.2b

4.3.1b

4.3.2b